The Dublin King

THE TRUE STORY OF
EDWARD, EARL OF WARWICK,
LAMBERT SIMNEL AND THE
'PRINCES IN THE TOWER'

JOHN ASHDOWN-HILL

The History Press

In memory of my dear cousin, Valerie Ashdown (Enkelaar) 1931–2014 – whose life also linked England and the Low Countries.

First published 2015

This edition published 2017 by
The History Press
The Mill, Brimscombe Port
Stroud, Gloucestershire, GL5 2QG
www.thehistorypress.co.uk

British Library Cataloguing in Publication Data.
A catalogue record for this book is available from the British Library.

ISBN 978 0 7509 6694 8

Typesetting and origination by The History Press
Printed in Great Britain

Contents

Part 4 – The Aftermath

Acknowledgements

I should like to give my profuse thanks to those people in Ireland who, in various ways have helped me with my research. These include James Harte, Samm Coade and the other very kind staff of the enormously helpful Irish National Library, together with Professor McGing and Eileen Kelly of Trinity College, Dublin, and Kate Manning, of the Archives of University College, Dublin. I should also like to record a heartfelt posthumous thank you to Professor F.X. Martin, whose publication on Lambert Simnel first brought to my attention the existence of the surviving (albeit damaged) seal of the Dublin King.

I also have debts of gratitude in the U.K. I am enormously grateful to Dr Emily Kearns, who has very kindly checked my Latin (and Greek) translations in an attempt to ensure that no mistakes have crept in. My thanks are also due to the Essex Library service; to the staff of the Albert Sloman Library of the University of Essex; to Marie Barnfield, of the Richard III Society Non-fiction Papers Library; to the Staff of the Guildhall Library in London; and to Dave Perry, who helped me check through the *Great Chronicle of London*. Dave Perry and Annette Carson also checked the proofs of my text to remove typographical and other errors and ensure that my meaning was clear. Finally, my thanks also go to the living Essex 'Lambert Simnel' who figures on *Facebook*, and who responded to my enquiry – even though, sadly, his *Facebook* identity proved to be a pseudonym!

Introduction

Anyone seeking information about Lambert Simnel will easily discover that this rather unusual name refers to a late fifteenth-century pretender to the English throne. His career is seen as marking one of the final chapters of the so-called Wars of the Roses. The word pretender was originally a neutral term, merely meaning claimant. Thus, for example, the eighteenth-century Old Pretender and Young Pretender, though they made the unspeakable error of professing the wrong religion in terms of the England (and Britain) of their day, were certainly not in any sense false claimants to the throne. However, since the word pretender tends to be applied mainly to failures, it is now often seen as implying 'fake claimant', and this is definitely its generally perceived meaning in the case of Lambert Simnel. To most historians – and to most of the general public – Simnel was nothing more than an impostor.

The name relates to a boy put forward by Yorkist leaders as the figurehead for their first campaign against Henry VII, a year or two after the latter's usurpation of the English throne in 1485. Incidentally, the word 'usurpation' is another term which might benefit from some analysis. Properly, it means taking something over without a legal right. Yet although it has frequently been applied to the accession of Richard III (who, in reality, was offered the throne of England by the Three Estates of the Realm), curiously it is not generally applied to the violent seizures of power by Edward IV and Henry VII. Apparently in the case of a violent but successful seizure of power, the use of the term usurpation is not now seen as appropriate!

If the general perception of 'Lambert Simnel, the impostor' is correct, the story of his 1487 adventure would be the first (and perhaps the only) incident in English history which involved a serious attempt at putting a totally fake claimant on the throne.[1] If that is the case, then it certainly needs some explanation. It has therefore been suggested that, thanks to Richard III's alleged murder of his nephews, the 'princes in the Tower', followed by the natural death of Richard's son, there was no clear and genuine Yorkist claimant to the throne to head the new campaign against Henry VII. Thus the only solution for the defeated and ousted Yorkists was to train a young impostor for the role of their figurehead leader. This impostor was then crowned as king in a unique ceremony held in the building generally known today as Christ Church Cathedral Dublin. However, the boy's real name was then revealed to be Lambert Simnel by Henry VII's spokesmen – or by some of them – for in actual fact even the official Tudor sources offer conflicting information regarding the pretender's true identity.[2]

Since his alleged name of Lambert Simnel sounds somewhat improbable – and has, in fact, sometimes been described as having a pantomime-like quality – it has also been suggested by some historians that the boy might perhaps have had a non-English (possibly Flemish) ancestry. However, no proof has ever been produced to show that the surname Simnel originated in the Low Countries. In fact, the true evidence relating to the history of this surname will be revealed in Chapter 6.

In addition to positing a misleading modern invention in respect of the origins of the name 'Lambert Simnel', the widespread current standard interpretation of his story also often includes misleading statements relating to the lives and deaths of the so-called princes in the Tower. Actually, there is no real evidence that those two sons of Edward IV were murdered. Although it has been widely credited, the very detailed but unsubstantiated account of their slaughter written by Sir Thomas More dates from thirty years after the alleged event.

In fact Thomas More himself was an insignificant boy of five in 1483, when the drama which he later reported in such detail was alleged to have occurred.

As for the contemporary fifteenth-century sources on the fate of the 'princes', they are conflicting, and very much lacking in detail. However, as we shall see, according to one near-contemporary source, the 1487 pretender was himself supposed to have claimed to be the younger of the two.[3] It is true that, when we examine it carefully, the evidence on this point in relation to Lambert Simnel will prove to be somewhat questionable. Nevertheless, there is no doubt whatever that a subsequent Yorkist pretender, known to history as Perkin Warbeck, advanced a similar claim on his own account, and was quite widely believed. Thus the Warbeck case proves incontrovertibly that the death of the sons of Edward IV was by no means universally accepted as a fact in the late 1480s and the 1490s. Indeed, Sir Thomas More himself later acknowledged that belief in the survival of at least one of them still persisted in his day.

The legal situation in respect of the so-called 'princes' was somewhat complex. An unofficial Parliament (meeting of the Three Estates of the Realm) in 1483, followed subsequently by the official Parliament of 1484, formally declared these two boys and their sisters illegitimate and unable to claim anything by inheritance. Thus from the summer of 1483 until the summer of 1485 (i.e. during the reign of Richard III) neither of Edward IV's sons was a genuine, legal prince – in consequence of which, neither of them possessed any claim to the English crown. This legal decision was significant in several ways, as we shall see later. However, one important side effect was that Richard III – who had been recognised as the legitimate sovereign by the same piece of legislation – would have had absolutely no logical reason for killing these two sons of his elder brother in order to obtain the throne, since they had already officially been declared bastards and excluded from the line of succession.

Subsequently, however, that legislation was revoked by the first Parliament of Henry VII. The new king's purpose in having the Act of Parliament of 1484 rescinded was to enable himself to present Elizabeth of York – the elder sister of the 'princes' – as the Yorkist heiress to the throne – and then marry her himself. However, one unfortunate but inevitable side effect of Henry's repeal was that it also restored the rights to the throne of his bride's brothers. Thus, if either of them was alive in 1486–87, as the now-reinstated legitimate son of a former king, that boy's claim to sovereignty would once again have been a strong one – far superior to the virtually non-existent blood claim of Henry VII himself. A surviving son of Edward IV (if there was one) would therefore arguably have been in a strong legal position to reassert a claim to represent the house of York.

One consequence of this is that after 1485 Henry VII's motivation for ending the lives of his brothers-in-law (the elder of whom would by then have been aged at least 15 and able to reign in his own right) would have been very strong. Indeed, it would have been far more compelling than Richard III's earlier motivation to do away with a pair of minor children who were legally excluded from the succession. The most significant proof of this statement lies in the fact that Henry VII did indeed put to death Perkin Warbeck, who had advanced a powerful (and, to some people, convincing) claim to be the younger of the two 'princes'.

However, the second point regarding the Yorkist claim in 1486–87 is that, even if both of Edward IV's sons by Elizabeth Woodville were dead, there were numerous other Yorkist claimants to the throne in existence. These comprised various nephews of Richard III and Edward IV. At least one of these Yorkist royal nephews – John de la Pole, Earl of Lincoln – was both adult and at liberty. Moreover, he had been promoted to high rank and groomed for government service during the reign of Richard III. Indeed, in terms of the norms of inheritance, he was probably the strongest Yorkist contender for the throne, because, unlike his cousins – the sons of Edward IV, and of the attainted Duke of Clarence – Lincoln's claim had never been impugned by any parliamentary legislation. If the Yorkists were in search of a leader and a claimant to the throne, Lincoln, the eldest surviving Yorkist prince, would have been an obvious candidate.

But, strangely, instead of putting forward his own claim, the 25-year-old Lincoln chose instead to back the supposed impostor. Why on earth would a genuine – and adult – Yorkist prince such as Lincoln have chosen to back a false claimant who (according to the surviving contemporary accounts) was a minor, instead of advancing his own valid claim? This unanswered question is by no means new, for it reportedly preoccupied Henry VII himself, in 1487.[4] Henry is said to have expressed regret at the death of Lincoln at the Battle of Stoke, since that precluded any possibility of interrogating the earl on this very subject. For about five hundred years, then, the issues surrounding the motivation underlying Lincoln's recorded conduct have been carefully glossed over by those who view Lambert Simnel as a spurious claimant to the throne. Indeed, those historians who accepted the Tudor accounts of Lambert Simnel had little other option, because if Simnel was an impostor, Lincoln's actions were a complete mystery, utterly lacking any credible explanation.

Despite this problem, most historians have nevertheless maintained that Lambert Simnel claimed – falsely – to be Edward, Earl of Warwick, another (and younger) nephew of Richard III and Edward IV, and the son of George, Duke of Clarence. It is intriguing, therefore, to discover that several surviving contemporary sources actually report that Simnel really *was* the Earl of Warwick. The geographical location of the writers appears to be highly significant in determining their attitude on this point. While official English (Tudor) sources maintained that Simnel was an impostor, Burgundian sources took the opposite view. Irish sources also held the opposite view until the Tudor victory at Stoke began the slow process of bringing Ireland back under English rule. Thus, consciously or unconsciously, by maintaining that Simnel was a fake, modern historians are following the official Tudor line.

Another intriguing point is the fact that the boy known as Lambert Simnel began advancing his claim in Ireland, with support from Flanders. These locations are significant, because the Earl of Warwick's father, the Duke of Clarence, had been accused in 1477–78 of attempting to smuggle his son and heir to either Ireland or Flanders. Why was this accusation levelled against Clarence at some length and in considerable detail, despite the fact that an official conclusion was then reached that his attempt had failed? Could it possibly be that – despite the fact that the government of his brother, Edward IV, proclaimed publicly that the 3-year-old Earl of Warwick was still at home – the Duke of Clarence actually succeeded in having his son sent out of England? As for the reason for the official government statement, it may have been that Edward IV and his advisors genuinely believed what they said.

As we have seen, the name 'Lambert Simnel' is supplied to us by official mouthpieces of Henry VII – who, of course, had every incentive for attempting to discredit the 1487 claimant. It is those same mouthpieces who also provide us with the alternative story of the pretender's childhood – as the son, not of a king or a royal duke, but of a tradesman of some kind (there are various conflicting accounts of the father's employment), who may have lived in Oxford. This story – as told, for example, by Polydore Vergil – superficially sounds clear and authoritative. In reality, however, when examined carefully, just like the other possible accounts of the boy's childhood, the 'Simnel of Oxford' version appears to contain some puzzling elements and a number of contradictions.

Thus, in every respect, the story of Lambert Simnel is far from straightforward. In this re-examination of the pretender and his claims, I shall try to offer a thorough exploration of every piece of evidence – including some new or little-known material – and I shall attempt to avoid proposing any facile

conclusions. To avoid prejudging any of the issues, hencefor-
ward I shall generally refer to the individual at the centre of
the investigation, neither as 'Lambert Simnel', nor as the Earl
of Warwick or the Duke of York, but as 'the Dublin King'.

My re-examination begins with the conflicting versions of
the Dublin King's five possible childhoods. The first of these
versions is the childhood of the younger son of Edward IV,
Richard of Shrewsbury, Duke of York and Norfolk. Many
people may feel that they know the basic outline of Richard's
story well. As we shall see, however, the widespread use of
the collective term 'princes in the Tower' in itself proves very
clearly that the life history of Richard of Shrewsbury is quite
widely misunderstood. As for the later stages of Richard's real
story, they are full of question marks.

Exploring Richard's life necessarily involves a re-examination of whether or not the sons of Edward IV really were
murdered. This leads inevitably to the theory advanced by
some modern writers that perhaps the Dublin King was in
reality none other than King Edward V. Although no fifteenth-
century accounts explicitly proposed such a theory, this second
possible childhood also has to be explored.

The third and fourth stories are two alternative versions of
the life history of Edward of Clarence, Earl of Warwick, the son
of the Duke of Clarence. The Earl of Warwick's story has been
very little studied and is generally not well understood. Even
the entry under his name in the *Oxford Dictionary of National
Biography* (*ODNB*) contains at least one glaring inaccuracy.

A quick glance at the timeline at the end of this book
reveals how young Warwick was when some of the key events
took place in which he was allegedly involved. This suggests
one very important point which seems generally to have been
overlooked. How many people would easily have been able
to recognise and identify him? In 1487 Warwick would have
been 12 years old. In 1476–77, when his father had tried to
smuggle him out of England (and had perhaps succeeded),
the little boy had been only 2. How easy is it, even today, to

recognise a boy of 12 whom one last saw when he was 2? When considered in this light, Henry VII's parading through the streets of London of the young person whom he held in custody under the name of the Earl of Warwick, in an attempt to undermine the claims of the Dublin King, appears ridiculous and meaningless.

In fact, what will emerge, as we shall see, is that the life history of the Earl of Warwick actually has two potential – and quite different – versions. The first of these is the authorised version, as publicised by successive English governments. The second is an alternative, unauthorised and unfamiliar version; nevertheless, evidence for its possible authenticity does exist.

The fifth childhood story to be considered is that of the mysterious boy who seems to have borne the name Lambert Simnel – though one contemporary account by a rather important witness tells us that the boy's real Christian name was actually John. This boy may have been brought up in Oxford, by his father, who may have been an organ maker – or a baker – or some other kind of tradesman. Possibly the boy was not brought up in Oxford, but was taken there by a clergyman who had evil intentions in respect of King Henry VII. Reportedly taken from his menial background (wherever that was) around the end of 1485, at the age of about 8, because he looked so much like the 10-year-old Earl of Warwick (whom most people had probably never seen) – or possibly because he resembled the even older Duke of York – Simnel was then allegedly trained to impersonate a royal prince by an insignificant – but obviously very enterprising – young Oxford priest. One account tells us that this priest was called William Symonds. However, another version of the story reports his name as Richard Simons. According to one source, Symonds/Simons was a prisoner of the Tudor government by the beginning of 1486. Confusingly, other sources report that he was only captured by Henry VII's forces about fourteen months later, after the Battle of Stoke. It will probably already be apparent that, despite its widespread acceptance, in actuality this official Tudor account of events contains at least as many confusions and potential contradictions as the other versions of the pretender's story.

Identifying for certain which of these four – or possibly five – boys was where, when and with whom, is by no means easy. The trail becomes increasingly complex as the story progresses. Nevertheless, a serious attempt to track down the true life histories and fates of all the boys in question is the only possible way of embarking upon the quest to shed new light on the story of Lambert Simnel and the Dublin King.

Note

In the Middle Ages the English calendar operated differently from the one we know today, in that the New Year began not on 1 January but on 25 March (Lady Day). Thus events which occurred in the months of January, February or March would have been counted by medieval English writers as occurring in the last months of the previous year. Some foreign writers, however, would have dated them in the modern manner. To avoid any possibility of confusion over year dates, all events which occurred in January, February or March are dated here in the following way:

February 1486/87

This means that in terms of the English medieval reckoning, the event in question took place in February, the penultimate month of 1486 – though in terms of the modern calendar we would date this as February, the second month of 1487.

The Historical Background

The background to the story of the Dublin King is the episode of English history popularly known as the Wars of the Roses. It is essential to understand the basic outline of this complex struggle for power within the royal family in order to be able to comprehend what took place in 1486–87.

The story of the Wars of the Roses started almost a century before the coronation of the Dublin King. It began in about 1390, with controversy over who was the true heir to the throne of the childless reigning monarch of the day, King Richard II. The rival contestants were, first, the descendants of Richard II's senior uncle, Lionel of Antwerp, Duke of Clarence and, second, the family of a younger uncle, John of Gaunt, Duke of Lancaster. As a result of the marriage of Anne Mortimer, great-granddaughter of Lionel, to her cousin, Richard, Earl of Cambridge, the Clarence descendants eventually evolved into what is known as the royal house of York, while John of Gaunt's descendants were the house of Lancaster.

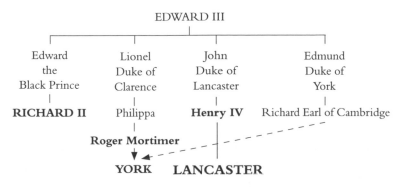

Who was the true heir of Richard II?

Historical attempts at analysing the rights and wrongs of the rival Mortimer/Yorkist and Lancastrian/Tudor claims to the throne are often based on the rather naïve assumption that the basic modern rules governing succession to the English throne also applied in the medieval period. The fact that the modern rules have only recently been altered should warn us against making any such assumption.

An examination of practice in relation to succession issues during the five centuries from 1000 to 1500 shows that the seizure of power by force, followed by subsequent Parliamentary ratification, was not infrequently the basis of a sovereign's authority during this period. It accounts for the accessions of William I (the Conqueror), King Stephen, King John, Henry IV, Edward IV and Henry VII. The accessions both of Stephen and of Henry II also prove beyond any shadow of doubt that a royal daughter could transmit rights to the throne if there was a lack of royal sons. At the same time, however, the civil war between King Stephen and Henry II's mother, Stephen's cousin Matilda, demonstrates that prior to 1500 the right of daughters to succeed to the throne in person remained unclear.

In 1399 John of Gaunt's son forcibly resolved the succession issue of his day by deposing, imprisoning and probably ultimately murdering King Richard II, and by seizing the crown for himself, under the royal title of King Henry IV. Thus began the reign of the house of Lancaster, which lasted for sixty-two years.

Of course, such behaviour invites retaliation. Its effect in this instance was that, from the very beginning of the Lancanstrian era, there were attempts to change the situation in favour of Richard II's alternative heirs, the descendants of Lionel, Duke of Clarence. The early attempts were unsuccessful, of course, and the house of Lancaster remained on the throne throughout the reigns of Henry IV and Henry V. However, the position of the dynasty was weakened by the death of Henry V, followed by the succession of the third Lancastrian king, his baby son, King Henry VI.

Henry VI was a weak king even when he grew up. His position was further undermined by a tendency to mental instability, which he may have inherited from his grandfather, King Charles VI of France. Doubts about the legitimacy of his supposed son and heir also helped to undermine the Lancastrian cause. Thus, after various vicissitudes, which later came to be called the Wars of the Roses, the Yorkist attempts to displace the house of Lancaster were finally successful. First, Parliament decided that the Yorkist line must succeed to the throne after Henry VI. Then in 1461, after this decision had been contested unsuccessfully by a Lancastrian army, Henry VI was deposed by one of his Yorkist cousins, who founded the Yorkist dynasty and became King Edward IV. Edward IV's claim to the throne was a strong one, based on three very solid arguments: first, his superior blood right (via his female-line descent from Edward III's second surviving son); second, his very effective seizure of power; third, the subsequent ratification of his succession by Parliament.

Ultimately, the death of Henry VI in the Tower of London left the Lancastrian dynasty with no clear heir, and the Yorkist takeover would almost certainly have proved to be a long-term success if Edward IV had had a sensible marriage policy. Unfortunately, by involving himself in two secret weddings, the king laid himself open to the accusation of bigamy. In 1461 he married Eleanor Talbot, daughter of the late first Earl of Shrewsbury,[1] but in 1464, while Eleanor was still alive, he also secretly married Elizabeth Woodville. Unfortunately for Edward, since only the second of these two secret marriages produced offspring, those children then became liable to accusations of illegitimacy. Matters came to a head when Edward IV died unexpectedly in April 1483.

Notionally Edward IV's heir was his eldest son, Edward, Prince of Wales, the elder of the so-called 'princes in the Tower'. Following his father's death, in April 1483, this Prince of Wales was initially proclaimed king as Edward V. However, the subsequent revelation of Edward IV's bigamy provoked

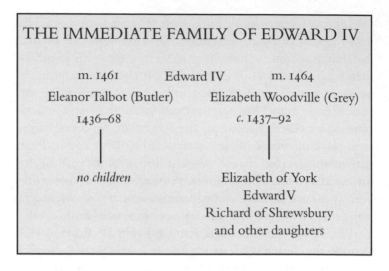

THE IMMEDIATE FAMILY OF EDWARD IV

m. 1461	Edward IV	m. 1464
Eleanor Talbot (Butler)		Elizabeth Woodville (Grey)
1436–68		*c.* 1437–92

no children

Elizabeth of York
Edward V
Richard of Shrewsbury
and other daughters

a new controversy between those members of the nobility, such as Lord Hastings, who were prepared to hush up the young king's technical illegitimacy, and those like the Duke of Buckingham, who believed that it should not be hushed up, and who insisted that the order of succession should be altered, either to maintain the principle of absolute legitimacy upon which the Yorkist claim to the throne had always been based, or perhaps to ensure the exclusion from any position of power of the parvenu and upstart Woodville family.

The immediate outcome of Hastings' opposition was his execution. Then, on the basis of the evidence of Edward IV's bigamy (and the consequential illegitimacy of his children by Elizabeth Woodville), coupled with the fact that George, Duke of Clarence had been attainted and executed in 1478, thereby excluding *his* children from the succession, the throne was offered to Edward IV's only surviving brother, the Duke of Gloucester, who thus became King Richard III. Since a Parliament had not, at that stage, formally been opened, the offer of the crown to Richard III was made initially by the Three Estates of the Realm – those noblemen, bishops and abbots, and representatives of the commons, who were in London waiting for the opening of Parliament. However, the following year, when a full Parliament was sitting, the offer was formally encapsulated in legislation, citing both the evidence of bigamy, and also the offer made to Richard III the previous summer.

As at every stage since the usurpation of Henry IV in 1399, the new change in the order of succession to the throne was not universally accepted. In France there was a remote descendant of John of Gaunt living in exile. The French, always happy to undermine the existing government in England, supported this obscure claimant, and to their – and probably his own – surprise, in August 1485 at the Battle of Bosworth, he suddenly found himself King of England, with the royal title of Henry VII.

Henry rapidly repealed the parliamentary decision which had declared Edward IV's children bastards. This was done in order that he himself could marry Edward IV's eldest daughter, Elizabeth of York, whom he wished to present to the nation as the Yorkist heiress. In this way he hoped that his marriage would be seen as having brought to an end the rivalry between the houses of Lancaster and York.

As a result of Henry VII's action, the legal position regarding the Yorkist succession reverted to what it had been during

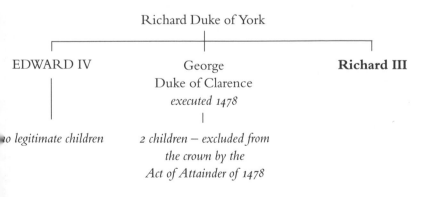

The heirs of Edward IV in 1483.

the reign of Edward IV. By rescinding the decision which had
declared Edward's Woodville marriage bigamous and its children illegitimate, Henry restored his bride, Elizabeth of York,
to the position of a legitimate princess, which she had enjoyed
during the lifetime of her late father. It was also now possible
for Henry to claim that Richard III had been a usurper.

But unfortunately, if Elizabeth's legitimacy had been
restored, so had that of her two brothers. Arguably, therefore,
from the Tudor viewpoint, the rightful Yorkist claimant was
now either Edward V or Richard, Duke of York – if either of
them was still alive. Whether those Yorkists who had supported
the late King Richard III would also have seen things in that
way is perhaps more questionable. *They* may still have perceived the sons of Edward IV as bastards, in which case they
would presumably have been seeking a new Yorkist leader
from among the other surviving nephews of Richard III.

Fortuitously from Henry VII's point of view, Edward IV's
two sons appeared to have been lost sight of in the meantime.
Thus, they were not on hand as immediate contenders for the
throne. Now that the legal situation in the autumn of 1485 has
been explained, some readers may feel that the boys' absence
was so much to Henry VII's advantage that it is very tempting to
believe that either Henry himself or one of his leading supporters
was behind their disappearance. However, Henry VII's apparent
uncertainty as to what had become of his young brothers-in-law
constitutes quite a strong argument against this. The possible fate
of the so-called princes will be considered in more detail later.

Meanwhile, from the Yorkist viewpoint, Henry's repeal of
the Act of *Titulus Regius* of 1484 had done absolutely nothing to restore the claim to the throne of the children of the
Duke of Clarence, since their father's attainder had not been
reversed. Thus it might appear that the official legal position in
Tudor eyes should logically have been that the 8-year-old Earl
of Warwick and his elder sister represented no real threat.

However, there was also an alternative *Lancastrian* viewpoint. Ironically, according to this the Earl of Warwick was the

rightful Lancastrian heir to the throne. This complex argument will also be explored in greater detail later. For the moment, suffice it to say that the new king was obviously taking no risks with potential rivals. He rounded up all the young Yorkist heirs that he could find, and made sure that they were placed under very careful supervision. Later, many of them were to be more permanently removed from the political arena by means of execution, either by Henry VII himself, or by his son Henry VIII.

In spite of his careful precautions, about a year after winning the crown Henry VII found himself confronting one possible Yorkist contender for the throne. The claimant was a boy who was recognised by those members of the house of York who were free to express their opinions, as a young but very high-ranking prince of that dynasty. Whoever he really was, all the surviving accounts speak quite well of him. They tell us that 'the child ... was handsome, intelligent and of courtly manners. ... *Lambertus erat vultu membrisque decorus* [Lambert was handsome of face and limbs],' says John Herd. '*Puer aspectu decoro et docile* [a boy of dignified appearance, and teachable],' writes Ware. 'Of a gentle nature and pregnant wit,' says the Book of Howth.[2]

Precisely who this boy really was, and what was his true life history, comprises the central subject matter of this book. One fact, however, is beyond dispute: the boy was crowned as King of England at Christ Church Cathedral in Dublin. As for which royal name and number this Dublin King used, various answers have been offered by previous writers. In reality, though, the true position (like so many aspects of the Dublin King's story) has not been clear. The relevant surviving evidence on this point will therefore be very carefully reviewed in due course. Before that, however, the fascinating quest for the true identity of the Dublin King has to begin by exploring all the possible – and conflicting – accounts of the boy's childhood.

PART 1

Possible Childhoods of
The Dublin King

Richard, Duke of York

About fifteen years after the death of King Richard III at the Battle of Bosworth, Bernard André (1450–1522), a French Augustinian friar and poet from Toulouse, who is also sometimes referred to under the Latin form of his surname as *Andreas*, and who was employed by Henry VII, wrote a history of the new king's reign. This is often called by its abbreviated Latin title, *Historia Henrici Septimi*. André's history of Henry VII offered the following account of the rebellion of 1487:

> While the dire death of King Edward's sons was still a fresh wound, behold, some seditious fellows devised another new crime, and so that they might cloak their fiction with some misrepresentation, in their evilmindedness they gave out that some base-born boy, the son of a baker or tailor, was the son of Edward IV. Their boldness had them in its grip to the point that out of the hatred they had conceived for their king they had no fear of God or Man. Thus, in accordance with the scheme they had hatched, rumor had it that Edward's second son had been crowned king in Ireland. And when this rumor was brought to the king, in his wisdom he elicited all the facts from the men who had informed him: namely, he sagely discerned how and by whom the boy had

been brought there, where he had been raised, where he had lingered for such a long time, what friends he had, and many other things of the same kind. In accordance with the variety of developments, various messengers were sent out, and finally [—],[1] who said that he could easily divine whether the boy was what he claimed to be, crossed over to Ireland. But the lad, schooled with evil art by men who were familiar with Edward's days, very readily replied to all the herald's questions. In the end (not to make a long story of it), thanks to the false instructions of his sponsors, he was believed to be Edward's son by a number of Henry's emissaries, who were prudent men, and he was so strongly supported that a large number had no hesitation to die for his sake. Now see the sequel. In those days such was the ignorance of even prominent men, such was their blindness (not to mention pride and malice), that the Earl of Lincoln [—] had no hesitation in believing. And, inasmuch as he was thought to be a scion of Edward's stock, the Lady Margaret, formerly the consort of Charles, the most recent Duke of Burgundy, wrote him a letter of summons. By stealth he quickly made his way to her, with only a few men party to such a great act of treason. To explain the thing briefly with a few words, the Irish and the northern Englishmen were provoked to this uprising by the aid and advice of the aforementioned woman. Therefore, having assembled an expedition of both Germans and Irishmen, always aided by the said Lady, they soon crossed over to England, and landed on its northern shore.[2]

There are several interesting points to note in André's account, and we shall return to his narrative to consider some of the issues that arise later. However, the first key point to notice is that André believed the Dublin King to be an impostor. Of course, this was a natural viewpoint for an employee of Henry VII. It would be astonishing if André – or anyone else writing from the official point of view of the Tudor king and his regime – were to tell us that the Dublin King was a genuine royal personage. We need to keep that fact in mind later, when reviewing the accounts of other historians of the reigns of Henry VII and Henry VIII.

The second point is that André states that one of Henry VII's heralds journeyed to Ireland on the king's behalf and interviewed the pretender. Although this herald clearly expected to be able to expose without any difficulty the boy's imposture, it is also evident, from André's report of what took place, that in actual fact, on meeting the pretender, the herald did not find himself in quite the straightforward situation which he had anticipated. His questions were apparently answered without hesitation, and it seems that, in the end, the herald may have concluded that the boy might indeed be the person he claimed to be. Indeed, André states quite clearly the interesting fact that the Dublin King 'was believed to be Edward's son by a number of Henry's emissaries' even though they were 'prudent men'.

The name of the herald who made this trip to Ireland on Henry VII's behalf is left blank in André's account, which suggests that André's report is probably at second hand, and that he had not spoken to the herald directly. However, Henry VII's Garter King of Arms (who had also previously served both Edward IV and Richard III), was John Wrythe (Writhe), who held this post from 1478 until 1504. It seems likely that Wrythe, who had been close to the Yorkist court, and who would have been in a good position to identify a surviving Yorkist prince – or disprove the pretentions of an impostor – may well have been the herald who visited the Irish court of the Dublin King. He is known to have made at least one visit to Ireland.[3] If John Wrythe was the herald in question, that might help to explain why André did not interview him in person. At the time when André was writing his account, Wrythe may already have been dead (for he died in 1504). If he was still alive, he was certainly an old man, and probably in a poor state of health. However, it is clear from André's account that the herald apparently found his mission a less simple matter than he had anticipated. Further evidence on the identity of the Dublin King, taken directly from the contemporary *Heralds' Memoir 1486–1490*, will be examined later (see Chapter 5).

As for the nature of the claims made by the Dublin King, André states quite specifically and unequivocally that he was a young impostor, who was attempting to pass himself off as one of the sons of Edward IV and Elizabeth Woodville. Two sons of this couple outlived their father. They are often known, both to historians and to the general public, as 'the princes in the Tower'. However, since by June 1483 they were officially no longer princes; since it is not certain how long they spent in the Tower of London, and since for the purposes of this study it is very important to stress that the two individual brothers experienced two quite separate and very different life histories, use of that popular collective term will, as far as possible, be avoided here.

The two boys in question were Edward (who was Prince of Wales until 1483, and then briefly 'King Edward V'), and his younger brother, Richard of Shrewsbury, Duke of York and Norfolk. André claims that both sons had suffered what he characterises as a 'dire death' at some time prior to (but not long before) 1486–87. However it is also his contention that the Dublin King put forward a false claim that he was the younger of these two sons of Edward IV, namely Richard, Duke of York. If André was correct in his assertion, we should hopefully be able to find further near-contemporary accounts which tell us the same story. Moreover, we should also be able to find evidence that the boy-king in Dublin used the royal name of Richard.

For the moment it will suffice to say that Polydore Vergil does confirm André to the extent of stating that, initially at any rate, the Dublin King claimed to be Richard of Shrewsbury. Moreover, there are certainly Irish coins in existence bearing the royal name of Richard which could possibly date from about this period. Unfortunately, however, fifteenth-century coins do not bear any date of issue. In the present case, this makes their significance somewhat difficult to interpret correctly. The Irish

The first Yorkist king, Edward IV, with his two wives: Eleanor Talbot and Elizabeth Woodville. Edward and Elizabeth are the first possible parents of the Dublin King.

Richard coins could simply date from the reign of Richard III. We shall return to both these points to examine the relevant evidence in greater detail in due course.

First, however, if this hostile historian of Henry VII is correct when he tells us that the Dublin King claimed to be Richard, Duke of York, it follows that in the eyes of historians from a non-Tudor background, the boy might conceivably have been seen as telling the truth. We therefore need to begin by examining the life history of the young Richard of Shrewsbury in so far as that is known. The clear evidence of his life story comes to an end in 1483. However, we shall also have to confront the very complex evidence of what became of him after 1483, and the question of when, where and how he died.

As his toponym indicates, Richard was born in Shrewsbury on 14 August 1473, the second son of Edward IV and Elizabeth

Woodville. The reign of the Yorkist dynasty, which had first formally claimed the throne in the person of Richard of Cambridge, Duke of York, had finally been made a reality by that duke's eldest son, Edward IV, in 1461. The Yorkist claim was founded upon the principle of legitimacy, which arguably gave the princes of York a better right to the English crown than their Lancastrian cousins. As we have seen, however, it then becomes difficult to establish whom Edward IV married.[4]

It appears to be the case that Edward IV contracted two secret marriages. The first of these, which probably took place in June 1461, was with Eleanor Talbot (Lady Butler), daughter of the first Earl of Shrewsbury. The second, reportedly in May 1464, was with Elizabeth Woodville (Lady Grey). The first union was childless, but its enduring consequence was that it made the second union bigamous, because the two marriages overlapped. As a result, the children born to Edward IV and Elizabeth Woodville were all technically illegitimate – and hence were ultimately excluded from succession to the throne. These, at any rate, were the conclusions reached by the Three Estates of the Realm in 1483, and formally enacted by Parliament in 1484. Thus, ironically, the marital conduct of the first Yorkist king did much to undermine the principle of legitimacy upon which his family's claim to the throne had been based.

At the time of his birth, however, Edward IV's son Richard of Shrewsbury was generally assumed to be legitimate, and was seen as the new second in line to the throne – thereby pushing his senior royal uncle, the Duke of Clarence, one step further from the prospect of ever wearing the crown of England. Richard was created Duke of York on 28 May 1474, when he was less than 1 year old, and he was knighted just under a year later, at which time land formerly held by the Welles and Willoughby families was settled upon him. In May 1475 both Richard and his brother, Edward, were made knights of the Garter.

The death of John Mowbray, Duke of Norfolk, in January 1475/76,[5] offered Richard's parents an unexpected further opportunity to improve their second son's future. Plans were made to marry him to Norfolk's only living child, his daughter, Anne Mowbray (1472–81), who, incidentally, was also the niece of Eleanor Talbot. A papal dispensation was required for the marriage of Richard and Anne, because they were close relatives through their mutual Neville ancestry.

Richard's marriage to Anne was celebrated with great splendour in January 1477/78, at the Palace of Westminster. On Wednesday, 14 January 1477/78, the 5-year-old bride, accompanied by the king's brother-in-law, Earl Rivers, was escorted into the king's great chamber in the Palace of Westminster, where she dined in state in the presence of a large assembly of the nobility and gentry of the realm.[6] The following morning Anne was prepared for her royal wedding ceremony in the queen's chamber, from which she was escorted by the queen's brother, Earl Rivers, on her left. At her right hand side was the king's nephew, the Earl of Lincoln. Her procession passed through the king's chamber and the White Hall to St Stephen's Chapel, the site of which is occupied today by the House of Commons. This Chapel Royal, brightly painted and gilded more than a century earlier by King Edward III, was also adorned for the occasion with rich hangings of royal blue, powdered with golden fleurs de lis.

In St Stephen's Chapel, under a canopy of cloth of gold, the royal family was assembled to await Anne. The king and queen were there, with both their sons – possibly one of the rare occasions on which the two princes found themselves in the same place at the same time. Their sisters, Elizabeth, Mary and Cecily of York, were also present. So was their grandmother – Anne Mowbray's great-great-aunt – Cecily, Duchess of York, mother of the king, and the 'queen of right', as she was called.

Anne's local Ordinary, Bishop Goldwell of Norwich, richly vested in a cope, waited at the chapel door to receive the bride. However, her procession was halted by Dr Coke, who ceremonially objected to the marriage on the grounds that the couple were too closely related, and said that the ceremony should not proceed without a dispensation from the pope. Dr Gunthorpe, the Dean of the Chapel Royal, then triumphantly produced and read the papal dispensation.

Once it had thus been formally established that the Church permitted the marriage contract, the Bishop of Norwich led the little bride into the chapel and asked who was giving her away. The king himself stepped forward to perform this office. High Mass was then celebrated, and the king's brother, the Duke of Gloucester, distributed largesse to those present, after which the bride was escorted to the wedding banquet by the same Duke of Gloucester and by the king's cousin, the Duke of Buckingham – a relative of Anne's paternal grandmother, Eleanor Bourchier.

The wedding banquet was held in St Edmund's Chapel. At the high table, with the bride and groom, were the Duke and Duchess of Buckingham, together with the bride's mother, Elizabeth Talbot, the young widow of the last Mowbray Duke of Norfolk. The young dowager Duchess of Norfolk was escorted on this occasion by Richard, Duke of Gloucester, who was the husband of her first cousin, Anne Neville. Two side tables were presided over respectively by the king's stepson, the Marquess of Dorset, and by the king's second cousin, the Countess of Richmond (mother of the future Henry VII).

The celebrations did not end with the wedding banquet. Three days later, in honour of his son's marriage, the king created twenty-four new knights of the Bath, and a week after the wedding a great tournament was organised at Westminster by Earl Rivers, with jousting of three kinds, and much splendid display. Anne Mowbray, Duchess of York and Norfolk, was queen of the festivities, and awarded prizes to the victors in the form of golden letters set with diamonds. The letters were 'A', 'E' and 'M'.

'A' and 'M' were for Anne Mowbray, of course. The 'E' was pleasantly ambiguous, standing for the names of the king, the queen, the Prince of Wales, the king's eldest daughter and the bride's mother. It even stood for the name of the bride's long-dead aunt, Eleanor Talbot, though her name was probably not one that the king wanted to recall just at this moment. It seems likely that the recent activity of his brother, the Duke of Clarence, had confronted the king with an unpleasant reminder of his relationship with Eleanor. Indeed, even as his son's wedding was being celebrated, Clarence was in prison, and Edward IV was grappling with the consequences of that reminder.

Young Richard of Shrewsbury was invested with all the main Mowbray titles: Duke of Norfolk, Earl of Nottingham, Earl Warenne and Earl Marshal, not to mention Lord Seagrave, Mowbray and Gower. Edward IV also enacted legislation of dubious legality to ensure that even if Anne Mowbray died her young husband would retain both the Mowbray property and the Mowbray titles.[7]

In May 1479, when he was still not yet 6 years old, Richard was appointed Lord Lieutenant of Ireland. Although officially he now had his own household, the members of it were his father's retainers. Thus it seems probable that, on the whole, both Richard and his young bride were brought up by and with his parents and sisters – unlike his elder brother, Edward. Sadly, however, Anne Mowbray died shortly before her ninth birthday, in 1481, leaving Richard a very young widower – and in somewhat dubious legal possession of the Mowbray inheritance.

Edward IV's notional direct heir, Richard's elder brother, Edward, Prince of Wales (born in November 1470), was almost three years older than his younger brother, Richard. In 1473 – the year of Richard's birth – Edward had been established in a household of his own at Ludlow Castle. There the little boy presided – in name, at least – over the newly established Council of Wales and the Marches. In reality, he was living and acting under the guardianship of his maternal uncle, Anthony, second Earl Rivers. Rivers was a well-educated man, and, under careful instructions laid down by the king, he seems to have brought up the Prince of Wales as a cultivated child. As a result of young Edward's separate household establishment at Ludlow, however, it is doubtful how much Richard, Duke of York saw of his elder brother during their childhood. This makes the traditional picture of the princes in the Tower – which groups the brothers together as though they were a single item – very misleading.

In April 1483, when Edward IV died unexpectedly, the Prince of Wales was still resident at Ludlow with his uncle, Lord Rivers. On the instructions of his sister (now the Queen Mother), Rivers made arrangements to bring the new young king – proclaimed as Edward V – to London, in preparation for his early coronation at Westminster. In effect, this amounted to an attempted coup, plotted by the Queen Mother and her family in order that the Woodvilles might seize power through their control of the young king.

There was no legal precedent in England for what Elizabeth Woodville was hoping to achieve. It is true that, about one and a half centuries earlier, Isabelle of France had overthrown her husband, King Edward II, and had briefly wielded power in the name of her young son, Edward III. However, no one would have regarded that as a model to be followed.

According to English custom, during the reign of a minor sovereign, authority normally resided in the hands of the young king's senior surviving male-line relative, the highest ranking adult prince of the blood. Thus, a hundred years earlier, during the minority of Richard II, councils had wielded power, though the young king's senior surviving uncle, John of Gaunt, had been the chief figure of authority. During the minority of Henry VI, earlier in the fifteenth century, the office of Lord Protector of the Realm had been created to be held by his paternal uncle the Duke of Gloucester (and by the Duke of Bedford when he returned from offices abroad), though once again his actions were subject to the approval of the royal council. In the present instance this model meant that the protector of the realm during Edward V's minority should have been his only surviving paternal uncle, Richard, Duke of Gloucester.

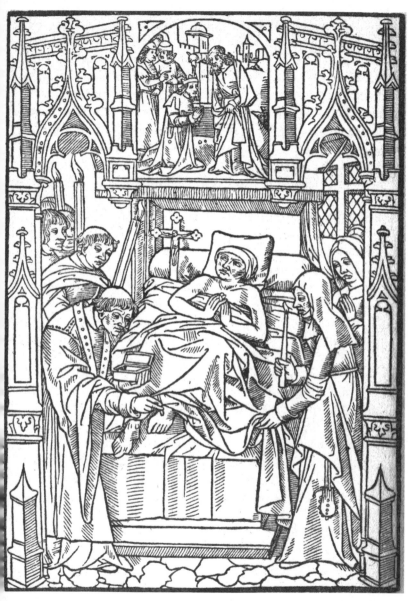

A deathbed scene.

At the time of Edward IV's death, Richard of Gloucester
was far away in the north of England. The Queen Mother
made no special effort to inform him of what was happen-
ing in London. However, certain key members of the nobility,
including Gloucester's cousins, the Duke of Buckingham,
and Lord Hastings, informed him of his brother's demise.
Gloucester accordingly summoned the nobles of the north
to York to take oaths of allegiance to his nephew, the new
king, Edward V. Then, alerted by the Duke of Buckingham
and Lord Hastings to the fact that Lord Rivers was taking the
new king to London, Richard moved south and met the royal
party at Stony Stratford. Buckingham seems to have joined
them there a few hours later.[8] Perhaps it was Buckingham
who then encouraged Richard to arrest, and later to execute,
Lord Rivers. Henry Stafford, Duke of Buckingham is a rather
significant character in our story. He was a descendant of
Edward III's youngest son, Thomas of Woodstock, Duke of
Gloucester and hence a cousin of the Yorkist kings.

Although Gloucester's role under Edward IV had been
to rule the north of England – which had, in a sense, been
his homeland – he had visited the court in London and
Westminster from time to time. Thus he undoubtedly knew his
younger nephew, Richard, Duke of York, and also Edward IV's
daughters. On the other hand, his elder nephew, the new king,
was probably a virtual stranger to him. Gloucester would have
met Edward V as Prince of Wales occasionally – for example at the Duke of York's wedding to Anne Mowbray – but
because young Edward had been brought up at Ludlow, such
meetings will have been quite infrequent. Thus, for young
Edward (brought up by his maternal uncle, Lord Rivers, aided
by Richard Grey and John Alcock), his paternal uncle, the
Duke of Gloucester, was an unfamiliar figure. However, the
two of them, forced together at Stony Stratford by the change
in circumstances, now made their joint way to London. There,
Edward V was initially received at the Bishop of London's
palace.[9] Later, however, the Duke of Buckingham suggested

that the most appropriate residence for the boy-king in the lead-up to his coronation would be the Tower of London.

Unlike his elder brother, Richard, Duke of York found himself at the centre of things when their father died, on 9 April 1483, for he was living at the Palace of Westminster with his family. At the end of April, when the news reached London that the Duke of Gloucester now had control of Edward V, it became apparent that the attempted Woodville coup had failed and, for the second time in her life, Elizabeth Woodville claimed sanctuary at Westminster Abbey. The young Richard, Duke of York accompanied his mother and sisters into sanctuary. He remained with his family at Westminster Abbey for more than six weeks. During that time his uncle the Duke of Gloucester established himself as Lord Protector of the Realm. Meanwhile plans were going ahead for Edward V's coronation.

On Monday, 9 June, an important council meeting was held from 10 a.m. until 2 p.m., at which plans for the coronation were due to be discussed. In the event, however, the council meeting appears to have found itself side-tracked by a serious question as to whether the coronation could go ahead, which had been raised by the Bishop of Bath and Wells. The bishop had declared that Edward IV's marriage to Elizabeth Woodville had been illegal, and that the new king was therefore technically illegitimate. Bishop Stillington's evidence was quite specific. He revealed that he himself had secretly married Edward IV to Eleanor Talbot, the former Lady Butler, daughter of the Earl of Shrewsbury, and sister of the Duchess of Norfolk, approximately three years prior to the same king's second secret marriage to Elizabeth Woodville.[10]

Since the late Duke of Clarence may have raised this issue earlier (in 1477), the question of the validity of Edward IV's Woodville marriage was probably not a complete surprise to all members of the royal council.[11] However, Clarence's evidence for Edward IV's Talbot marriage had probably been slight. That, together with Clarence's subsequent execution, may have persuaded most people to give the illegitimacy of

Edward IV's children as little credit as the French legend of Edward IV's own illegitimacy.

Now, however, the situation was rather different. For the person now recounting the story of Edward IV's Talbot marriage was none other than a priest who claimed that he himself had officiated at the marriage of Edward and Eleanor. This priest was now not only a bishop, but also an expert in marriage law. Thus, when he told the council that Edward IV's Woodville marriage was bigamous and that the children born of it were illegitimate, he had to be taken seriously.

Even if some of the council members had heard this story before, Bishop Stillington's new and authoritative announcement probably shocked them – and also the Duke of Gloucester. Initially, opinions differed as to how the new situation should be handled. The Duke of Buckingham and others argued strongly that Edward V must now be set aside and the throne offered to the Duke of Gloucester as the senior surviving Prince of the Blood Royal. Other noblemen, led apparently by Lord Hastings, felt more inclined to hush up Stillington's revelation and allow the plans for Edward V's coronation to go ahead.

Unbeknown to Richard, Buckingham may have had his own axe to grind in this dispute. Although, as a young orphan of royal descent, he had been brought up by Elizabeth Woodville and her family, and had been married off to one of the younger Woodville sisters, the Duke of Buckingham by no means favoured the Woodvilles and their cause. As we have seen, he had already firmly supported Richard, Duke of Gloucester for the role of protector. Now he was pushing for the setting aside of Edward IV's bastard children by Elizabeth Woodville, and for the throne to be offered to Richard of Gloucester.

The next scheduled session of the council seems to have been split into two separate meetings, reflecting the two rival factions, so that Hastings and his contingent met at the Tower of London whereas Buckingham's supporters assembled at the Palace of Westminster. The Duke of Gloucester, Protector of the Realm, apparently visited both groups. Mancini states that Hastings entered the council meeting bearing concealed arms in an attempt to launch an attack on Richard, and that he was therefore executed for treason. Apparently Gloucester had been convinced by his cousin, Buckingham, that decisive action on his part was now called for. The execution of Hastings effectively silenced – at least temporarily – those council members who had been supporting his views.

Incidentally, the fact that Buckingham had opposed Lord Hastings over the succession issue was probably no accident. Earlier, Edward IV had allowed – and indeed encouraged – Lord Hastings to establish himself as the leading magnate in Staffordshire. But that was a role which, in Buckingham's eyes, should rightfully have belonged to *his* family – the Staffords. Although Hastings had certainly taken the wrong side, politically, over the question of whether or not Edward V should be set aside, for Buckingham the execution of Hastings also had a definite personal advantage. It meant that *he* was then able to re-establish his own position in Staffordshire.

The decisive action taken at the council meeting logically required that the alternative Woodville heir – young Richard, Duke of York – should be removed from the control of his mother as urgently as possible. Probably the fear was that once she learned that her marriage had been set aside – and her children, bastardised – the Queen Mother and her family would step up their opposition by using the young Richard as another rallying point for rebellion.

The Duke of Buckingham – who had been the first to propose that Edward V should be lodged at the Tower – was also a leading member of the delegation which was now sent to persuade Elizabeth Woodville to allow her younger son to join his brother there. Interestingly, Buckingham is regarded by contemporary Continental sources as the person responsible for the subsequent fate of the two 'princes' (whatever that fate really was).

On 16 June the Queen Mother was persuaded by the delegation, including the Duke of Buckingham, but actually led by
another royal cousin, the Archbishop of Canterbury, Cardinal
Bourchier, to allow the Duke of York to join his brother at
the Tower of London. Ironically, their period of residence
at the Tower was probably the first time that the two boys,
Edward and Richard, had ever spent any significant amount of
time together.

Edward's coronation, scheduled for 22 June, had now been
postponed, and on 26 June the crown was formally offered by
the Three Estates of the Realm (no actual Parliament having as
yet been opened) to Richard, Duke of Gloucester. However,
in spite of Hastings' execution, his view of things had not been
totally quashed. There is even evidence to show that – curiously – his former opponent the Duke of Buckingham may
have taken over the cause of Richard's two nephews, the sons
of Edward IV, after Hastings' death. At all events, as we shall see,
towards the end of July 1483 an attempt was made to break
into the Tower of London and seize the two boys.[12]

What subsequently became of Edward IV's sons is one of the
great historical mysteries, and more will be said about this in
the next chapter. Even at the time, very few people knew their
fate for certain. However, this uncertainty constitutes one of
the strongest reasons for doubting those later accounts which
suggest that they were murdered by – or at least on the orders
of – their uncle, the new king, Richard III. If Richard had any
motive for killing them, it would presumably have been to
ensure that they could no longer be used to challenge his right
to the throne. But to achieve that it would have been essential
for everyone to know for certain that the two boys were dead.
Mystery about their fate would not have been helpful.

Whatever became of them, it would have been in
Richard III's best interests to ensure that what had happened
to his nephews (or, at least, an official version thereof) became
public knowledge. Thus, he would have been best advised to
make a public statement of some kind regarding what had

occurred. Even if the boys were really dead, a risk would have remained that substitute claimants might subsequently be brought forward to impersonate them. Indeed, this may possibly have happened later, in the case of Perkin Warbeck. If Bernard André's account of Lambert Simnel were to prove correct, the situation might even have arisen twice.

The fact is that, if he was truly in control of the fate of his two nephews, Richard III's conduct is completely mysterious. Consequently the most obvious and logical explanation of Richard III's silence seems to be that the fate of the two boys was somehow taken out of his hands. As a result, he no longer knew whether they were alive or dead, or, if they were living, where they were located. How this may have been done, and by whom, will be reviewed in the next chapter.

A nineteenth-century depiction of the alleged murder of the 'Princes in the Tower'. There is no surviving contemporary representation of Richard of Shrewsbury, Duke of York and Norfolk, the second of these so-called princes.

Another significant point is the fact that when Henry VII took the crown he initially levelled no accusation against Richard III of having had his nephews killed. A specific accusation to that effect only surfaced many years later, after Henry had been been forced to deal with the second Yorkist pretender – who was a rather convincing claimant for the role of the younger of the two sons of Edward IV. Henry then allowed it to be rumoured that Sir James Tyrell (who was executed in 1502 for other activities) had confessed to having killed the boys on Richard III's instructions. No text of James Tyrell's confession was ever published, and no such document appears to survive. Probably none ever existed. Nevertheless, the enormous practical value of the story of the murder and of the executed Tyrell's confession was that they would hopefully help to make it impossible for any future Yorkist pretender to claim to be a son of Edward IV.

The detailed circumstantial account of Thomas More, penned long after the events to which it claimed to refer, was written specifically in the light of the alleged (but probably mythical) confession of Sir James Tyrell. More's account is not worthy of serious attention. As for the earlier accounts referring to the murder of the two boys, both in England and abroad, all of them are hearsay, nothing more than reports of contemporary gossip. They lack detail, they lack witnesses, and they were based partly on the fact that no one knew where the sons of Edward IV were, and partly upon the personal objectives of those who produced the stories.

However, it is surely significant that at least one pretender certainly appeared, claiming to be Richard of Shrewsbury. On the basis of the surviving fifteenth-century evidence (as we shall see), he was quite widely accepted and believed. It is also significant that no pretender ever claimed to be Edward V.

These two key facts appear to indicate that in the last decade and a half of the fifteenth century the most widespread belief was that Edward V may have been dead, but that his younger brother, Richard, Duke of York, could well be still alive.

Against this, of course, one must set the allegation of some modern writers that the Dublin King either was, or claimed to be, Edward V. *That* case, together with the rather limited evidence relating to it, will be examined in the next chapter.

Here, the focus of our attention is upon the case of Edward IV's younger son, Richard, Duke of York. According to Bernard André, that was who the Dublin King claimed to be. One key point in respect of the young Richard is that there is absolutely no clear evidence that he died – or was believed to have died – in 1483. This assertion is offered here in spite of the existence of a document known as the 'Cely note', which some modern historians have sought to interpret as proving the death of Richard, Duke of York. In my view, such interpretations are incorrect. They are highly subjective, and are based upon a misunderstanding of the document in question, coupled with an incorrect assessment of its dating. Nevertheless, the claims made for the 'Cely note' cannot simply be ignored. Let us briefly examine this example of the many theories surrounding the alleged murder of the so-called 'princes'.

The Cely family were middle-class Londoners. A selection of their family papers, covering the years 1472–88 was presented as evidence in the Court of Chancery in 1489, during the course of a family dispute. As a result, the papers are now preserved in The National Archives. The undated 'Cely note' which concerns us here was written by George Cely.[13] Armstrong dates it tentatively to 13–26 June 1483 and characterises it as possibly expressing fears for the life of Edward V.[14] Alison Hanham likewise assumes that George Cely's reference to 'the king' is to Edward V, on the basis that mention in the note of the death of the 'chamberlain' must relate to the execution of Lord Hastings.[15]

In fact, however, it is impossible to date the Cely note with any degree of certainty. Indeed, some earlier historians assigned it to August 1478, based on its reference to the death of an unnamed Bishop of Ely.[16] In reality, though, it is extremely unlikely to have such an early date, since the text is inscribed upon the reverse of a document which seems to have been written in late 1481 or early 1482. The note, which is reproduced below, following as closely as possible the layout and format of the original manuscript text, includes a number of strange symbols, the meaning of which is not clear. Earlier publications of the 'Cely note' seem simply to have ignored these symbols:

⊗　　　　　　　　　　　　　　　　　　？
Ther ys grett romber in the Reme/ the scottys has done grett

⚕
yn ynglond/ schamberlayne ys dessesset in trobell the chavnse

+
ler ys dyssprowett and nott content/ the boshop of Ely is dede

++
yff the Kyng god ssaffe his lyffe were dessett/ the dewke of Glo

lll
sett[er] wher in any parell/ yffe my lorde prynsse, wher God

ooo
defend, wher trobellett/ yf my lord of northehombyrlond

ll
wher dede or grettly trobellytt/ yf my lorde haward wher

o
slayne

　　　De movnsewr Sent Jonys.

This note is more than a little mysterious. Since its text is quite difficult to read in the original form, a second version is offered here, the spelling and punctuation of which have been modernised:

There is great rumour in the realm. The Scots has done great [*sic*] in England. Chamberlain is deceased in trouble. The chancellor is disproved [? *dyssprowett*] and not content. The bishop of Ely is dead.

If the King, God save his life, were deceased, the Duke of Gloucester were in any peril, if my Lord Prince wh[ich] God defend were troubled, if my lord of Northumberland were dead or greatly troubled, if my lord Howard were slain.

De Monsieur Saint John.

The note falls naturally into two parts. The first part states what purport to be facts, while the second contains obvious speculations, introduced by the word 'If'. However, the opening sentence should warn us that we are dealing with rumour and gossip throughout the note. The meaning of some of the supposed 'facts' is far from clear, and one of the note's clearest statements appears to be false.

In terms of dating, the 'facts' are mutually incompatible. Only by selecting one 'fact' and ignoring others can any date be assigned to the note. Early attempts to date the note selected the 'Bishop of Ely' statement, thus producing the date of August 1478. Subsequently Armstrong and Hanham selected the 'Chamberlain' statement and dated the note to June 1483. However, it would be equally valid to select the 'Chancellor' statement, and this would suggest a date *earlier* in 1483. Obviously any dating arrived at in this way can only be subjective and must remain potentially contentious.

Neither Edward IV nor Edward V is referred to by name. The same applies to Lord Hastings. The 'Chancellor' statement (the precise meaning of which has itself been debated) may refer to Archbishop Thomas Rotherham. He, however, was dismissed at the beginning of May 1483. If the 'Bishop of Ely' statement refers to John Morton, it was certainly false. Far from being dead, John Morton survived to plot against Richard III, ultimately becoming Henry VII's chancellor and cardinal archbishop of Canterbury. As for the speculations in the second part of the note, some, such as the one relating to the possible death of Lord Howard, are also demonstrably in error. Lord Howard was about to become Duke of Norfolk and he was subsequently killed with Richard III at Bosworth. In short, there is absolutely no guarantee that any part of the note is accurate.[17]

This evidence is in one way very significant, since it demonstrates clearly that the fact that something was written down by a contemporary cannot, by itself, guarantee that the writer knew what (s)he was talking about. A modern comparison would be if I were to write a statement about the death of Diana, Princess of Wales. I count as a contemporary, since I was living in England at the time of her death. However, I possess no specific, first-hand knowledge of what occurred. Thus anything I wrote would reflect nothing more than my own opinion. Unfortunately the writer of the Cely note seems to have been equally ill informed.

The fact remains that the note could well have been written earlier than Armstrong and Hanham suggest. In that case, the king to whom it refers would have been Edward IV, who died in April 1483. If so, the note must certainly have been written before the public proclamation of his death, since it mentions the king's decease only as a speculation, not as a fact. Moreover, if the 'king' of the note is indeed Edward IV, then it follows that 'my lord prince' refers to the Prince of Wales (the future Edward V), who was then very much alive.

Based on her later assessment of the date of writing, however, Hanham concludes that the 'prince' of the note must be Richard of Shrewsbury, the younger son of Edward IV. This seems a highly unlikely interpretation. As we have seen, Richard of Shrewsbury possessed his own proper titles, including Duke of York and Duke of Norfolk. One would expect reference to him to be by one of these – as it seems to be in Lord Howard's household accounts for 30 January 1482/83, when Lord Howard gave 2s 6d 'to Poynes that dwellyd with my Lord of York, for to bye with a bowe'.[18] Other references to Richard of Shrewsbury during his father's lifetime, and after his creation as Duke of York, are generally to 'the right high and mighty prince, the duke of York'.[19] There seems to be no surviving example of a document which omits his ducal title and calls him 'prince' only.

ג On the other hand, during his father's lifetime the future Edward V was Prince of Wales. 'My Lorde Prynsse' is therefore far more likely to refer to him than to his younger brother. If the 'king' of the note is indeed Edward IV; and the 'prince', the future Edward V; the only thing that George Cely has to say about Edward V (then still Prince of Wales) is to speculate whether he 'were troubled'. This certainly does not establish that he was dead at the time – or even rumoured to be so.

Armstrong goes on to associate the questionable evidence of the Cely note with the inference that Edward V's younger brother, Richard of Shrewsbury, may have been dead by 28 June 1483. Armstrong's inference has been drawn from the elevation of John, Lord Howard, to the dukedom of Norfolk (previously held by Richard of Shrewsbury) on that date.[20] In this connection Armstrong raises the very interesting concept of the distinction between legal and physical death. He argues that in acknowledging Edward IV's prior marriage to Eleanor Talbot, and the consequent illegitimacy of his children by Elizabeth Woodville, the Three Estates of the Realm created a situation in which Edward V and Richard of Shrewsbury were legally dead. As princes of the realm they did not exist and all their titles were extinct. This is an important concept to bear in mind. It is also a proposition which appears to receive some support from the petition of Elizabeth Talbot, dowager Duchess of Norfolk, to Henry VII, dated 27 November 1489.[21]

The dowager Duchess of Norfolk was Richard of Shrewsbury's mother-in-law, and Eleanor Talbot's younger sister. Her petition relates to the confiscated manor of Weston, Baldock, Herts. Elizabeth Talbot sets out in detail the transmission of this manor as part of the Mowbray inheritance, including Edward IV's provision for its reversion (in the event of her own death, and that of her daughter, Anne) to Richard of Shrewsbury. However, she then makes no reference whatsoever to the latter's death, merely stating: 'afterwards, the said

Anne dying, the reversion of the manor descended to John
Howard, last duke of Norfolk ... and to William, then viscount, now marquis of Berkeley'.[22] The omission is interesting,
because if Richard of Shrewsbury was known to have died
in June 1483, and John Howard had acquired the manor in
consequence of the boy's death, there was no possible reason,
in 1489, why Elizabeth Talbot should not have said so. On the
other hand, if the reversion of the manor had been held to
descend to John Howard because of the *illegitimacy* of Richard
of Shrewsbury, that was a matter to which it would certainly
have been extremely unwise for the duchess to make reference in 1489, during the reign of Henry VII – the husband
of Richard of Shrewsbury's sister. This may very well explain
why the dowager duchess chose to gloss over the point.

It is certainly possible that Edward V died in the summer or
autumn of 1483, under circumstances which will be explored
in the next chapter. But if we reject the interpretations of
the 'Cely note' arrived at by Armstrong and Hanham, there
is absolutely no reason to assume that Edward V's younger
brother, Richard of Shrewsbury, shared the same fate, or
died at that time. Indeed, there is no proof that Richard of
Shrewsbury died at any time between 1483 and 1485, or that
he died in the Tower of London. As we have seen, the so-called
princes in the Tower were not a single item.

Moreover, late fifteenth-century Yorkists showed very
clearly by their conduct that at least some of them believed
the young Richard to be still alive after 1485. It was for this
reason that they supported the second Yorkist pretender. He is
usually referred to by later writers as Perkin Warbeck, but he
himself used the royal styles of 'Richard of England' or 'King
Richard', and he undoubtedly claimed to be the younger son
of Edward IV.[23] This is the context within which we need to
consider Bernard André's suggestion that the Dublin King also
claimed to be Richard.

So was Bernard André's account of the Dublin King correct? Could the boy crowned in Dublin's cathedral have been

the real Richard of Shrewsbury – or an impostor pretending
to be Richard of Shrewsbury? In point of fact, both of these
suggestions appear improbable. According to those who saw
him, the Dublin King was reported in the most official surviving sources to be a boy of about 10 years of age.[24] Since
no one can possibly have seen any record of the boy's birth
this estimate of the child-king's age was presumably based
upon his height and appearance. More will be said about this
in Chapter 4, while contradictory (but less contemporary and
official) evidence which assigns to the Dublin King a different
age will be examined in Chapter 15.

For the moment, however, it is worth noting that the average height for a boy of 10 today is said to be 137cm (55in).[25]
In 1487 Richard of Shrewsbury would have been 14, not 10,
years old. The average modern height for a 14-year-old boy is
163cm (65in). Moreover, since Edward IV was unusually tall,
it seems unlikely that he would have fathered a short son.[26]
If anything, given the identity and physical appearance of his
father, one would probably expect Richard of Shrewsbury to
have been of above-average height. Yet the Dublin King was
apparently at least 26cms (10in) shorter in 1487 than Richard
of Shrewsbury should have been, were he merely of the average height for his age. This seems to suggest it is unlikely the
boy was Richard, Duke of York – or even that he claimed
to be.

As a result of André's text, some historians, led by Polydore
Vergil, have contended that the Dublin King underwent a
change of identity during his career. It is proposed that at first
he (or his supporters) said that he was Richard of Shrewsbury,
but that later he changed his identity and claimed instead to
be Edward of Clarence, Earl of Warwick. This has sometimes
been used to suggest that silver 'three crowns' coins from
Ireland that bear the name Richard might perhaps refer to
'Lambert Simnel'. However, this argument is very weak. The
issue of the Irish coinage of this period and what it shows will
be explored in greater detail later. For the moment, though,

it will suffice to point out that we have no way of knowing whether these coins refer to King Richard III, or to Perkin Warbeck, who styled himself as Richard of England.

As for the story of a change of identity, of course that was a useful weapon for official government spokesmen, whose principal objective was to undermine the credibility of the Dublin King. Thus, as we shall see, Polydore Vergil – who basically had an entirely different account of the pretender's assumed identity than that of his colleague, Bernard André – nevertheless mentioned the same notion as André, namely that the Dublin King claimed to be Richard of Shrewsbury. In Vergil's version of events the identity of Richard of Shrewsbury was assumed at first, but later changed.

All the evidence relating to the reign of the Dublin King, both from Ireland and from England, will be examined in detail in Part 3. As we shall then see very clearly, this evidence shows that, despite Polydore Vergil's suggestion that he underwent a change in his royal identity during the course of his 'reign', in fact all the surviving contemporary evidence appears to show that the Dublin King consistently used the royal name of Edward. There is absolutely no evidence that he ever used the royal name of Richard.

The more or less inevitable conclusion is that, in his account, Bernard André simply made a mistake regarding the pretender's royal identity. All the surviving evidence indicates that the name of Richard of Shrewsbury was never claimed by, or for, the Dublin King, either before or during his 'reign'. This conclusion is reinforced by the fact that André's account is unique among the early sources referring to the Dublin King. No other contemporary writer – whatever his political background – suggests that the boy's long-term royal identity was based upon the claim that he was Richard of Shrewsbury. Perhaps André was confused by the later events involving Perkin Warbeck.

At present we possess no certain knowledge of the fate of Richard of Shrewsbury, Duke of York. One possible way to improve our understanding would be to re-examine the remains of children found at the Tower of London in 1674, and later reburied by Charles II in Westminster Abbey as Richard, Duke of York and his elder brother, Edward V. At present there is no certainty whether these remains really are those of the 'princes'. It is not known whether they are the remains of males or females; nor is it known from what historical period they date. Despite this, claims have been put forward that the remains belong to two boys of about the right age who were closely related to one another. Of the two skulls, the elder one displays a congenital absence of teeth. The owner's missing teeth were four in number, namely the second premolars on both sides of the upper jaw and the wisdom teeth on both sides of the lower jaw. It is not unusual for these particular teeth to be absent. Indeed the present author shares the congenital absence of both the wisdom teeth of the lower jaw! Nevertheless, it has been suggested by some writers that the younger skull also showed the congenital absence of a tooth, namely the deciduous last molar on the right side of the lower jaw. It has therefore been argued that the owners of the two skulls might well have been siblings. Moreover, the remains of Anne Mowbray, wife of Richard of Shrewsbury, Duke of York, were accidentally found in London in 1964, and Anne also had congenitally missing teeth. Since she was related to her young husband via their shared Neville ancestry, Dr Jean Ross proposed that Anne's missing teeth proved that the bones found at the Tower of London were the remains of her husband and his elder brother.[27]

However, the present writer pointed out in 2009 that other evidence exists which suggests that Anne Mowbray's inheritance of hypodontia could well have descended to her, not via her father's Neville ancestry, but through her mother's Talbot bloodline.[28] If that was the case, Anne's congenital absence of teeth would prove nothing in respect of the Tower bones, because the sons of Edward IV had no Talbot ancestry. Moreover, in a recent publication I also highlighted a new piece of evidence derived from the remains of King Richard III (which were rediscovered in Leicester in 2012, thanks to my research, and the work of Philippa Langley and other members of the Looking For Richard Project). The new discovery is the fact that Richard III had no hypodontia. The implication of this fact is that, despite the shared Neville ancestry of King Richard III and his nephews, Edward V and Richard of Shrewsbury, no blood relationship appears to exist between King Richard and those young individuals whose remains were dug up in the Tower of London. In other words, this questions whether the bones found at the Tower, and reburied by King Charles II at Westminster Abbey, really are the remains of Richard III's nephews.

It is also not known for certain whether the bones in the urn at Westminster Abbey comprise the remains of only two individuals. In 2013, together with bone expert Dr Joyce Filer, I took part in a re-examination of the Clarence vault at Tewkesbury Abbey, where Richard III's brother George, Duke of Clarence and his wife, Isabel, had been buried. This re-examination revealed that the remains preserved in the vault, which had previously been thought to represent two individuals, actually comprise parts of at least three, and possibly four people.[29]

DNA testing and carbon dating could potentially clarify such issues in respect of the alleged bones of the 'princes' at Westminster. In the meanwhile, all we can say, based upon the evidence currently available, is that Richard of Shrewsbury may have survived both the Tower of London and the reign of his uncle King Richard III. However, the most important point in our current context is that it seems that there was never any connection between Richard of Shrewsbury and the persona of the Dublin King.

2

Edward V – and the Wider Problems of the Fate of the 'Princes'

Even if we have now dismissed the notion that the Dublin King either was, or claimed to be, Richard of Shrewsbury, it remains the case that the fate of the princes in the Tower is of enormous and very widespread interest. What is more, although no fifteenth-century sources advanced the claim that the Dublin King was the elder son of Edward IV, some modern writers have nevertheless put forward that suggestion. For this and other reasons, more will be said in this chapter about the probable fates of Edward IV's two sons, bearing in mind that the issue of the alleged survival of at least one of these boys subsequently impinged adversely upon the fate of the official 'Earl of Warwick' imprisoned by Henry VII in the Tower of London.

Let us not waste time repeating the well-known stories of Thomas More and other Tudor writers, since these are not contemporary and have no basis in fact. Instead, we should concentrate on the surviving real evidence. In particular one important fifteenth-century documentary source will be cited here, which has hitherto been more or less ignored by historians. Let us begin, however, by briefly considering the suggestion of some modern authors that the Dublin King may either have been – or have claimed to be – Edward V. One obvious point in favour of this suggestion is the evidence considered briefly in the previous chapter, namely the fact that the Dublin King apparently consistently used Edward as his royal name.

In all but one of the surviving fifteenth-century sources, this royal name of the Dublin King is unaccompanied by any numeral. This was by no means unusual at that period. Medieval English coins of Edward III, Edward IV and Edward V, for example, all typically employ Latin inscriptions such as: *Edwardus Dei gratia Rex Anglie et Francie et Dominus Hibernie* ('Edward, by the grace of God King of England and France and Lord of Ireland'), or abbreviations thereof. And while official documents sometimes add a royal numeral for these Edwards – accompanied by the necessary Latin clarification *post conquestum* (because the numbering of England's medieval Kings called 'Edward' took no account of the existence of such pre-Conquest monarchs as Edward the Confessor) – even written documents do not always include royal numbering.

Generally, historians who are aware of extant references to the Dublin King as King Edward have taken the initiative of adding the royal numeral 'VI' after his name. Michael Bennett, in particular, did this consistently. But of course, unless specific evidence can be presented to show that the Dublin King really did call himself 'Edward VI', it would be unscientific to refer to him in that way.

Presumably most writers who have assigned to the Dublin King the royal numeral 'VI' have done so chiefly because it appears logical. One potential problem, however, is that, as we have seen, the accession of Richard III in 1483 was based upon the parliamentary decision that Edward V was illegitimate, and therefore not a valid king. There is also clear evidence of various kinds that during the reign of Richard III, the brief reign of Edward V was not treated as valid. For example, documents issued in the name of Edward V had to be re-issued. In addition, one specific piece of surviving evidence from the reign of Richard III, showing the unique way in which the son of Edward IV was cited at that time, will be presented shortly.

One possible consequence of all this which needs to be considered is the question of whether, if the Yorkist supporters of the Dublin King believed that Richard III had been the rightful king of England, they might have decided to discount the brief reign of Edward IV's elder son. Had they followed that course, they would presumably have ignored the royal title and numeral of the 1483 'Edward V' as invalid. In that case they might possibly have counted their new, 1487, Dublin King Edward as the true King Edward V. The only possible way to check whether or not this was done is to find some contemporary fifteenth-century evidence of the royal numeral employed by and on behalf of the Dublin King.

The only specific piece of evidence in respect of the Dublin King's title and royal numeral which survives from the period of his reign consists of a reference in the York city archives, relating to a letter received by the City Council of York from the Dublin King in 1487. Unfortunately the way in which this has been handled in previous publications has merely served to perpetuate the confusion. However, the issue will now finally be resolved.

As published by Angelo Raine in 1941, this York city archives entry was transcribed as follows:

> Copie of a letter direct to the Maire, etc. from the lords of Lincoln, Lovell and othre, late landed in Fourneys in the name of ther King calling hymself King Edward the V.[1]

But while Raine's official publication states that the letter was from the 'King calling himself King Edward the V' (employing the Roman numeral 'V'), Michael Bennett's published text of the same letter states that it is a 'letter of "King Edward the Sixth"' (with 'Sixth' in word form).[2] Which (if either) of these two opposing statements is correct? Obviously this point is of the utmost significance, and the conflict between the two modern published versions of the manuscript can only be resolved by referring back to the original.

Fortunately, the fifteenth-century annotation above the manuscript copy of the letter as preserved in York House Book B6, fol. 97, is absolutely clear and unequivocal, and an image of the original manuscript is reproduced below, so that readers can check it for themselves. It reads:

> Copie of a lettə [*letter*] direct to the Maire, &c.
> from the Lords of Lincoln + Lovell &
> othre Late Landed in fforneys in
> the name of þə [*ther*] King calling
> hymself King Edward the vj[t].

From this unique York manuscript reference – the *only* fifteenth-century record now surviving of the Dublin King's full royal name and number – it therefore seems certain that the boy was referred to by his supporters as King Edward VI. In which case, whoever he was, he was not the elder of the two sons of Edward IV.

In its surviving form, the transcript of the letter itself (as opposed to its heading, written presumably by a York city clerk) contains no reference to the boy-king's royal name or

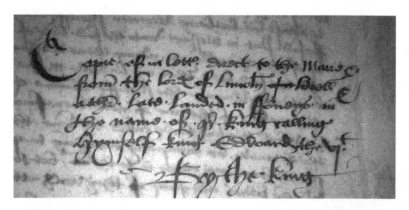

The contemporary heading above the copy of a letter from 'King Edward VI', York city archives, 1487 (*York House Book* 6, f. 97r). Reproduced courtesy of York city archives.

number. Possibly the actual letter sent from the Dublin King's camp to the mayor of York (as opposed to the surviving copy of it inscribed in the York archives) was headed simply by the Dublin King's name (with no number) and titles, as outlined earlier. The original heading may thus have read:

> Edward, by the grace of God, king of England and France and lord of Ireland, to the mayor and council of the city of York, greetings

or something similar.[3] In other words, even if the manuscript copy of the original letter sent by the Dublin King had been preserved, it might not have provided any further information in respect of the boy-king's royal numeral.

Presumably those modern writers who had thought that the Dublin King might have been – or have claimed to be – the elder son of Edward IV were either unaware of the evidence from York in favour of the royal style of 'Edward VI', or had only seen the erroneous transcript of that document, published in 1941 by Angelo Raine. In favour of their contention, however, they also cited:

> a) 'The consistency in the behaviour of Elizabeth Woodville and Dorset, mother and stepbrother [*sic* for half-brother] to the little princes, seems to suggest that they believed in the survival of at least one of Edward IV's sons … it seems possible, then, that the Dublin pretender was claiming to be Edward V'.[4]

> b) Claims that the Dublin king was aged 15 in 1485 (see below) – and was therefore of exactly the right chronological age to be Edward V.[5]

Smith, for example, asserts that 'the conclusion that the king from Dublin was Edward V not only fits the events of the so-called Simnel rebellion of 1487, but also explains the differences

in the narratives of Molinet, André and Vergil, and in their candidates for the Irish pretender'.[6]

However, this rather dubious contention needs to be set
against the basic fact outlined above, namely that if surviving
Yorkists in 1486 and 1487 still considered that Richard III had
been the true and rightful King of England, they were possibly unlikely to have counted the elder of the 'princes in the
Tower' as his rightful successor. The key difficulty here is that
the claims to the throne of Richard III and of Edward IV's
children by Elizabeth Woodville were, and forever are, mutually incompatible. If Edward V was a valid sovereign, then
Richard III must logically have been a usurper. On the other
hand, if Richard III was a valid sovereign, then Edward V was a
bastard with no valid claim to the throne.

Of course, another significant point, which would completely undermine any possibility that the Dublin King could
have been the elder son of Edward IV, would be any evidence
suggesting that by 1486 Edward V was dead. We have already
seen how surviving contemporary evidence appears to imply
that Edward may generally have been considered to have died
in about 1483. Since at least three other children of Edward IV
and Elizabeth Woodville are known to have died young and
of natural causes (see the table below), the idea that Edward V
may have suffered a similar fate is by no means improbable.
However, specific evidence exists which suggests that this may
well have been what occurred.

One of the earliest references to the death of Edward V
appears in Domenico Mancini's account 'concluded at
Beaugency in the County of Orleans, 1 December 1483'.[7]
A member of a religious order, possibly the Augustinian
(Austin) friars, Mancini was in the service of Angelo Cato,
Archbishop of Vienne, on whose behalf he visited England
for some months in 1483. Indeed, some historians believe that
he may have arrived in England in the second half of 1482.
It was for Cato that he wrote his subsequent account of the
state of affairs he had found in England, under the Latin title

The Children of Edward IV and Elizabeth Woodville

	Age at death	Key events
Elizabeth	37	b. 11 February 1465/66
		d. 11 February 1502/03
		Married Henry VII
Mary	14	b. 11 August 1467
		d. 23 May 1482
Cecily	38	b. 20 March 1468/69
		d. 24 August 1507
		Married 1. Ralph Scrope; 2. John Welles, 1st Viscount
		Welles; 3. Thomas Kyme or Keme
Edward	12?	b. 4 November, 1470
		d. August 1483
		Betrothed 1480 to Anne of Brittany
Margaret	8 months	b. 10 April 1472
		d. 11 December 1472
Richard	?	b. 17 August 1473
		d. ?
		Married Anne Mowbray
Anne	36	b. 2 November 1475
		d. 23 November 1511
		Married Thomas Howard (later 3rd Duke of Norfolk)
George	2	b. March 1476/77
		d. March 1478/79
Catherine	48	b. 14 August 1479
		d. 15 November 1527
		Married William Courtenay, 1st Earl of Devon
Bridget	37	b. 10 November 1480
		d. 1517 Probably four of Edward IV's ten children
		died naturally before the age of 15.

The average life of Edward IV's eight children by Elizabeth Woodville whose age at death is on record was 26.6 years.

- To maintain this average, if Edward V died naturally aged 12, then the natural lifespan of Richard, Duke of York should have been about 41 years.
- Edward IV's age at death was 41 years.

De occupatione regni Anglie per Ricardum tercium [Richard III's take-over of the Kingdom of England]. This report was submitted in December 1483. Mancini, who had departed from England in July 1483, reported:

> I have seen many men burst forth into tears and lamentations when mention was made of him [Edward V] after his removal from men's sight; and already there was a suspicion that he had been **done away with** [*sublatum*]. Whether, however, he has been done away with, and by what manner of **death** [*mortis*], so far I have not at all discovered.[8]

My highlighting of part of Armstrong's published English translation of Mancini's text is because it is misleading. The literal meaning of the Latin word *sublatum* is not 'done away with', but rather 'removed' or 'taken away'. Mancini's subsequent use of the word *mortis* in the following sentence shows clearly that he is talking about death, therefore his text really means:

> there was a suspicion that death had carried him off.

In other words, the original Latin text does not imply that Edward had been murdered.[9] Mancini merely reports that Edward V's death was the subject of rumour and gossip during the summer of 1483 – the period when he himself was still in England. This does not establish Edward's death as a concrete fact. It certainly does not establish the cause of his death (if indeed he had died). In other words, Mancini's account merely offers contemporary evidence of public speculation on the subject.

However, he names one specific source for his information on Edward. That source is extremely interesting because it was Dr John Argentine, who was young Edward's physician (*medicus*), and who clearly visited Edward on a regular basis while he was in the Tower. Indeed, Mancini tells us that Argentine was

Funeral brass of Dr John Argentine.

'the last of his attendants whose services the king enjoyed'.[10] Apparently Dr Argentine reported to his friend Mancini that Edward made daily confession because he considered 'that death was pressing upon him'.[11] This phrase is usually interpreted as a sign that Edward expected every day to be murdered. Obviously this is a rather slanted view. After all, the source for the information has already been specified as Edward's *doctor*, who was visiting him regularly. Surely a more logical interpretation would therefore be that the young boy was seriously ill, and believed that he was dying – rather like his elder sister, Mary of York, who had died at about the same age just over a year earlier.

It is also interesting that Dr Argentine apparently had not a word to say about the health – or the death – of Edward's younger brother, Richard, Duke of York. A later account by Jean de Molinet suggests that Richard was in good health at the time of Edward's putative illness, and tried to encourage his melancholy and depressed elder brother to be cheerful and even to dance. Of course, Molinet's text dates from about twenty years after 1483. Indeed the author even made mistakes concerning the names of the two sons of Edward IV, so they do not appear to have been of any great importance to him, and Molinet is no more to be regarded as the horse's mouth on the subject of what happened to the boys than Sir Thomas More.[12] Nevertheless, a contemporary letter, written by Simon Stallworth to Sir William Stonor on the 21 June 1483 also reports that Richard, Duke of York was in a cheerful mood at the Tower of London in the summer of 1483:

> On Monday last was at Westm. gret plenty of harnest men : ther was the dylyveraunce of the Dewke of Yorke to my lord Cardenale, my lord Chaunceler, and other many lordes Temporale : and with hym mette my lord of Bukyngham in the myddes of the hall of Westm. : my lord protectour recevynge hyme at the Starre Chamber Dore with many lovynge wordys : and so departed with my lord Cardenale to the toure, wher he is, blessid be Jhesus, mery.[13]

An entry in the Anlaby cartulary (written, however, after 1509) assigns the date of 22 June 1483 for the death of Edward V.[14] Unlike Mancini's, this is a far from contemporary account, and the precise date which it gives may not be correct. It would have been much more intriguing if it had suggested that Edward had died just one month later – on 22 *July* 1483 – the day following Richard III's departure from London. Nevertheless, further contemporary evidence that Edward V was thought to have died before the end of September 1483 does exist – though it had been largely overlooked until recent years. It is in the borough records of Colchester, in the collection now generally known as the *Oath Book*.[15] This volume comprises various records, including indexes containing listings of burgesses, wills proved in the borough courts, and enrolments of property grants covering the period 1327–1564. The folios relating to the fifteenth century are in the form of a year-by-year listing of the bailiffs and burgesses, together with a summary of documents registered by the borough during the year in question.

Typical entries in the *Oath Book* to mark the start of a new civic year simply give the names of the two bailiffs for that year. However, 1483 was the highly unusual year of three kings. The Colchester town clerk at that time – the local lawyer, John Hervy, who had served both John Howard (Duke of Norfolk), and the family of Howard's cousin by marriage, John de Vere, 12th Earl of Oxford[16] – clearly thought it desirable to add some note of explanation. Thus he supplies specific (if slightly inaccurate) accession dates for both Edward V and Richard III.[17] From this one can deduce that in broad terms Hervy knew what he was talking about.

The form of the annual Colchester borough records at this period shows that these were written up retrospectively, at the end of the civic year, which ran from Michaelmas Day (29 September).[18] This is clear from the fact that the listing of deeds and wills is normally continuous and in the same hand.[19] If a bailiff or a king died in the course of a year, that fact is recorded under the bailiffs' heading for the year, and before the list of deeds for the year commences. In the present instance, this implies that John Hervy's 'three kings' note for 1482–83 was written on or shortly after 29 September 1483.

The *Oath Book* was published in the form of a calendar, in English, in 1907.[20] This calendar version is the one now most often cited, since it is more generally accessible than the original text. Even the calendar version clearly implies that Edward V died in 1483, since it refers to him quite specifically as the 'late son of Edward IV'.[21]

The full original Latin entry in the Oath Book itself runs as follows:

Tempore Iohannis Bisshop & Thome Cristemesse, Ballivorum ville Colcestrie a festo Sancti Michelis Archangeli Anno domini Edwardi quarti nuper Regis anglie, iam defuncti, vicesimo secundo, usque octavum diem Aprilis tunc primo sequentem, Anno regni Regis Edwardi --- ------ [Regis spurii?]*22* quinti nuper filii domini Edwardi quarti post conquestum primo, usque vicesimum diem Iunij tunc primo sequentem, Anno Regni

Regis Ricardi tercij post conquestum primo incipiente, et
abinde usque ad festum Sancti Micheli Archangeli extunc
primo futuro quasi per unum Annum integrum.*23*

[In the time of John Bisshop and Thomas Cristemesse,
Bailiffs of the town of Colchester from the feast of St
Michael the Archangel in the 22nd year of the reign of the
Lord Edward IV, late king of England, now deceased, up
until the 8th day of April first following; [and] in the first
year of the reign of King Edward [*erasure*; see note 22] V,
late[24] son of the lord Edward IV after the Conquest, up to
the 20th day of June then first following; [and] in the first
year of the reign of Richard III after the Conquest, from the
beginning, and thence until the first feast of St Michael the
Archangel thereafter as for one complete year.][25]

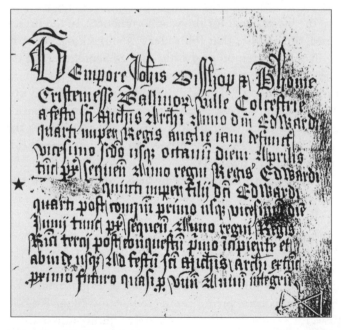

The Colchester record of the 'year of the three kings', written in September 1483.
The star marks the point at which words were later erased. (Colchester *Oath Book*,
D/B 5 R1, f.107r, modern foliation – old page no. 156). Reproduced courtesy of
Essex Record Office.

Like all the year headings naming the bailiffs, this record is inscribed in red ink, while the yearly record of burgesses, deeds and wills which follows is in black ink. There is no doubt, therefore, that this note was entered in the record as an entirety, and that the entry was made on or about 29 September 1483.

The proposed format of the erased phrase, '*Regis spurii*', is highly unusual, and is not elsewhere attested with reference to any other supplanted monarch. For example, the terminology employed by the functionaries of Edward IV to describe Henry VI was quite different. He was characterised as *rex de facto, non de iure* ('king in fact but not in law'). However, as we have seen, the situation of Edward V was fundamentally different from that of Henry VI. The personal legitimacy of the latter was never in question. Only his right to be king was at issue. Edward V, on the other hand, was adjudged illegitimate by

The same document, with the probable missing words *Regis spurii* ('illegitimate king') conjecturally reinserted, to show how they would fit in the gap.

birth. His exclusion from the throne – for he was excluded, and not deposed[26] – depended upon that judgement. It would not be surprising, therefore, to find him referred to in a different and unique manner. In Edward's case the phrase *rex de facto, non de iure* would have been utterly inappropriate.

The erasure of the words which seem likely to have characterised Edward V as an illegitimate (i.e. illegal) king, would presumably have been carried out in the autumn of 1485, following the repeal by Henry VII's first Parliament of the *Titulus regius* of 1484. The repeal and destruction of this Act automatically re-established the legitimacy of Edward IV's children by Elizabeth Woodville.[27] In this connection, it is noteworthy that Thomas Cristemesse, one of the two bailiffs for 1482–83, served as a member of Henry VII's first Parliament. The enactments of this Parliament in respect of the title to the throne were clearly well known in Colchester at the time, and are recorded in precise and accurate detail in the borough records.[28] Thus the erasure of offending words implying the bastardy of Edward IV's children might well have been ordered by the Colchester bailiffs in September 1485, as a politically correct move.[29] Even more interesting is the fact that in September 1485, in addition to his role as Member of Parliament, Thomas Cristemesse was approaching the end of yet another term of office as one of the two town bailiffs.[30]

As for the wording of the original entry in respect of Edward IV and Edward V, the former is characterised both as *nuper Regis* and as *iam defuncti*. Clearly, he was known to be dead. In the case of Edward V the entry is somewhat more intriguing. Despite the absence of the word *defuncti*, the obvious interpretation of the phrase *nuper filij Edwardi quarti* ('late son of Edward IV') seems to be that Edward V was dead (or at least that the writer believed him to be so).[31] Thus the Colchester *Oath Book* record is consistent with Mancini's reported rumour. Both sources permit the conclusion that Edward IV's elder son died before the end of September 1483. This evidence also concurs with the general Yorkist belief current in the 1490s, which apparently regarded Edward V as dead, but the fate of his younger brother, Richard, as uncertain.[32]

Interestingly, there is documentary evidence to show that a requiem mass was offered for the repose of the soul of an English king called Edward at the Sistine Chapel in Rome on Tuesday 23 September 1483.

The notice occurs in the *Diary* kept by Iacopo Gherardi of Volterra, apostolic secretary and 'secret chamberlain' to Pope Sixtus IV. The *Diary* is largely a record of papal ceremonies, strictly speaking not a diary, since it was put together after Gherardi left papal service in 1492. Nevertheless it seems generally accurate and must have been written up from notes taken at the time. The entry reads:

> *Eduardo Anglie regi parentatum hodie septembris XXIII in maiori sacrario, pontifice et patribus presentibus, rem divinam egit Christophorus episcopus Modrusiensis. Sed novissima persolvit pontifex, vaparato thure et aqua sancta inspersa, non pluviali sed purpurea cappa circumdatus.*[33]

Gherardi's Latin text means:

> For King Edward of England a mass for the dead was celebrated today, 23 September, in the greater [= Sistine] chapel, with the pope and fathers present, Bishop Christopher of Modruss celebrated the divine service, but the pope performed the final part, after the offering of incense and the sprinkling of holy water, wearing not his pluvial [ordinary cope], but a purple *cappa* [more elaborate cope].

The date is interesting. It was and is normal practice for prayers and masses for the dead to be celebrated at specific regular intervals after the date of death of the person being commemorated. The standard long-term custom is to pray on the yearly anniversary of the death. In the third century

Tertullian spoke of observing the anniversary of a death in this way. In the fifteenth century there are clear surviving examples of such commemorations. Thus Eleanor Talbot arranged for annual memorial services for her father and mother, the Earl and Countess of Shrewsbury, on the precise anniversaries of their respective deaths.[34]

But in addition to the annual commemoration ('Year's mind'), it was also standard practice to commemorate the 'month's mind' (late Middle English 'moneth–mynde') and to precisely focus prayers for the dead on the date of their deaths in other ways. For example, John, Lord Howard (later Duke of Norfolk) paid for a mass celebrated for King Edward IV (who had died at Westminster about the end of the first week of April 1483) on Wednesday 16 April.[35] Later, on Saturday 3 May Howard commissioned a second mass. Presumably that was to be celebrated as the king's 'month's mind'.[36] Similarly, in Rome, the death of King Louis XI of France, which occurred on Saturday 30 August 1483, was commemorated by Pope Sixtus exactly two weeks later, on Saturday 13 September.[37]

It was noted earlier (see above) that the Anlaby cartulary assigns 22 June 1483 (a Sunday) as Edward V's death date. However, the cartulary comprises a later account, and the question was raised that maybe it records mistakenly the *month* of the death. It seems more likely that Edward V may have died on Tuesday 22 July 1483 (the fourth Tuesday of July) – just after Richard III's departure from London. As we shall see shortly, Richard III clearly received significant news at Reading on 22 or 23 July, and hastily sent John Howard, Duke of Norfolk, back to London as a result. If Tuesday 22 July is the correct date for the death of Edward V, then the celebration of a requiem mass for the boy in Rome, on Tuesday 23 September (the fourth Tuesday of September) would have been highly appropriate, as it would very precisely have marked the 'two-month's mind' of his death.

In any case, the date of the mass in the Sistine Chapel makes it unlikely that it was a belated papal commemoration of the death of King Edward IV. Given that Edward IV had died around the end of the first week of April, if Pope Sixtus had chosen to commemorate *that* English king in September 1483 the date chosen would almost certainly have been towards the end of the first week of September. Or he would have celebrated the mass about the end of the first week of October, commemorating the 'six-month's mind' of Edward IV.

Thus, the most likely fates of the sons of Edward IV appear to be that Edward V died during the late summer of 1483, possibly from natural causes. If, however, Edward's death was not natural, then it was probably orchestrated by someone other than Richard III – someone in a position of power, who simply took the matter into his own hands. As some historians have previously suggested, the most likely contender for such a role is probably Richard III's cousin, former supporter and ultimate enemy, the Duke of Buckingham. As we saw at the end of the previous chapter, one obvious way of advancing our knowledge regarding the fates of the sons of Edward IV would be to re-examine their famous putative remains in the urn created by Sir Christopher Wren in Westminster Abbey.

As for Richard of Shrewsbury, there is no evidence to suggest that he died in 1483. On the other hand there *is* specific evidence that Yorkists in the late 1480s and in the 1490s thought that young Richard was still alive. However, his uncle, King Richard III, made no statement as to his whereabouts. The only logical explanation for King Richard's silence seems to be that the younger boy's fate had also, in some way, been taken out of the king's hands. Once again, the most likely contender for the role of orchestrator of the Duke of York's removal from the Tower of London is the Duke of Buckingham.

What was done with Edward IV's younger son, if indeed he did survive, remains a mystery. Various fates have been suggested for Richard of Shrewsbury, both in the fifteenth century and subsequently.[38] However, it is intriguing that the story later recounted by Perkin Warbeck (who claimed to be Richard of Shrewsbury) was generally consistent with the potential fates of the 'princes' as proposed here. Of course, by itself this does not necessarily prove that Warbeck was Richard. But it does very strongly suggest that, if Warbeck was not the genuine Richard, but an impostor, then whoever prepared and trained him for his royal role had inside knowledge of the true fate and whereabouts of the younger of Edward IV's two sons. Unfortunately there now seems to be little chance of examining the remains of Perkin Warbeck or of using DNA as a way of clarifying whether or not he was whom he claimed to be.

As we have seen, the story of the fate of the two 'princes' as recounted by Perkin Warbeck matches, on the whole, the picture which emerges from surviving scraps of contemporary evidence, dating from the time of the curious event known as Buckingham's Rebellion. The Duke of Buckingham certainly took part in this rebellion, but it seems highly unlikely that he was the orchestrator of the entire movement, which, in the end, comprised at least three different – and mutually incompatible – aims.

When he became king, Richard III rewarded Buckingham for his support by returning to him and his family lands formerly held by the Lancastrian kings. Then on Monday, 21 July, Richard set off on a royal tour of parts of his kingdom. He, the queen and their party rode first from Windsor to Reading. Three days later they were in Oxford. By the beginning of August they had reached Gloucester, and it was there that the Duke of Buckingham last saw his cousin, the king, face to face.

One key factor in the events of July 1483 was that, during Richard III's absence from the capital, attempts were definitely made in London to access the sons of Edward IV, who, at that point, were still living in the Tower. Whether these attempts were intended to rescue the boys or to kill them, and whether the attempts succeeded or failed, is far from clear, but from the meagre evidence which survives, there is no doubt that such attempts took place.

It is interesting, therefore, that Continental sources tell us that it was none other than the Duke of Buckingham who was responsible for the disappearance of the two boys from the Tower. In his role of Constable of England, Buckingham would potentially have had sufficient authority to send men into the Tower of London. It is possible, therefore, that, taking advantage of Richard III's departure on his royal tour, Buckingham sent men to the Tower on or about Tuesday, 22 July 1483, either to kill the sons of Edward IV, or to extract them from their place of detention.

Buckingham might well have wanted the boys in his hands as living hostages. Perhaps his plan was to use them later, in some way, for his own advantage. We have already seen that he often seems to have had his own axe to grind. And it could well have been his discovery of Buckingham's involvement in the mysterious disappearance of the two sons of Edward IV which caused Richard III to describe his cousin as 'the most untrue creature living'.[39]

A small beam of light – though it is still a very murky light – is shed upon what took place in London by Richard III's rapid decision to send John Howard, Duke of Norfolk (the Earl Marshall of England) back to London, either on Tuesday 22nd, or on Wednesday 23 July 1483. It appears that Howard had originally intended to accompany the king throughout his royal tour, but in the end he only travelled with the royal party as far as Reading and Caversham. The king then sent him back to the capital on a very important mission, which seems to have been connected with some men who had been apprehended, and who were detained at Richard III's former London home as Duke of Gloucester – Crosby's Place in Bishopsgate.

The warrant which Richard III subsequently issued on Tuesday, 29 July, at Minster Lovell, was almost certainly linked with Howard's mission. It refers to prisoners detained for their recent involvement in some 'enterprise'. No details of the alleged crime are specified in the warrant. However, we know from other sources that there had been unauthorised attempts both to extract the late King Edward IV's daughters from sanctuary at Westminster and also to remove his sons from the Tower of London.

A plot by a number of Londoners in favour of the sons of Edward IV was reported by the Frenchman Thomas Basin, who probably wrote down his account early in 1484. Later, the sixteenth-century chronicler John Stow also speaks of a plot to abduct Edward V and his brother by setting off incendiary diversions in the neighbourhood of the Tower of London.

It seems probable that, upon receipt of the king's instructions from Minster Lovell, The Chancellor, Bishop Russell, and the royal council, deferred to the Duke of Norfolk, whom the king had sent to sit in judgement upon those prisoners who had plotted to secure some or all of Edward IV's children. It appears that the trial of at least some of these individuals

The Great Hall of Crosby's Place, Bishopsgate (on the right of the picture). Here John Howard, Duke of Norfolk, tried some of the men who had rescued – or attempted to rescue – the sons of Edward IV from the Tower of London in 1483.

took place at Crosby's Place, during the following month. References to the expenses incurred in preparing Crosby's Place for such a trial are to be found in John Howard's accounts for the beginning of August.

So something definitely happened in London on or around 22 July 1483, which involved the sons of Edward IV. There appears to be no way now of establishing for certain whether the person responsible for the plot (probably the Duke of Buckingham) succeeded in securing the persons of Edward V and his brother the Duke of York, but it is certainly possible that he did so. It is therefore significant that the event known as Buckingham's Rebellion began in the south and south-west of England, and that its initial and openly declared aim was to restore Edward V to the throne.

The supporters of this movement were a very mixed bunch. Some were men who had been loyal to Edward IV, but who had now been dismissed and replaced with his own loyal servants by the new king, Richard III. Others were members of the Woodville family and its supporters. Presumably both these groups felt either a genuine loyalty to, or a self-interest in, Edward IV's son. Probably they also either did not understand the complex reasoning behind the pronouncement of his illegitimacy, or they did not care about it.

At the same time, other people involved in Buckingham's Rebellion had a very different political background. Some of them were former Lancastrians. These men presumably had a totally different idea of who should now be King of England. Indeed, they were probably behind the subsequent change in the focus of the rebellion – from support for the cause of Edward V, to support for the cause of the Beaufort descendant Henry Tudor.

Moreover, one thing is certain. It was this Lancastrian group which began to spread a rumour that the sons of Edward IV were dead. Of course, this was a story very much in their interest, since it would hopefully persuade the former supporters of Edward V to transfer their allegiance to Henry Tudor.

As for the Duke of Buckingham himself, his place in all this is totally unclear. Possibly he was hoping to make himself protector, with one of Edward IV's sons on the throne as king. It is also possible that, since Edward V had formally been declared illegitimate, Buckingham may have considered it better to dispose of the elder boy, while retaining Edward IV's younger son, Richard, Duke of York as a living potential claimant to the throne. In either case, Buckingham's longer-term aim might well have been to claim the throne for himself.

However, later Tudor accounts tell us that Buckingham was then won over by Margaret Beaufort, Countess of Richmond and Derby, to give his support to *her* son, Henry Tudor. Certainly Buckingham wrote to Henry Tudor on 28 September. By this time the sons of Edward IV seem to have somehow disappeared, and the plan – reshaped by such cunning Lancastrians as Bishop Morton of Ely – was now to enthrone Henry Tudor and to marry him to Edward IV's eldest daughter.

It was not until Saturday, 11 October, that Richard III discovered that Buckingham himself had betrayed him. On Wednesday, 15 October, Buckingham was formally proclaimed a rebel and traitor. On Saturday, 18 October, Buckingham openly unfurled his rebellious banners. But London was defended against him by the loyal John Howard, Duke of Norfolk. Based on the news received from Howard, Richard III then focussed his personal attention on dealing with the rebels in the south-west. On Friday, 24 October, the king led his army to Coventry. Meanwhile Buckingham's banners had attracted little support. Bishop John Morton therefore abandoned the Duke, fleeing first to the fenlands around his own cathedral at Ely, and then taking ship to the Low Countries. Buckingham, now in despair, disguised himself in peasants' clothing and tried to conceal himself in Shropshire.

By the end of October he had been captured. He was brought to Richard III at Salisbury, where the panic-stricken Duke begged the king to see him, but Richard absolutely refused.

Whether, if Richard had agreed, Buckingham would have been able to reveal to the king the hiding place of Edward IV's living sons – or the location of their buried remains – we shall now never know. On Sunday, 2 November 1483, Henry, Duke of Buckingham was beheaded in Salisbury Market.

Of course, in the present context, the prime aim of our investigation is not to resolve the issue of the fate of Edward IV's sons, or to reinvestigate the claims of Perkin Warbeck. Our objective is to examine the true identity of the Dublin King. From our investigation of the story of the sons of Edward IV, fascinating new evidence of what might have happened to the two boys has hopefully emerged. However, no evidence whatsoever has come to light to connect either Edward V or Richard of Shrewsbury with the boy crowned in Dublin in 1487. It is therefore time to move on from the stories of these two 'princes' and to explore alternative accounts and evidence relating to the true identity of the Dublin King.

3

Edward, Earl of Warwick
– Authorised Version

No fifteenth-century writer ever attempted to identify the Dublin King with Edward V, the elder son of Edward IV. With the exception of Bernard André, none of them seriously attempted to identify him with Edward IV's younger son, Richard of Shrewsbury, Duke of York – or with an impostor claiming to be Richard. It is true that Polydore Vergil (perhaps influenced by André's account) does suggest that the boy's puppet masters considered at one point the possibility of a Richard of Shrewsbury imposture. But Vergil then goes on to say that they rapidly abandoned the idea.

Before considering Vergil's account in detail, let us first turn back to the Burgundian chronicler Jean de Molinet, who wrote in, or just before, 1504. In respect of the sons of Edward IV, Molinet proved to be not very accurately informed – and perhaps not very deeply interested. However, in the case of the Dublin King, one of whose key supporters was Margaret of York, Duchess of Burgundy, the Burgundian background of Molinet makes him a potentially very interesting source. It is fascinating, therefore, to discover that Molinet reported that:

> one little branch, engendered by a Royal tree, had been nurtured amongst the fruitful and lordly shrubs of Ireland … this very noble branch is Edward, son of the Duke of Clarence, who, based upon the advice and moral deliber-

ation of the nobles of Ireland, and with the support of a number of barons of England, his wellwishers, decided after due debate to have himself crowned king, and to expel from his royal throne the Earl of Richmond, who was then in possession of the crown of England.[1]

Two interesting points emerge immediately from Molinet's statement. The first is that the boy who was crowned as the Dublin King was 'Edward, son of the Duke of Clarence', in other words the genuine Earl of Warwick. As we shall see in due course, Molinet is not the only contemporary Burgundian chronicler who reported that the Dublin King was the real Earl of Warwick. The second point made by Molinet is that this Yorkist princeling had been 'nurtured amongst the … lordly shrubs of Ireland'. This gives the impression that the boy had been in Ireland for several years at least. We shall review the implication underlying that notion in detail, and also review other Burgundian and Irish sources which back up Molinet's version of events, in the next chapter.

About ten years after Molinet penned his version of events, Henry VII's leading historian, Polydore Vergil, wrote his account, which runs as follows:

[There was] a popular rumor that Edward's sons survived and had secretly fled somewhere, and that Edward Earl of Warwick, the son of the Duke of Clarence, had either been murdered, or soon would be. These rumors, although quite false, encouraged Richard Simons [*sic*], so that he fancied the time would come when Lambert could plausibly assume the guise of one of those royal boys and claim the kingdom, being assured that he would not lack helping hands, since most of the hatreds arising from factions are everlasting (for he measured others according to his own standard). And so, led by this hope, he took his Lambert to Oxford, where he studied letters and with wonderful zeal began to acquire royal manners, the goodly arts, and to memorize the royal pedigree, so that, when the need should arise, the common people might admire the boy's character and more readily believe this lie. Not much later a rumor went abroad that Earl Edward of Warwick had died in prison. When Simons learned this, thinking the time had come for his intended crime, he changed the lad's name and called him Edward, the name of the Duke of Clarence's son, *who was of the same age, so that neither was older than the other*, and immediately took him and crossed over to Ireland. There he secretly met with some of the Irish peerage whom he had learned by rumor to be disaffected towards Henry, and when they had taken an oath of secrecy he told them that he had saved from death the Duke of Clarence's son and had brought him to that land, which he heard had always uniquely loved King Edward's name and stock. This matter gained their ready credence and was then revealed to others, and was taken as Gospel truth to the point that Thomas Fitzgerald, the island's Chancellor, was especially deceived by this show of truth and offered the boy his hospitality, as if he were born of the royal blood, and began to help him with all his might.[2]

Four significant questions arise from Vergil's account. These questions will be highlighted now, and then re-examined in subsequent chapters. The first question concerns Vergil's statement that the priest, whose name he gives as Richard Simons, *took* Lambert Simnel to Oxford. The implication is that Simnel (and therefore presumably his family) were not inhabitants of that city.

Second, Vergil states that there were rumours of the death of the Earl of Warwick. From its context in his account the implication would appear to be that these rumours were in the air in about 1486. However, no other evidence survives to support this allegation.

Vergil's third questionable point is his statement that Lambert Simnel and the Earl of Warwick were of the same age. This definitely appears to be an error, for the contemporary official statement in the Rolls of Parliament gives Lambert Simnel's age in 1487 as 10 years,[3] whereas the Earl of Warwick would have been 12 years old at that time. In fact, Vergil seems sometimes to have been in a muddle about the ages of both boys, since he specifically (but incorrectly) suggests at one point that in August 1485 Warwick was aged 15.

Since there were no such things as birth certificates in the fifteenth century, no one can possibly have seen written evidence of Lambert Simnel's age. Thus, the figure of 10 years given in Henry VII's Parliamentary records was presumably an estimate, based on the boy's height and appearance. That makes the age estimate, and the two-year difference between it and the real chronological age of the Earl of Warwick, potentially rather interesting. This is a point which will be explored in greater detail in the next chapter.

Finally, Vergil states explicitly that Lambert Simnel was only taken to Ireland (by Richard Simons) after rumours began to circulate of the death of the Earl of Warwick in prison – i.e. presumably in 1486. This conflicts with Molinet's evidence (see above), which clearly implies that the Dublin King had spent at least part of his childhood in Ireland, where he had been brought up in noble houses. Of course, there is also another obvious difference between the accounts of Molinet and Vergil. Whereas Molinet states explicitly that the Dublin King was Edward of Clarence, Earl of Warwick, Vergil says that he was not Warwick, but merely impersonated him.

From what has already begun to emerge about the childhood of the Earl of Warwick, it must already be apparent that, whereas initially it appeared that his might be *one* of the possible alternative stories of the childhood of the Dublin King requiring consideration, in fact the true picture is rather more complex. For the childhood of Warwick seems to have at least *two* possible versions. First, there is what might be termed the authorised version of Edward's life – the version officially endorsed by three successive kings: Edward IV, Richard III and Henry VII. According to this version of Edward's story he was brought up in England, passing, after the death of his father, through the hands of various high-born English guardians.

However, after recounting that officially recognised story – and before we can begin to review the account of the Dublin King's possible childhood identity as Lambert Simnel – we must also consider an alternative version of the life of Edward, Earl of Warwick. According to this second version, Warwick may have left the land of his birth at a very young age, and been brought up across the sea, in Ireland. Before considering that alternative account, however, let us first resume and conclude the authorised version of Warwick's life.

Warwick's father, George, Duke of Clarence, born in 1449, had been the middle of those three sons of Richard and Cecily, Duke and Duchess of York, who survived the vicissitudes both of a medieval childhood and the Wars of the Roses to

George, Duke of Clarence and his wife, Isabel Neville, Duchess of Clarence – the second possible parents of the Dublin King.

attain adult status. His elder (and indeed, much older) brother was Edward, Earl of March – later Edward IV. His younger brother, who was quite close to George in age, and with whom he spent much of his childhood, was Richard, Duke of Gloucester (Richard III). Of these three brothers, George was, in worldly terms, the least successful. He never attained the throne of England – or indeed any throne – despite the fact that his ambitions included the possibility of attaining an independant realm of his own in the Low Countries.

Politically, George was very close to his much older cousin, Richard Neville, the Kingmaker, Earl of Warwick. As a result – and despite the initial opposition of his brother, King Edward IV – George eventually married the Kingmaker's elder daughter and co-heiress, Isabel Neville. By Isabel, George had four children. However, his first child was born dead, or died soon after birth, and his youngest son also died very young. In his father's eyes, that final little baby boy – together with his mother, the Duchess of Clarence – were poisoned at the instigation of his enemy, Elizabeth Woodville, the bigamous second wife of his brother the king, and the mother of the two boys who had displaced George from the prospect of succession to the English throne.

One ironic outcome of the marriage of the Duke and Duchess of Clarence is the fact that this fifteenth-century couple has a large number of living descendants in the world today. Their second daughter, Margaret, Countess of Salisbury, born at Farleigh Hungerford Castle in Somerset, lived long, and, by her marriage to Sir Richard Pole, produced a number of children. Had Henry VIII not decided to have her head cut off on 27 May 1541, Margaret's life would have been even longer. Every known living descendant of George and Isabel is also a descendant of their daughter Margaret.

However, it is the third child – and first son – of George and Isabel, born at Warwick Castle on 25 February 1474/75, who is the focus of our attention in the present context. This little boy's two godfathers were his uncle, King Edward IV, and John Strensham, Abbot of Tewkesbury. It was in honour of the senior godfather, his uncle, the king, that the little boy was baptised Edward. The king then went on to create him Earl of Warwick.[4] Edward is one of the boys at the centre of this book, for in the opinion of many of those who attended the coronation of the Dublin King in 1487, that king was none other than Edward of Clarence, Earl of Warwick. Indeed, even the majority of those who do not accept that identity nevertheless believe that the Dublin King at least *claimed* to be Warwick – even if he was, in reality, a poor boy from Oxford.

Christine Carpenter's bizarre statement about his title not-withstanding,[5] in fact, despite the attainder and execution of his father, the young Edward always retained the rank of Earl of Warwick. This was because it had not come to him via a paternal line inheritance. Rather, it had been specifically granted to him by the king in right of his maternal descent. On his mother's side the little boy was the Kingmaker's grand-son. As we shall see presently the surviving household accounts of Edward IV prove incontrovertibly that the little boy always continued to hold the Warwick title, and that his tenure was completely unaffected by his father's attainder and execution.

The precise movements of the Duke of Clarence following his wife's death are a matter which we shall need to review in greater detail in the next chapter. For the moment, however, it is sufficient to note that when the Duke was arrested, in the summer of 1477, his son, the Earl of Warwick, would have been only 2½ years old. Presumably the little boy was then residing at Warwick Castle, which had been his parents' main home since 1471. Like all children of his rank he must have had a staff of nurses and other servants to care for him. He had probably seen little of his mother, who had died when he was less than 2 years old. It is also somewhat doubtful how well he will have known his father, given his still very young age at the time of the Duke's arrest. When Clarence was executed, on 18 February 1477/78, Warwick was a week away from his third birthday. His awareness of what had happened must therefore have been very slight.

Because his father's execution had left him an orphan, in 1478 the boy required a guardian, and in 1481 his wardship was assigned by the king to the latter's own stepson, Thomas Grey, Marquess of Dorset, son of Elizabeth Woodville by her first marriage. Although Edward IV had stood as godfather to the little boy, it is not certain that he had actually attended the baptism in person. It is therefore also not certain whether he had ever set eyes on his nephew. Even if he had seen him at the baptism, however, that would have been when the boy was less than a month old. Edward IV's personal ability to recognise that same nephew three years later must therefore be open to question.

Since the Marquess of Dorset held the governership of the Tower of London, it seems likely that, having been assigned to his care, the little boy was brought to London, where he then probably spent the greater part of the years from 1478 until 1483 at the Tower – ironically the very building in which his father had been executed. Whether the Marquess of Dorset had ever seen the Earl of Warwick before the little boy was given into his charge is completely unknown.

Having accepted the child who had been delivered to them by the servants of the dead Duke of Clarence, Edward IV and his family in London naturally treated the little boy as a relative; as a member of the royal family, and as a person of potential future importance. The king's surviving household accounts include the following entries:

> To th'Erle off Warrewyk to have for his were and use, iiij peire of shoon double soled and a peire of shoon of Spaynyssh leder single soled, by virtue of a warrant under the Kinges signe mannuelle and signet bering date the second day of Juyn in the xxti yere of the moost noble reigne of our said Souverain Lorde the King [2 June 1480].[6]

To th'Erle of Warrewyk to have of the yifte of oure said Souverain Lorde the Kyng for his use and were, a peire of shoon single soled of blue leder; a paire of shoon of Spaynyssh leder; a paire of botews of tawny Spaynyssh leder; and ij paire shoon single soled … and unto the Maister off the Kinges Barge ayenst the commyng of the righte high and right noble Princesse Lady Margarete the Duchesse of Bourgoingne suster unto our saide Souverain Lorde the Kyng, a gowne of blak chamelet, by virtue of a warrant under thye Kynges signet and signe manuelle bering date the xxiiijti day of Juylle in the xxti yere of the moost noble reigne of oure said Souverain Lord the Kyng [24 July 1480].[7]

These accounts show that, following the execution of Clarence, Edward IV continued to take some interest in his nephew, the Earl of Warwick. They also demonstrate incontrovertibly that the young boy definitely did hold the title of 'Earl of Warwick', despite the curious comments on this point in his *ODNB* entry. In addition, the interesting fact emerges that the little boy may well have seen and been seen by his aunt, Margaret, Duchess of Burgundy during her visit to England in 1480. At the time of Margaret's visit the Earl of Warwick was 5 years old.

In 1483, following the death of his uncle and godfather, King Edward IV, and in the aftermath of the attempted Woodville plot to take over the government of England – and its eventual failure – the little boy's guardian, the Marquess of Dorset, fled the country to join Henry Tudor. As a result, the young Earl of Warwick was once again briefly left without a guardian. However, his younger paternal uncle, the new king, Richard III, took charge of him. Warwick attended Uncle Richard's coronation in July 1483, and was knighted on the occasion of the investiture of his cousin, Edward of Middleham, as Prince of Wales, in September of that same year. After his coronation, Richard III established Warwick, together with the daughters of Edward IV, and possibly some other young Yorkist scions, at the Castle of Sheriff Hutton in Yorkshire.

This castle was situated 10 miles from the city of York. It had originally been built in the reign of King Stephen, and was christened Sheriff Hutton because its builder was the sheriff of Yorkshire. However, it was subsequently inherited by the Neville family, and Ralph Neville, Earl of Westmorland, the brother-in-law and supporter of Henry IV, 'rebuilt, enlarged, and strongly fortified the castle'.[8] Sheriff Hutton remained in the hands of the Nevilles until Richard Neville, Earl of Warwick was killed fighting on the wrong side at the Battle of Barnet. All the Kingmaker's possessions were then seized by Edward IV, who granted the castle and manor of Sheriff Hutton to the late owner's younger son-in-law, his own brother, Richard, Duke of Gloucester.

In 1483, following the death of Edward IV, Richard used Sheriff Hutton Castle initially to imprison Anthony Woodville, Earl Rivers. But this was for a short time only, for Rivers was then sent on to Pontefract, where he was beheaded. According to the mid nineteenth-century account of William Grainge:

> After Richard had cleared his way to the throne by the murder of his brother's children, he imprisoned in this castle, Edward Plantagenet, son of his brother, the duke of Clarence, earl of Warwick, and Elizabeth, eldest daughter of his late brother, king Edward.[9]

This sentence is full of the most amazing Ricardian mythology, for, of course, Richard attained the throne by judgement that Edward's children were bastards, and not by murder. Likewise there is no reason whatever for describing young Warwick's residence at Sheriff Hutton as an imprisonment.

Grainge is more useful when it comes to his description of Sheriff Hutton Castle itself. First he quotes Leland, who had seen the castle before it was ruined:

Ther is a base court with houses of office besides the enter-
ing. The Castell itself in front is not ditched, but it standeth
in loco utcunque edito. I marked in the front part of the first
area of the castell three great and high Towres, of the which
the Gatehouse was the middle. In the second area be five or
six towers, and the statlie stair up to the Haul is very mag-
nificent, and so is the Haul itself, and all the residue of the
House; insomuch that I saw no house in all the north so like
a princely lodging.[10]

The fact that this was the most princely of the northern
castles presumably provides the true explanation as to why
Richard III chose to house (not *imprison*) his nephews and
nieces there.

Sadly, Sheriff Hutton Castle has been in ruins since the
seventeenth century:

The ruins stand on a hill, to the south of the village, and
consist of the remains of four large corner towers, with a
part of the warder's tower over the entrance on the east
side. The towers are of considerable elevation, especially
that at the south-west corner, which is one hundred feet
in height; square, massive, perpendicular, and plain, without buttresses, or architectural ornament of any kind. In
the base of this tower, is a vault or dungeon … Above, is
another room, arched in a similar manner, and in a tol-
erable state of preservation. The rooms above are broken
down, and in a state of ruin. The circular stair which led
to the top of the tower, has been entirely taken away. …
The principal entrance has been on the east side; the not
very lofty pointed arch of the gateway yet remains, with
four shields carved on stone above it. The inner area of the
castle is overgrown with grass … The castle has not been
moated in front, and only partly on the northern side; on
the southern, are the remains of a double moat, about two
hundred yards in length, each division being about five

yards wide, and full of water; these meet at an acute angle
on the west, with another fosse, partly filled with water
from the north side of the castle.[11]

At Sheriff Hutton Castle the young Yorkists came under
the supervision of their older cousin John de la Pole, Earl of
Lincoln. A figure of great importance in this story, Lincoln
was born in about 1460. He was the eldest son of Elizabeth
of York and her husband, John de la Pole, Duke of Suffolk.
The Duchess of Suffolk was the middle sister of Edward IV
and Richard III. Edward IV had created her eldest son Earl of
Lincoln on 13 March 1466/67. Later, the young Earl had been
knighted, together with Edward's own sons, on 18 April 1475.
On the occasion of Anne Mowbray's marriage to Edward IV's
second son, Richard, Duke of York in January 1477/78,
Lincoln had attended the child bride. Subsequently he had
borne the salt at the baptism of Edward's daughter Bridget
in November 1480. In the absence of the future Richard III
himself, Lincoln had acted as the chief mourner at the funeral
of King Edward IV in 1483. Finally, at Richard III's coronation
Lincoln was given a position of honour, and carried the orb.[12]
By 1485 he was already a young adult:

> Lincoln supported Richard against the rebels of October
> 1483 and was rewarded the following April with land
> worth £157, and the reversion of Beaufort estates worth
> a further £178 after the death of Thomas, Lord Stanley,
> who had been granted a life interest in the land which
> his wife, Margaret Beaufort, had forfeited for her part in
> the rising. In the following month Lincoln was granted an
> annuity of £177 13s. 4d. from the duchy of Cornwall until
> the reversion materialized.[13]

The new king, Richard III, who might possibly have encountered the real Earl of Warwick as a baby, had probably not seen
much of him since, because Richard himself had spent the

greater part of the intervening years in the north of England, while Warwick, as we have seen, had probably been based in London under the care of the Marquess of Dorset. Therefore in the summer of 1483, by which time Warwick was 8 years old, neither Richard, nor his wife, Anne Neville (who was the younger sister of Warwick's late mother, the Duchess of Clarence – and therefore Warwick's aunt by blood as well as by marriage), would have been in any position to personally recognise their nephew when they met him. As in the case of Edward IV and the Marquess of Dorset, five years earlier, the new king and queen must simply have accepted the boy who was presented to them under the Warwick title. Richard then took charge of this boy, and treated him as of noble and royal status. Both Warwick and Lincoln were promoted by Richard III, who saw these royal nephews as potentially important future figures within the Yorkist royal family.

Following the deaths of his own son, Edward of Middleham, and of his wife, Anne Neville (which both occurred in 1484, according to the medieval year reckoning), Richard III found himself with no direct heir. As a result, throughout 1485 (right up until his death at the Battle of Bosworth) he was planning a second marriage, to an infanta.[14] His preference was for the Infanta Joana of Portugal. However, a second possible choice was the Infanta Isabel of Spain (an elder sister of Catherine of Aragon). Both of these possible brides were descendants of the house of Lancaster. Clearly, what Richard had in mind was to reunite the houses of York and Lancaster – just as Henry VII later claimed to do.

As far as Richard was aware, he still had many years of kingship before him in 1485. He must therefore have had every hope of producing another legitimate son of his own, as the future heir to the throne. Nevertheless, it is conceivable that, if he failed to produce such a son, Richard had the two Earls of Lincoln and Warwick in mind as potential future Yorkist kings. Indeed, it has often been said that he actually named one of them – either the Earl of Warwick or the Earl of Lincoln – as heir to his throne.[15] In fact there is no evidence that either nephew was ever formally designated as heir presumptive. Indeed, the conflicting accounts of different writers on this point merely serve to underline the lack of certainty.

It remains possible that, in August 1485, on the eve of what proved to be his final battle, Richard may have made some statement about the succession.[16] Moreover, if he did make such a statement, that could perhaps provide a clear explanation for the subsequent conduct of the Earl of Lincoln. Richard's marriage negotiations with Portugal had made excellent progress, and the marriage with the Infanta Joana would probably have taken place had Richard survived the battle. But the fact is that in August 1485 he had no queen and no son to succeed him. Some statement about the succession under these circumstances would perhaps have seemed logical.

But whatever plans Richard may have had for the future, during his short two-year reign he never got around to revoking the Act of Attainder against his brother, Clarence. This left the Earl of Warwick in a somewhat equivocal position as a potential heir. Logically, whether or not Richard III made any pre-battle statement on the subject, the heir presumptive to the throne prior to August 1485 should have been John de la Pole, Earl of Lincoln because the Act of Attainder against Clarence and his line was still in force.

However, Richard's own claim to the throne was based not only upon the bigamy of his elder brother, Edward IV, but also upon a wider range of criticisms of Edward, as outlined in the Act of Parliament of 1484. Although Edward IV's treatment of his brother, Clarence, was not specifically mentioned in that Act, Richard III and his supporters may have perceived the wider criticism of Edward IV as implying that the late king's actions against Clarence and his heirs were invalid.

It is therefore possible that on the eve of Bosworth Richard III named the Earl of Warwick as heir to the throne. If so, such a decision on the part of his uncle, taken on the eve of his death at Bosworth, could well explain the subsequent conduct of the Earl of Lincoln. It has already been noted that Lincoln amazed Henry VII by backing the claim of the Dublin King (whom Lincoln explicitly recognised as Warwick), rather than seeking to win the crown for himself. In this apparently puzzling situation, most historians offer cynical explanations of Lincoln's conduct, which they see as certainly intriguing, but probably sneaky. Maybe this tells us more about the mentality of the writers in question than it does about Lincoln. If King Richard III had announced, or stated in his will, just before he was killed, that, in the event of his death, Warwick should be the next King of England, surely that might possibly explain Lincoln's subsequent loyalty to the Dublin King.

Leaving on one side their respective claims to the throne, in the eyes of Richard III both Lincoln and Warwick were promising bulwarks who could – and hopefully would – support and maintain the royal house of York on the English throne well into the coming century. Richard III therefore had every reason to train and promote them as future key supporters for the throne. Richard III's son, Edward of Middleham, Prince of Wales, had briefly held the important post of Lieutenant of Ireland before he died.[17] After Edward of Middleham's death, Richard appointed Lincoln to the same post (21 August 1484). Lincoln was also created president of the Council of the North. This was a body established in

A representation of Edward of Clarence, Earl of Warwick. This is not a true 'portrait' since he was only a child when the picture was drawn.

the summer of 1484 'as the successor to the prince's council, which had itself replaced Gloucester's ducal council as a way of maintaining Richard's authority in the north'.[18]

Like Lincoln, Warwick was also a member of the Council of the North.[19] In Warwick's case (given his youth) his membership was probably largely nominal in 1485, but it certainly indicates Richard III's intention that this younger nephew, too, should be trained to play some role in the politics of the future.

Following the Battle of Bosworth, in August 1485, Warwick's situation changed yet again. Having seized power, the new king, Henry VII, sent at once to Sheriff Hutton. Naturally, his first objective was to secure the person of his potential bride, Elizabeth of York, eldest daughter of Edward IV and Elizabeth Woodville. As we have seen, Henry intended to reverse Elizabeth's bastardy, in order that he might marry her and present her to his people as the Yorkist heiress. But Elizabeth of York did not journey to London alone. She was almost certainly accompanied by her sisters and by some of her cousins.

Naturally, all the surviving Yorkist heirs were perceived as potential threats by Henry VII. They therefore had to be rounded up and placed under secure control. Moreover, interestingly, in spite of the Act of Attainder passed against his father, Clarence, which was arguably still in force, Henry VII seems to have perceived the young Earl of Warwick as a particularly strong danger. Could it be that Henry had been informed that, on the eve of the Battle of Bosworth, Richard III had designated Warwick as his heir?

That is one possibility. However, a much more likely source for Henry VII's fear of Warwick was the new king's own uncle, Jasper, Earl of Pembroke. In the period 1470 to 1471, during the Lancastrian Readeption, George, Duke of Clarence had sided with the Lancastrians against his own brother, Edward IV. Jasper knew this very well, since he had been in regular contact with George at that time. He also knew the precise consequences of George's Lancastrianism: one result of the Duke of Clarence's support for the restoration of Henry VI was that

George had been formally recognised by the last Lancastrian king as second in line to the throne, after Henry VI's alleged son, Edward of Westminster, Prince of Wales. When this information was coupled with the fact that subsequently Henry VI and Edward of Westminster had both died, leaving no surviving children – and with the fact that George himself had also died – legally, the Lancastrian heir to the throne in 1485 was not Henry VII, but George's only surviving son – namely the Earl of Warwick. In other words, according to the agreement sealed by Henry VI, it was the Earl of Warwick who should now be king. Arguably, this Lancastrian claim would have been completely unaffected by the Act of Attainder passed by the Yorkist usurper, Edward IV, in 1477.

His inherited – and unassailable – Lancastrian claim to the throne therefore made Warwick the most dangerous surving member of the house of York from Henry VII's point of view. And indeed, it is absolutely clear that in the new king's opinion, 'Dynastically the young Plantagenet offered the greatest threat to Henry's claim to the throne … One of Henry's first acts after Bosworth was to fetch the earl of Warwick from Sheriff Hutton, and keep him securely guarded'.[20] The new controller of the little prince was initially Henry VII's own very determined and forceful mother, Margaret Beaufort, Countess of Richmond and Derby. She was granted custody of Warwick in 1485, as this later note proves:

24 February 148[5/]6
Henry, by the grace of God, king of England and of Fraunce, and lord of Irland. To the tresourer and chambrelains of oure Eschequier greting. Forasmoche as oure moste dere moder, at our singuler plesure and request of late hadde the keping and guiding of the ladies, doughtres of King Edward the iiijth, and also of the yong lordes, the duc of Buk,[21] therles of Warwik and of Westmerland,[22] to her grate charges, For the which oure right trusty servaunt Maister William Smyth, keper of oure hanaper within oure

Chancery, at oure special commaundement, hath paied and delivered unto oure saide moder the somme of cc, Ii., for the which he hath not hadde of us any warrant or othre matier suffisaunt for his discharge in the premises. [*The text went on to say that king would now reimburse Smyth.*].[23]

Later, as we shall see, Warwick was permanently confined in the Tower of London by Henry VII. In effect, he became the third 'prince in the Tower'. Indeed, we have already noted that Vergil alleges that there were rumours of Warwick's death in the Tower in about 1486.[24] However, no other sources survive to confirm Vergil's statement.

Thus the official account of his life tells us that the real Earl of Warwick remained in England from before his father's death in 1477, until 1485. Could he then have escaped and gone to Ireland? Was the later prisoner in the Tower – who supposedly suffered from mental deficiency, and who was held (and later executed) by Henry VII – the authentic earl? All these are issues to which we shall return later. First, however, it is now necessary to consider an alternative childhood history for the Earl of Warwick. This is a completely different story from the official version. However, it is the story hinted at by the intriguing words of Jean de Molinet.

4

Edward, Earl of Warwick
– Alternative Version

We have already noted that the Burgundian chronicler Molinet reported unequivocally that the Dublin King was 'Edward, son of the Duke of Clarence', and therefore the young Earl of Warwick. Not only did Molinet state the Dublin King's true identity as a matter beyond question; he also believed that the boy had been 'nurtured amongst the … lordly shrubs of Ireland'

Interestingly, one contemporary Irish version of the events, as recorded in the *Annals of Ulster*, appears to confirm Molinet's account in both respects:

> A great fleet of Saxons came to Ireland this year [1487] to **meet** the son [*sic* = grandson] of the Duke of York, **who was exiled at this time with the Earl of Kildare**, namely, Gerald, son of Earl Thomas. And there lived not of the race of the blood royal that time but that son of the Duke and he was proclaimed King on the Sunday of the Holy Ghost [3 June – Feast of Pentecost], in the town of Ath Cliath [Dublin].[1]

Despite a slight error in the date,[2] the wording of this report is highly significant. Not only do the *Annals of Ulster* confirm the view that the Dublin King was a genuine member of the royal house of York (and indeed the key surviving member of that family), but they also make it very clear that he was already living in Ireland before his supporters from England came to join him, having himself been 'exiled' in Ireland at some earlier date (not specified). Since the date of his 'exile', he had been residing in Ireland with the Earl of Kildare.

This version of the boy's history clearly echoes Molinet's statement that he had been brought up by Irish nobles (*'nourri entre les fertils et seigneurieux arbrisseaux d'Irlande'*). Even more significantly, it also calls to mind one of the charges which had been brought against the Earl of Warwick's father, George, Duke of Clarence, in 1477/78. That charge against Clarence will be examined in detail in just a moment.

First, however, we should also note that although both the Burgundian chronicler Jean de Molinet and the writer of the Irish *Annals of Ulster* believed that the Dublin King really was the Earl of Warwick, they are not the only surviving sources which offer this opinion. Another Burgundian chronicler, Adrien de But, also states unequivocally that the Dublin King was the son of George, Duke of Clarence. During the 1440s De But, later the prior of the Benedictine Abbey of the Dunes, had spent part of his youth at school in Mechelen, where he had relatives. Mechelen was later the home and power-base of Margaret of York, dowager Duchess of Burgundy. As we shall see, another contemporary source shows that it was in Mechelen that Margaret received the Duke of Clarence's son in 1486. Through his family connections with the town, De But had every chance of accessing the views of the court of Margaret of York more or less straight from the horse's mouth. De But makes one very small error in his account, in that he calls the boy the *Duke* of Warwick. This error in the title probably stems from a slight confusion between Warwick's rank and that of his late father. Nevertheless, De But was clearly knowledgeable in some respects. For example, he was well aware that the young boy's right to the Warwick title had been inherited from his mother, Isabel Neville, and not from his father. Adrien de But's clear statements on the identity of the Dublin King are quoted *verbatim* in Chapter 6.

While Adrien de But confirms the statements of Molinet and of the *Annals of Ulster* in respect of the Dublin King's identity, unfortunately he has nothing to tell us about where young Warwick had been brought up. However, as we have seen, both the other sources thought that Warwick had not spent his childhood in England, as the authorised account of his life would have us believe, but had instead been brought up in Ireland. As has already been noted, this story, from two separate and more or less contemporary sources, calls to mind very strongly the fact that in 1478 Edward IV had accused Warwick's father, George, Duke of Clarence of attempting to smuggle the little boy out of the country.

The Act of Attainder against the Duke of Clarence expressed the charge in the following words:

> And also, the same Duke purposyng to accomplisse his said false and untrue entent, and to inquiete and trouble the Kynge, oure said Sovereigne Lorde, his Leige People and this his Royaulme, nowe of late willed and desired the Abbot of Tweybury, Mayster John Tapton, Clerk, and Roger Harewell Esquier, to cause a straunge childe to have be brought into his Castell of Warwyk, and there to have be putte and kept in likelinesse of his Sonne and Heire, and that they shulde have conveyed and sent his said Sonne and Heire into Ireland, or into Flaundres, oute of this Lande, whereby he myght have goten hym assistaunce and favoure agaynst oure said Sovereigne Lorde; and for the execucion of the same, sent oon John Taylour, his Servaunte, to have had delyveraunce of his said Sonne and Heire, for to have conveyed hym; the whiche Mayster John Tapton and Roger Harewell denyed the delyveraunce of the said Childe, and soo by Goddes grace his said false and untrue entent was lette and undoon.[3]

As reported here, the first part of Clarence's plot required John Strensham (or Streynsham), Abbot of Tewkesbury,[4] John Tapton and Roger Harewell to bring a child to Warwick Castle, with the intention that this substitute boy should then impersonate Clarence's little son, the Earl of Warwick. The second part of the plan was to send the real Earl of Warwick either to Ireland or to the Low Countries, either for his own safety, or in order to provide a focus for future rebellion against Edward IV (depending on how one interprets the planned getting of 'assistaunce and favoure agaynst oure said Sovereigne Lorde'). The Abbot of Tewkesbury was apparently a friend of the Clarence family, and as we have already seen, he was one of the godfathers of the Earl of Warwick (the other being the boy's uncle, King Edward IV, after whom he had been named).[5]

As reported in the Act of Attainder, the plot to send the Earl of Warwick abroad was planned in precise detail, involving named individuals, some of whom had obviously been interrogated as part of the proceedings against the Duke of Clarence. Moreover, at least part of the planned operation actually took place, because Clarence's servant John Taylour was dispatched to collect the real Earl of Warwick, in order to transport the child out of England. Meanwhile, together with the Abbot of Tewkesbury, Tapton and Harewell were supposed to produce a substitute child who would take the young Earl's place. When they were interrogated, however, Tapton and Harewell denied that they had actually handed over their substitute child. Within the context of the legal case conducted against the Duke of Clarence, the implication appears to be that the attempt to smuggle the real Earl of Warwick abroad with the help of the named servants and affinity members had not succeeded. And this is certainly how most historians appear to have construed the text.

However, a careful reading of the precise words of the Act reveals nothing to show that the genuine Earl of Warwick was not taken out of England by John Taylour. Unlike Tapton and Harewell, Taylour is not reported to have denied carrying out his instructions. Indeed, if he was out of the country, he would have been unavailable for questioning. The Act of Attainder certainly states quite specifically that John Taylour was sent somewhere (possibly to Warwick Castle) by the Duke of Clarence, to take charge of the young Earl, whom he was then to convey abroad, either to Ireland or to Flanders.

The only other information contained within the Act can be interpreted in two possible ways, depending on how one understands the key word '*denyed*'. One possibility is that the proposed substitute child who was to have been produced by Tapton and Harewell was withheld. In that case, the *original* planned substitution would not have materialised. However, that does not prove that *no* substitution ever took place. It leaves open the possibility that some other substitute child, from a different source, had subsequently been installed at Warwick Castle to assume the role of the little Earl of Warwick, who had been handed over to John Taylour.

The second possible interpretation is that, when interrogated, Tapton and Harewell (wishing, presumably, to escape charges against themselves) denied that they had carried out their instructions. That would tell us absolutely nothing about what actually occurred. It would merely show that, when questioned, Tapton and Harewell were afraid, and wished to distance themselves as far as possible from any involvement. In that case, it remains entirely conceivable that, despite what they said under interrogation, in reality Tapton and Harewell carried out the instructions they received from the Duke of Clarence.

Interestingly, George, Duke of Clarence, who was born at Dublin Castle, had been appointed Lord Lieutenant of Ireland in 1462, and held that post until his death.[6] In 1477, following the demise of his wife, Clarence accused one of her servants, Ankarette Twynyho, of having poisoned her. Strangely, however, he did not act upon this belief immediately after Isabel Neville's death. It was not until about 3 months later that he took action against Ankarette. An eighteenth-century writer mentions that Clarence visited Ireland in 1477.[7] The source is, of course, far from contemporary, but if the account is correct, the only time during 1476/77 (in terms of the medieval calendar) when the duke could have made such a visit was in the three months following Isabel's death. Subsequently his whereabouts are on record, and there is no indication that Clarence then left England. Therefore, it is possible that Clarence visited Ireland in January–March 1476/77. In that case his trip across the Irish Sea may have been the reason for the delay in his prosecution of Ankarette Twynyho.

But what important consideration could have made him delay proceedings against his wife's believed killer, in favour of a visit to Ireland? Could it be that Clarence himself accompanied John Taylour and the little Earl of Warwick to Dublin – or made a personal advance visit to speak to his deputy, the Earl of Kildare, in order to request the latter to receive the Earl of Warwick from the hands of John Taylour, assume guardianship of the little boy, and take care of him, bringing him up in Ireland? Under such highly unusual circumstances, a personal visit from the Duke of Clarence may well have seemed a wise precaution. After all, if the proposed scenario is correct, what Kildare was being asked to do in respect of an infant prince of the blood royal would have been something unprecedented. Thus, even a sealed letter from the Duke of Clarence might not have seemed sufficient to assure Kildare that he really was being asked to receive his lord's young son as his ward.

There is no question of the fact that the Dublin King later enjoyed the unqualified support of Gerald Mór Fitzgerald, eighth Earl of Kildare, who on 25 March 1477 (the first day of the New Year, according to the medieval English calendar) had succeeded his father, the seventh Earl, as the Duke of Clarence's Deputy Lieutenant of Ireland. It is therefore not implausible to suggest that Gerald (on behalf of his dying father) had personally received George in Ireland in February–March 1476/77 – at the very time when the duke was reported to have been plotting to send his son abroad secretly. It is also possible that the Earl of Kildare subsequently acted as guardian to the young Earl of Warwick, bringing him up, as Molinet later wrote, '*entre les fertils et seigneurieux arbrisseaux d'Irlande*' ('amongst the fruitful and lordly shrubs of Ireland'). Naturally, if the Earl of Kildare really did receive the little Earl of Warwick in 1476/77, at the request of the boy's father, no one would have been in a better position than the Fitzgerald family to know for certain that the Dublin King really was the son of the Duke of Clarence.

Incidentally, at this point it may be worth saying something about whether or not the Duke of Clarence is at all likely to have sent his son away in secret. At first glance, such a suggestion may appear highly improbable. However, given that George believed his family to be in danger – probably at the hands of Elizabeth Woodville – he may well have taken steps to protect his son and heir. Indeed, the Act of Attainder passed against him proves beyond any question that the government of the day believed that George had at least attempted to send his son away in secret.

Nor would such action have been unique for a noble family with royal connections at that period. When John, the ninth Lord Clifford (the killer of Edmund, Earl of Rutland – brother of Edward IV and Richard III), was killed by a Yorkist arrow on the day before the Battle of Towton, his 7-year-old son and heir, Henry, was spirited away, on his mother's instructions, from his family home at Skipton castle. Initially he was concealed as a shepherd-boy, living with the peasant family of his former nurse. Henry Clifford remained in hiding for twenty-four years, until Richard III was killed at the Battle of Bosworth, and the Act of Attainder against his late father was repealed.

As we have seen, following George's execution his (alleged) son in England was consigned to the guardianship of Elizabeth Woodville's son, the Marquess of Dorset. However, we have also seen that Dorset probably didn't know the real Earl of

Warwick from Adam. Even Dorset's stepfather, the king, would probably have been incapable of recognising his real nephew. If presented with a child of about the right age, brought to him by former servants of his late brother, Edward IV would doubtless have accepted the little boy as the Earl of Warwick without question.

In the light of this suggestion, it is intriguing – and potentially very important – to note that the Dublin King was later stated in Parliament, by Henry VII's official spokesmen, to have been aged about 10 in 1487. Since they had no access to any record of the boy's date of birth, this estimated age can only have been based upon the child's height and appearance. Significantly, however, the real Earl of Warwick, born in 1475, would not have been 10 years old in 1487. He would have been 12.

In this context it is also important to note that evidence was recently published (by this author), indicating that Warwick's father, the Duke of Clarence, was probably of below-average height.[8] Burgundian observers who encountered the young George and his brother, the future Richard III, in 1461, when they were in exile in the Low Countries, made an error in estimating George's age. In reality, at the date in question George was approximately 11½ years old, while Richard was about 8½ However, the chronicler Jehan de Wavrin,[9] having seen the two young Yorkist princes, guessed their ages as 9 and 8 respectively.[10] This suggests that when he was 8 years old Richard (III) was of about the normal average height for a boy of his age. At the same time, however, George, at the chronological age of 11½ , looked about two years younger. Based on the average heights recorded for modern boys aged 10 and 12, the height difference implied by this evidence would have been of the order of about 12.7cm (5in).[11]

This information about the height of the Duke of Clarence is very important in the present context. We are dealing here with evidence which indicates that in 1487 the Dublin King – who was reputed to be George's son – also appeared to be about two years younger than his true chronological age. When these two pieces of information are considered side by side, they can be interpreted as indicating that the Earl of Warwick simply took after his father. The evidence implies that when they were approaching the age of 12, both the Earl of Warwick and the Duke of Clarence were about 5 per cent below the average height for typical boys of their age.[12] Presumably Warwick had simply inherited the genes which determined his stature from his father, with the result that both of them were of below-average height. In that case, those who claimed that the Dublin King was the true Earl of Warwick could well have been telling the truth.

So was the pretender of 1487 the genuine Earl of Warwick? If his father had succeeded in secretly sending the boy abroad in 1477, then the Dublin King might well have been the prince he claimed to be. As we have seen, the 1487 pretender certainly enjoyed the support of Gerald, Earl of Kildare, who had formerly been the Duke of Clarence's Deputy Lieutenant of Ireland. Had Gerald received George in Ireland in February–March 1476/77, at the very time when the Duke is said to have been plotting to send his son secretly to Ireland? Did he therefore know for certain that the pretender was a genuine Yorkist prince?

Sadly, for about five hundred years such questions have largely been ignored by the standard English historical accounts of the story of 'Lambert Simnel'. Such accounts have simply reiterated endlessly, as unquestionable facts, the official statements of the government of Henry VII – a body which had the strongest possible political motive for doing everything in its power to ensure that the Dublin King was written off as an insignificant fraud. The only way to move forward from that position is to seek fresh evidence.

The alternative account of the childhood of the Earl of Warwick offered in this chapter has sought to do precisely that. What has emerged is that contemporary Burgundian and Irish sources believed the Dublin King truly was the Earl of

Warwick. They also thought he might have been brought up in Ireland since the age of about 2. The Act of Attainder against the Duke of Clarence, when read with care, indicates that the real Earl of Warwick had possibly been removed from his nursery at Warwick Castle in 1476/77, on his father's instructions. And while no fifteenth-century source tells us explicitly that the Dublin King looked like the Duke of Clarence, the evidence contained in some of the sources strongly suggests that they might have resembled one another in respect of their height. Is this fresh evidence sufficient to prove that the Dublin King really was the Earl of Warwick?

5

Lambert Simnel

There remains yet one other potential childhood of the Dublin King to consider.

Despite evidence from both Ireland and the Low Countries that chroniclers in both of those places believed that the Dublin King was the genuine Earl of Warwick, the official account of the Tudor government in England produced an entirely different explanation. The surviving *Herald's Memoir 1486–1490* reports the Battle of Stoke as follows:

> on the morne, whiche was Satirday [16 June 1487, Henry VII] erly arros and harde ij masses, wherof the lorde John [*sic* for Richard] Fox, bishop of Excester, sange the ton. And the king had v good and true men of the village of Ratecliff, whiche shewde his grace the beste way for to conduyt his hoost to Newark, … of whiche guides the king yave ij to therle of Oxinforde to conduit the forwarde [vanguard], and the remenant reteynede at his pleasur. And so in good order and array before ix of the clok, beside a village called Stook, a large myle oute of Newarke, his forwarde [vanguard] recountrede his enemyes and rebelles, wher by the helpe of Almyghty God he hade the victorye. And ther was taken the lade that his rebelles called King Edwarde

(whoos name was in dede John) – by a vaylent and a gentil esquire of the kings howse called Robert Bellingham.[1]

This account states quite clearly that according to the information available to the heralds, the boy captured at the Battle of Stoke was an impostor. As we have already noted from other sources, his official royal identity was that of 'King Edward'. Thus the heralds presumably accepted that at the time of his defeat the Dublin King was claiming to be the Earl of Warwick, son of the Duke of Clarence. However, the account goes on to report that he was a false claimant, whose real Christian name was John. No surname is recorded for him by this source.

Confusingly, however, the *Heralds' Memoir* account is contradicted by other Tudor sources. According to the Act of Attainder against John de la Pole, Earl of Lincoln, preserved among the records of Henry VII's 1487 Parliament:

> on 24 May last, at the city of Dublin, contrary to his homage, faith, truth and allegiance, [the Earl of Lincoln] traitorously renounced, revoked and disclaimed his own said most natural sovereign liege lord the king, and caused one Lambert Simnel, a child of ten years of age, son of Thomas Simnel late of Oxford, joiner, to be proclaimed, set up and acknowledged as king of this realm, and did faith and homage to him, to the great dishonour and shame of the whole realm.[2]

This record, dating from November 1487, is the earliest surviving source which gives Lambert Simnel as the name of the Dublin King. It is the only source for the alleged first name of Lambert's father. It is also the only source which states that his father's profession was that of a joiner. As we have already seen, Bernard André asserted that the Dublin King's father was a baker or a tailor.[3] An alternative source which will be presented shortly tells us that he was an organ maker. The record

in Lincoln's Act of Attainder also appears to imply that Lambert
and Thomas Simnel were permanent inhabitants of Oxford.
However, other sources imply that this was not the case.

Much earlier in the same year, according to the modern
calendar (or at the end of the previous year according to
the calendar of the time), on 13 February 1486/87, at the
Convocation of the Province of Canterbury, at St Paul's
Cathedral, London:

> A certain Sir William Symonds, was produced, a priest, of
> the age of twenty-eight years, as he declared, in the presence
> of the said lords and prelates and clergy who were there,
> as well as the mayor, aldermen, and sheriffs of the city of
> London. He publicly admitted and confessed that he took
> and carried off to Ireland the son of a certain [blank], organ
> maker of the University of Oxford, the which son was there
> reputed to be the Earl of Warwick, and that afterwards he
> was with Lord Lovell in Fuvnefotts. These, and other things
> were admitted by him in the same place. The said most
> reverend father in Christ [Archbishop John Morton] asked
> the aforesaid mayor and sheriffs, that the above mentioned
> Will. Symonds be brought unto the Tower of London, to be
> kept there for him, since the same most reverend father was
> holding another of the company of the said William, and
> had [space for] but one person in his manor of Lambeth.[4]

This slightly earlier account, reporting what took place at the
convocation, had not named either the pretender or his father.
Presumably these points either had not been discovered, or
perhaps had not been invented, at that point. The convocation report did, however, name the priest who confessed to
having taken the boy to Ireland, and who, according to this
account, was already a prisoner in the hands of Archbishop
John Morton in February 1486/87. There is also the curious
statement that Morton did not have room to imprison William
Symonds at Lambeth Palace, since he only had room there to

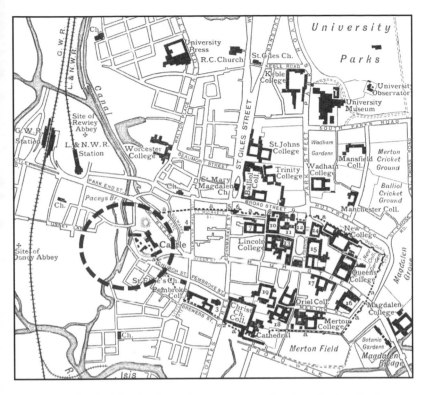

Map of Oxford, showing the area in which Thomas Simnel is said to have lived.

accommodate one detainee, and that space was already occupied by 'another of the company of the said William'. This
suggests that William Symonds either was, or was seen to be,
part of a group of conspirators. It may also suggest that he
was not perceived as being the most important member of the
conspiracy. At all events, another alleged member of the group
had also been detained, but was not made to appear before
the convocation – possibly because he was not a priest. The
name of this other detainee, and also his alleged role in the
conspiracy, remain unknown.

Curiously, as we have already seen, Polydore Vergil's
semi-official account of these events contradicts the earlier

convocation report in several respects. Vergil mentions a priest with a slightly different name: Richard Simons.[5] Moreover, Vergil says that Simons remained with his protégé until the Battle of Stoke. According to Vergil, it was only after their army's defeat in the battle that both Richard Simons and Lambert Simnel were captured together:

> Young Lambert the pretender was taken, together with his tutor Richard, but the lives of the both of them were spared, because the former was innocent and, thanks to his youth, had done no wrong, as being incapable of doing anything in his own right, and the latter was a priest.[6]

The obvious conflict between Vergil's account and the report from the Canterbury convocation is intriguing. The contemporary report of the convocation not only gives a different name for the priest but also states clearly that he was already a prisoner some months before the Battle of Stoke took place. Do both records refer to the same priest? And if so, how can the conflict between them be reconciled? Previous writers have tended to assume that a single priest called Simons or Symonds was involved, and that his first name was either William or Richard. Curiously, no one seems to have considered the possibility that there may have been two priests: William Symonds, who was arrested before February 1486/87, and Richard Simons, who was only captured later in the year, after the Battle of Stoke.

The discrepancies over the name and arrest date of the priest involved in the Lambert Simnel case also remind us of another issue, which was highlighted in Chapter 4. There, we noted Vergil's statement that 'Richard Simons … took his Lambert to Oxford'.[7] This wording clearly implies that the boy was not a native of Oxford, and that he had not previously been resident there. By contrast, the Canterbury convocation account states that William Symonds found Lambert Simnel already living in Oxford, where his father was reportedly employed by the university. These discrepancies and contradictions make it difficult to be sure of the true nature of Lambert Simnel's connection with Oxford.

Based upon its rather pantomime-like quality, it has also been suggested that the unusual name of Lambert Simnel may indicate a foreign – possibly Flemish – background.[8] However, when I asked a Dutch-speaking Belgian whether 'Lambert Simnel' sounded to him like a name derived from his homeland, his reply was negative. In fact such a suggestion seems to have been made only by native speakers of English – presumably because the name did not appear to be typically English.

It is important to recognise that, even in the early sixteenth century, surnames were not necessarily fixed in England, and there is evidence to show that men (particularly clergymen) often used more than one surname, even at that comparatively recent date.[9] Actually, no one seems previously to have undertaken much research into the various surnames which figure in the official Tudor version of the Simnel story. On the internet, however, the following rather interesting information is to be found under the surname 'Simnel':

Recorded in over one hundred surname spellings throughout Europe, this interesting surname is of pre- written historical origins. It ultimately derives from the Hebrew personal name 'Shimeon', meaning 'one who harkens' … In England the name generally takes the form of Simon … The surname first appears in the latter half of the 13th Century (see below), Pieter Ziemke, of Hamburg, Germany, in 1289, and William Simon in the 1291 Calendar of Letter Books of the City of London. Other recordings from medieval times include Ernest Symers of Bremen, Germany, in 1262, and John Simon in the Subsidy Rolls of County Sussex, England, in 1296. The first recorded spelling of the family name [in England] is shown to be that of John Simond, which was dated 1273, in the 'Hundred Rolls of Oxfordshire' … Throughout the centuries, surnames in

every country have continued to 'develop' often leading to
astonishing variants of the original spelling.[10]

The first thing which emerges is the fact that there is evidently
no reason to suggest that the surname Simnel was foreign. The
second important point is that Simnel is merely a variant form
of the English surname 'Simon'. More specifically, Simnel is a
diminutive form. Interestingly, other potential variants of this
surname in medieval England were Simons and Symonds.

The existence in the late fifteenth/early sixteenth century
of yet more variant forms of the surname Simons/Symonds
is clearly indicated, for example, in the following entry from
Emden's *Biographical Register of the University of Oxford*:

> Symonds, William (*Simondes, Symondes, Symondys, Symons,
> Symunds*), All Souls College, fellow adm. 1503, still in 1511,
> Warden of All Souls &c.; supplicated for M.A. 3 March
> 150[6/]7. Vicar of Bishops Tawton, Devon, adm. 11 June 1520.[11]

Although Emden does mention a priest who reputedly
trained Lambert Simnel, and whose name was said to be
William Symonds or Richard Simons, it is clear that Emden
found no specific evidence for the existence of either of these
individuals among the surviving records of the University of
Oxford. Whether the William Symonds listed by Emden in
1503–20 was in any way connected with the priest who reputedly trained Lambert Simnel in about 1485–86, and who was
made to appear before the Canterbury provincial convocation
in London there is no way of knowing.

However the variant recorded forms of the surname of
Emden's early sixteenth-century William Symonds, including
the mixture of 'i' and 'y' in the first syllable, and the presence
or absence of the final 'd' and 's', all help to make it clear that
Simons (as recorded by Vergil) and Symonds (as recorded at
the Canterbury convocation) are merely variant versions of
the same surname, and could either refer to the same person,

or – given the two alternative Christians names – to two different people, who were, however, possibly members of the same
family. Moreover, hopefully it is now also clear that Symonds
(and its variations) are probably a much more common spelling of the rather unusual surname Simnel.

Thus we find ourselves confronting a hitherto unrecognised
situation in which the surname of Lambert Simnel was merely
a variant form of Simons or Symonds – the surname(s) of the
priest(s) reported to have educated him. Moreover it was a
diminutive variant form, of the kind which might well have
been applied to a young boy.

Two possible interpretations might logically be formed
upon the basis of this evidence. The first would be that the boy
pretender and the priest or priests who trained him were in
some way related to one another. However, an alternative possible interpretation would be that when it became essential for
Henry VII's government servants to come up with (perhaps
invent) a name for the Dublin King in order to demonstrate that
he was a fraud, they may have done so by adopting a diminutive
form of the surname of that priest (or of those priests) whom
they were already accusing of acting as his instructors.

If the first of these interpretations is correct, neither of the
priests is likely to have been the pretender's biological father.
Priests, of course, were supposed to be celibate. While that in
itself does not absolutely guarantee that none of them had children, we also have to take some account of the fact that, for the
boy's father, we are supplied by the Lincoln Act of Attainder
with the Christian name of Thomas. However, it remains possible that the priest was (or the priests were) related to the boy.
It is therefore very interesting to note that in a significant and
intriguing marginal annotation to a manuscript copy of the
Book of Howth preserved in Trinity College, Dublin, we find
the pretender described as 'Simon's son'.[12]

As for the second interpretation, that offers one possible
added advantage, in that it also would provide a potential explanation for the fact that, as we have seen in another, less public

Reconstruction of late-medieval Oxford, showing Osney Abbey in the foreground, and the Castle Mound in the background. Thomas Simnel, the third possible father of the Dublin King, is reported to have held a tenement from Osney Abbey in the 1470s, which was located between the abbey and the castle, in the area shown here.

and less official Tudor source (the *Heralds' Memoir*), an entirely different *Christian* name is cited for the boy in question.

Michael Bennett, an earlier researcher on the 1487 claimant, who wrote the present *ODNB* entry for the Dublin King under the name of Lambert Simnel, does claim to have documented the existence of Thomas Simnel of Oxford:

> A Thomas Simnel worked in Oxford in the late 1470s and held a tenement on the conduit towards St Thomas's Chapel[13] from Osney Abbey[14] in 1479. [...] The organ builder William Wooton was a neighbour, suggesting Thomas Simnel was a carpenter by trade who built organs.[15]

Unfortunately, however, Bennett's claim cannot easily be verified, because, sadly, he failed to record his source for this information.

The poll tax records for Oxford dating from a century earlier (1381) record no organ makers as Oxford residents – though there were three harp makers in Oxford at that time.[16] It is, perhaps, also worth noting that no men from Oxford were recorded among the supporters of the Dublin King in 1486–87, despite the fact that, according to some sources, at least, Lambert Simnel was reputedly 'the son of an Oxford joiner and had been launched on his impostor's career by an Oxford priest'.[17]

It is interesting that Emden's assumption appears to have been that although William Symonds and/or Richard Simons may have been priests studying in Oxford, neither was necessarily a native of the city. This ties in with Vergil's implication (see above) that Lambert Simnel was not actually a native of

A late fifteenth-century organ. According to one account, Lambert Simnel's father was an organ maker.

Oxford, but was simply taken there by the priest who trained him, for the purpose of preparing him for the role he had to play. Thus we find that it is very unclear how long-lasting and permanent was the connection of the Simnel/Simons/Symonds family with the city of Oxford.

We have now examined in detail all the possible versions of the childhood of the Dublin King. The suggestion that he was one of the sons of Edward IV – either Edward V or Richard, Duke of York – appears to have no real evidence to support it. Thus, while it is quite possible that Richard, Duke of York outlived the reign of Richard III, the notion that either he or his elder brother subsequently re-emerged as the Dublin King has been firmly rejected. So too has the notion that the Dublin King was a fake claimant who attempted to assume the identity of either Edward V or Richard, Duke of York. At the same time, it has been shown that the official Tudor accounts of the identity of the Dublin King contain significant contradictions and uncertainties. Therefore, it cannot be asserted that anyone has ever proved that the Dublin King and Lambert Simnel were one and the same person. The further implications of that statement will need to be considered later.

What does now seem clear is that the Dublin King used the royal identity of Edward, Earl of Warwick, son of the Duke of Clarence. Of course, he may nevertheless have been a fake claimant. On the other hand a real possibility has emerged that he may have been the genuine Earl of Warwick. What is more, if he was Warwick, the further question then remains as to whether he was brought up in England, and only taken to Ireland in about 1486, or whether he was shipped to Ireland by his father when he was very small, and brought up there by the Earl of Kildare. And in either case, the question of what may have become of him after his army was defeated at the Battle of Stoke also still remains. That is another aspect of the story, which has yet to be explored.

But before we begin investigating the possibilities of the aftermath of his story we need to look at who supported the Dublin King, and who opposed him, and why. We also need to look at the short but fascinating history of his reign. Among other things, this will include a detailed enquiry into the intriguing story of how on earth his supporters managed to carry out a coronation when they had no access to St Edward's Crown – not to mention the lack of an orb and sceptre, the lack of a throne, and the impossibility of any access to Westminster Abbey.

PART 2

Supporters and Enemies

6

Lincoln, Lovell and Yorkists in England

The key active supporters of the Dublin King in England, in Ireland and on the Continent, included two leading members of the royal house of York, together with certain noblemen and gentry who had been among the prominent supporters of the Yorkist dynasty during the approximately twenty-four years of its rule. The leader of the Dublin King's cause on the Continent was the Earl of Warwick's youngest surviving aunt, Margaret of York, dowager Duchess of Burgundy. In Ireland his supporters were led by the Anglo-Irish Fitzgerald family, headed by Gerald Fitzgerald, Earl of Kildare, who, rightly or wrongly, may have considered himself to have been the Earl of Warwick's guardian for about nine years. We shall consider in greater detail the character and background of these Continental and Irish supporters presently. First, however, let us review the situation in England, where the Dublin King's key supporters included the Earl of Warwick's cousin John de la Pole, Earl of Lincoln, together with one of Richard III's greatest friends, Francis, Viscount Lovell.

Lincoln was born in about 1460, to Richard III's sister, Elizabeth of York.[1] He was the first child born to Elizabeth following her marriage to John de la Pole, Duke of Suffolk. As we have seen, his uncle, King Edward IV, created him Earl of Lincoln on 13 March 1466/67. Later, he was knighted. He had then fulfilled various ceremonial public roles, the most recent of which had been when he bore the orb at King Richard III's coronation.[2] The eldest grandson of Richard and Cecily, the Duke and Duchess of York, by 1485 Lincoln was already a young adult. He gave Richard loyal support during Buckingham's Rebellion – for which his uncle rewarded him with grants of lands, together with the reversion of estates held by Margaret Beaufort for her lifetime.

Richard III's son, Edward of Middleham, Prince of Wales, died, probably of tuberculosis, at the beginning of 1484,[3] Before his death, Edward of Middleham had briefly held the important post of Lieutenant of Ireland.[4] This post was normally exercised through a deputy, so that the boy's youth was not a problem. After Edward of Middleham's death, on 21 August 1484, Richard then appointed the Earl of Lincoln to the same post. Lincoln was also appointed to the presidency of the Council of the North.

The grant of the lieutenancy of Ireland may be one indication that, following the death of his son, Richard III initially regarded Lincoln as his interim heir. As we have seen, in connection with the life story of the Earl of Warwick, historians have sometimes claimed that, following his son's death, Richard specifically named one of his nephews as his heir. Some writers have suggested that Edward of Clarence, Earl of Warwick was the chosen prince, while others argue that the nephew selected was Lincoln.[5] Since there is no surviving written evidence that either nephew was ever formally designated as Richard III's heir, these conflicting stories could simply be later inventions. However, there is also another possible way of interpreting the statements that both Warwick and Lincoln were recognised as Richard's heir in 1485.

We have already noted that, until the eve of the Battle of Bosworth, there was no real necessity for King Richard to make any public statement about who should succeed him, for two reasons. First, he was still a young man, with every prospect of a long life before him. The death of Queen Anne Neville, in 1484/85, focussed government attention on the succession problem. However, it also offered the perfect long-term solution: a second royal marriage and the begetting of new and healthy sons.

Negotiations ensued for marriage with either a Portuguese or a Spanish infanta. Since the English proposal was very favourably received in Portugal, under normal circumstances the Infanta Joana of Portugal would shortly have become the new queen consort of England.[6] Assuming that many years of his own reign still lay before him, Richard III would then have had ample time to train a new son for future kingship. Therefore, it is difficult to see why he should have made any specific announcement about the identity of his heir presumptive prior to August 1485.

The second reason is that in April 1485, from a Yorkist point of view, the situation regarding the sucession was already quite clear. Apart from the death of Edward of Middleham, nothing had changed since Richard's own accession two years earlier. Thus, until the king remarried, and produced a new son and heir apparent, the heir presumptive was John de la Pole, Earl of Lincoln. No explicit statement about the succession was therefore required unless Richard III wished to alter the situation in some way.

The point is that Richard III's own accession had been based upon a decision made by the Three Estates of the Realm in 1483 (and subsequently confirmed by the formal Parliament of 1484). The prime factor behind this decision was that Edward IV had committed bigamy, in consequence of which his children by Elizabeth Woodville were illegitimate and therefore excluded from the succession. However, that first key point had been coupled with an almost equally important second one: the fact that in 1478 Edward had signed an Act of Attainder against his brother the Duke of Clarence thus excluding Clarence and his children from the succession. The fact that Clarence's heirs had been excluded by the Act of Attainder is stated quite specifically in the subsequent Act known as *Titulus Regius*, in the following terms:

> Moreover, we consider how afterwards, by the three estates of this realm assembled in a parliament held at Westminster in the seventeenth year of the reign of the said King Edward IV [1478], he then being in possession of the crown and royal estate, by an act made in the same parliament, George, duke of Clarence, brother to the said King Edward, now dead, was convicted and attainted of high treason, as is contained at greater length in the same act. *Because and by reason of which, all the issue of the said George was and is disabled and barred from all right and claim to the crown and royal dignity of this realm,* which they might in any way have or claim by inheritance, by the ancient law and custom of this same realm.[7]

Without this explicit statement regarding the status of Clarence's heir, Richard III himself would not have been the rightful heir to the throne in 1483. Instead, the ruling that the children of Edward IV and Elizabeth Woodville were illegitimate could have resulted in the crown passing to Clarence's surviving son, the young Earl of Warwick, since Warwick's line of royal descent was senior to that of Richard III.

Based upon the precise statement in the Act of *Titulus Regius*, however, it is obvious that in 1483, the young Earl of Warwick had been formally adjudged by Parliament to have no legal claim to the throne because of his father's attainder. As long as this remained the case – even following the death of Richard III's son, Edward of Middleham – there would have been no need for the king to make any formal statement about the identity of the heir presumptive to his throne. It should already have been perfectly clear to everybody that until the king either produced another son, or set aside the Clarence Act of Attainder of 1478, his legal heir was John de la Pole, Earl of Lincoln.

However, this logical analysis of the situation, together with the conclusion to which it inevitably leads, makes the subsequent support offered by Lincoln to the Dublin King appear utterly extraordinary. In fact, as we have already seen, it was considered extraordinary by some people – including Henry VII – *at the time*. And it is that which invited the suggestion that in August 1485 Richard III may suddenly have decided to re-instate the Earl of Warwick in the order of succession.

No documentary evidence of any such action on Richard's part now survives. Nevertheless, it is only if his uncle – the then-reigning king, and a sovereign whom he had always served with loyalty – had made some specific move, prior to his death, to proclaim Warwick as his heir, that the subsequent conduct of the Earl of Lincoln becomes understandable. Only then does Lincoln's subsequent loyal support for the Dublin King – whom he identified as the Earl of Warwick – make sense.

If my suggestion is correct – if in August 1485 Richard III chose to restore Warwick to his original place in the order of succession – Lincoln's conduct in 1486–87 would then be of a piece with his earlier conduct in 1483. Those who accept the argument I have put forward would then find themselves forced to the conclusion that in John de la Pole, Earl of Lincoln we find ourselves dealing with a member of the house of York whose actions were determined by one fundamental aspect of his character – his absolute loyalty.

Of course, when Henry VII seized the throne, the position of the de la Pole family suddenly changed. Previously they had been closely related to the reigning monarchs (Edward IV and Richard III). Now, suddenly, a much more distant and possibly hostile relative wore the crown of England. After the Battle of Bosworth 'Henry VII was lenient with John of Lincoln mainly because the de la Poles were too powerful a family to drive into opposition until the King had a secure hold on the Crown, so the de la Poles retained their titles and estates'.[8] Nevertheless, in the long term the aim of the new Tudor dynasty was to bring down the de la Poles – an objective which Henry VII and Henry VIII carried out slowly, but with complete success. There are now no living descendants of any of the seven sons of Richard III's sister, the Duchess of Suffolk.

But in 1486 and 1487 the Earl of Lincoln's public devotion to the Dublin King, 'Edward VI', was not widely reflected in his immediate family. His father, the Duke of Suffolk, was, of course, only related to the house of York by marriage. In fact the Duke's family background had originally been Lancastrian. Although he had served Edward IV and Richard III loyally during their respective reigns, the Duke's main concern after 1485 seems to have been to ensure the safety of his own family and the maintenance of its position by the retention of its lands and property. He therefore acknowledged Henry VII. Indeed, the assessment of Michael Hicks is that the Duke of Suffolk 'avoided supporting causes that were lost, quickly acquiescing in the successions of Richard III and Henry VII'.[9]

The position of Suffolk's wife, Elizabeth of York, may have been more equivocal. In fact for her there was now a new and even bigger problem, in that her namesake and niece, the younger Elizabeth of York, had married the recently enthroned king, Henry VII. Elizabeth of York junior was now Queen of England. Moreover, she was also on the way to producing a new heir to the throne.[10] The loyalties of the senior Elizabeth of York, Duchess of Suffolk, may therefore have felt somewhat split.

In the longer term it appears probable that, despite the political realism of her husband, privately Elizabeth of York, Duchess of Suffolk, took a rather different view. During her husband's lifetime, of course, she was not really free to express her own feelings. Nevertheless, it is reported that 'in the years after her husband's death, Elizabeth Plantagenet went to visit her sister in Burgundy'.[11] The Duke of Suffolk is thought to have died in 1492,[12] so Elizabeth's visit to her younger sister, Margaret, came much too late to be of any help to her son, the Earl of Lincoln, or to his chosen sovereign, the Dublin King.

But while it is true that in 1486 and 1487 only Elizabeth's eldest son, the Earl of Lincoln, came out openly in support of 'Edward VI', later some of Lincoln's younger brothers were also to make it plain to the world that the Tudor usurpation was completely unacceptable in their eyes.

But in 1486 and 1487, in terms of the actions they took, the surviving members of the royal house of York were divided. Elizabeth, based at Wingfield in Suffolk, did nothing to support 'Edward VI'. Her elderly mother, the dowager Duchess of York, now residing at Berkhamsted Castle in Hertfordshire, also did nothing. Of course, Cecily Neville was by that time very old, and her attention seems to have been entirely focussed on the future of her own immortal soul. Moreover, one of her grandchildren was married to the new king. On the other hand Cecily's other surviving daughter, Margaret, who resided in the safe haven of the Low Countries, was firmly and openly opposed to Henry VII, and backed 'Edward VI' up to the hilt. And, as we have seen, her nephew the Earl of Lincoln also showed unequivocal loyalty to the Dublin King.

Of course, Lincoln was not unique in this respect; the same loyalty to the legitimate heir of his chosen royal house is also apparent in that second key English supporter of the Dublin King Francis, Viscount Lovell.

Francis had lost his father, the eighth Baron Lovell, in 1463, when he was only 9 years old. As a result the boy had become a ward of the king. Edward IV had then consigned him to the guardianship of his cousin, Warwick the Kingmaker. In this way Francis eventually found himself growing up as a companion of the adolescent Richard Duke of Gloucester (Richard III), and the two youths became close friends.

Francis Lovell was married in 1466 to one of Warwick's nieces, a girl called Anne FitzHugh. Anne was the first cousin of Anne Neville, who eventually became the wife of Richard III. She was also the first cousin of Isabel Neville, Duchess of Clarence. This marriage consolidated Lovell's position in Warwick's entourage. As a result, in 1469–70, Francis (together with his father-in-law) seems to have supported the campaign of Warwick and the Duke of Clarence against Edward IV and the Woodville family. Later, when Edward IV had re-established himself as king and Warwick was dead, Francis Lovell received a royal pardon. Since he was still under age, he was then consigned to the guardianship of Elizabeth of York, and her husband, John de la Pole, Duke of Suffolk.[13] In this way the 17-year-old Francis was first brought into contact with Elizabeth's 11-year-old son, John, Earl of Lincoln.

Francis also had interesting connections through his father's family. In 1463 his paternal grandmother, Alice Deincourt, had married Ralph Butler, Lord Sudeley (she was his second wife). This made Francis Lovell a kind of cousin-in-law of Eleanor Talbot, the first secret wife of Edward IV.[14]

The death of his grandmother, Lady Sudeley, in February 1473/74, brought Francis a large inheritance, making him one of the wealthiest barons in the land. In 1480 he served under his friend Richard, Duke of Gloucester in the Scottish campaign. He was knighted for his service by Richard in 1480, and one of the last acts of Edward IV was to elevate Francis from the rank of baron to the rank of viscount (4 January 1482/83).[15]

Following the death of Edward IV in April 1483, Francis became one of Richard's strongest supporters. While he was still Lord Protector, Richard appointed Francis Chief Butler and Constable of Wallingford Castle. After Richard had been invited to take the throne, Francis carried one of the swords of state at his friend's coronation. He succeeded the executed Lord

The coat of arms of Francis, Viscount Lovell, redrawn from his Garter stall plate at Windsor Castle.

Hastings as Lord Chamberlain, and was created a Knight of the Garter. Towards the end of 1483, Francis helped Richard to defeat the rebellion of the Duke of Buckingham.

It was in July 1484 that William Collingbourne, an opponent of the Yorkist regime, attached to the door of St Paul's Cathedral in London a now famous couplet:

> The Catte the Ratte and lovell owyr dogge
> Rulyn all Engeland undyr an hogge.[16]

The *hogge* was Richard III, the reference being to his white boar badge. Likewise the mention of Lovell as a *dogge* referred to the white wolf which formed part of the crest above his coat of arms. The *Catte* referred to William Catesby, another of Richard III's servants, and yet another connection of Eleanor Talbot.[17] The *Ratte* was Richard Ratcliffe, who was killed with Richard III and the Duke of Norfolk at the Battle of Bosworth.

In 1485, when news came of the planned invasion of England by Henry Tudor, Francis Lovell was sent by Richard III to guard the south coast. Since Henry actually landed at Milford Haven, Francis was not able to intercept him, and although some historians maintain that Francis fought with Richard at Bosworth – and two contemporary reports actually listed him among the dead[18] – in fact it is by no means clear whether Francis had been able to reach Richard in time to take part in the battle. More will be said about this point – and about the subsequent history of Viscount Lovell – later, when we explore what actually occurred in 1486 and 1487.

Other Yorkists who actively supported the Dublin King included members of the gentry. Sir Henry Bodrugan from Cornwall was one of them.[19] Although he was about 60 years of age in 1486, Bodrugan, who, like Lincoln and Lovell, had previously been a very firm supporter of Richard III, attended the Dublin coronation. John Beaumont was another member of the Yorkist gentry who attended the coronation.[20] Like Bodrugan, Beaumont was based in Cornwall;

indeed it is possible that Beaumont was related in some way to Bodrugan, who had married Jane, the widow of William Beaumont, in about 1461.[21] Another member of the Yorkist gentry who is recorded as having supported the cause of the Dublin King is Sir Thomas Broughton.[22] Edward Franke or Franks, who had been sheriff of Oxfordshire and Berkshire in 1484, under Richard III, also gave his support to 'Edward VI'.[23]

Some members of the religious hierarchy in England also supported the Dublin King. One notable example is John Sant, the Abbot of Abingdon, who first helped the Stafford brothers in their unsuccessful rising of 1486, and whose name was well known to Margaret of York in Flanders. Later it was reported that Abbot Sant sent one of his servants abroad in January 1486/87, carrying funds for the Earl of Lincoln. Since this predated Lincoln's own departure it would suggest that plans for the Dublin King were well under way even while Lincoln was still at Henry VII's court.[24]

Curiously, however, the division of opinion over the contest between Henry VII and 'Edward VI' which we have already encountered within the royal house of York, also seems to have been present among the wider ranks of former Yorkist supporters. By no means did all the living Yorkists in England follow Francis Lovell, Bodrugan, Beaumont and Broughton in supporting the Dublin King. Even among those families which had earlier seemed very loyal to the house of York, the position adopted in 1486 was equivocal.

The Howard family are an excellent example of this, and possibly reveal the reason why some former Yorkists seemed reluctant. John Howard, Duke of Norfolk had, of course, been killed at the Battle of Bosworth, together with his king, Richard III. However, his son, Thomas, Earl of Surrey, though wounded in the fighting, survived – to be captured by Henry VII and subsequently imprisoned in the Tower of London.[25] It is reported that in 1486 Thomas Howard was offered a chance to escape from the Tower and fight for the

Dublin King.[26] But apparently Thomas felt that it was safer for him to remain in his cell. Of course, this in itself may indicate that the Yorkist loyalty of the Howards had not died completely, for 'while others prospered in serving the new king and in establishing the new authority, [Howard] led a passive existence'.[27] But since he had been stripped of all his lands and titles by the Tudor regime, he was probably frightened about taking any further risks. In the long run, of course, Thomas Howard's refusal to back the Dublin King does seem to have acted in his favour – as perhaps he had secretly hoped. Thus in May 1489, after the Dublin King had been defeated, Henry VII restored Thomas to the earldom of Surrey.

7

The 'Diabolicall Duches'

Outside of England, of course, the position was very different. Anyone with an interest in English politics who was resident in a foreign country was in a fairly safe position to say and do exactly what they felt. Thus, after the Earl of Lincoln, it is not surprising to find that the key surviving member of the royal house of York who most unequivocally supported the Dublin King was Margaret, dowager Duchess of Burgundy. According to Professor Mary Hayden, 'she was a woman skilled in intrigue, and was very popular in Flanders'.[1] Certainly the second part of this sentence is correct.

From the safety of her palace in Mechelen, Margaret vehemently opposed Henry VII. It is usually supposed that her opposition dated from the first moment when the news reached her of his victory over her brother, Richard, at Bosworth. However, Christine Weightman tentatively suggested a different and rather more mundane explanation:

> Margaret had benefitted from all the various trading licences granted by her brother Edward, and she had continued to enjoy these privileges during the brief reigns of Edward V and Richard III, but with the accession of Henry VII her trading activities appear to have ceased.[2]

Whatever the real reason for her opposition to Henry, in the year following his seizure of the English throne, Margaret invited to her palace in Mechelen the young future 'King Edward VI'. Once this boy had joined her there she recognised him as her nephew the Earl of Warwick and set in motion the initial planning of his future Dublin coronation.

Margaret was the third daughter of the Duke and Duchess of York, and the youngest of their daughters to survive to adulthood.[3] She was born on Tuesday, 3 May 1446, at Waltham Abbey in Essex.[4] Very close in age to her slightly younger brother, George, Duke of Clarence she seems always to have felt very close to him. She also appears to have been close to her youngest brother, Richard. It is therefore not surprising that, after the death of Richard III in August 1485, Margaret took an interest in Clarence's son, the young Earl of Warwick.

Incidentally Margaret's genuine devotion to the interests of her family – the house of York – makes it inherently improbable that she would deliberately have supported impostors. Like all her contemporaries in 1486 and 1487, she knew that her niece, Elizabeth of York the younger, was married to

Henry VII, and was therefore engaged in producing new royal children who would be partly of the bloodline of the house of York, and one of whom would eventually inherit the crown, assuming that Henry VII remained

Margaret of York, dowager Duchess of Burgundy, sister of Edward IV and Richard III, a supporter and a possible aunt of the Dublin King.

on the throne. It must therefore be the case that she genuinely believed that the Dublin King was her nephew Edward,
Earl of Warwick just as later she must genuinely have believed
that the claimant known as Perkin Warbeck really was Richard
of Shrewsbury.

In itself, of course, Margaret's belief is not sufficient to prove
the authenticity of either of the Yorkist pretenders. After all,
Margaret of York had left England in 1468, when the Duke
of York and the Earl of Warwick had not yet been born. She
may have met them both in 1480, when York was aged 7 and
Warwick was 5. But that does not guarantee that she would
have recognised Warwick six years later, at the age of 11, or
York some twelve years later, at the age of about 19. Margaret
could perhaps have been deceived – or have deceived herself.

As a girl, she was brought up in England, where she had
spent much of her early life in the care of her mother. She
was with the Duchess of York and her two younger brothers
at Fastolf's Place in Southwark in the autumn of 1460. After
her father was killed at the Battle of Wakefield, Margaret's two
younger brothers were sent to the Low Countries for safety,
but except for a possible period of residence in Ireland when
her father and mother held court there in her early childhood,
Margaret herself never left England until the time came for
her marriage. In 1460/61, while her brothers were in exile in
Utrecht, Margaret seems to have remained at her mother's side.
In the early days of the reign of her eldest brother, Edward IV,
Margaret and her mother were resident at Baynard's Castle
in London. Later, Edward IV established a household for
Margaret, George and Richard at the Palace of Pleasaunce
(Greenwich Palace).

Like other members of her family (some of whom were
probably reluctant to do so) Margaret was required to attend
the coronation of Elizabeth Woodville as Edward IV's queen
in May 1465. During the following two years she spent a good
deal of her time in the new queen's company. Margaret, the
only unmarried princess of the house of York at that time, was

potentially a valuable pawn in the hands of her brother's government. There was talk of a possible Scottish royal wedding, followed later by discussion of a possible Portuguese alliance. Most serious in the mind of her brother, the king, however, was the prospect of a possible alliance between Margaret and the widowed Count Charles of Charolais, son and heir of the Duke of Burgundy.

Negotiations for a Burgundian match began almost as soon as Charles lost his second wife, in 1465. The process was delayed somewhat by the innate Lancastrian predilections of Charles' parents, the Duke and Duchess of Burgundy. Progress was also hindered in England by the opposition of Edward and Margaret's cousin, Richard Neville, the Kingmaker Earl of Warwick, who much preferred the idea of an alliance with France. By 1467, however, a marriage between Margaret and Charles was agreed.

Margaret left London on 18 June 1468, and was escorted by her brothers and a large selection of the nobility with great splendour. She set off on a slow procession through the county of Kent which finally took her to the port of Margate. There she embarked for the Low Countries. Her marriage to Charles the Bold was celebrated at Damme on 3 July, followed by another splendid process, this time a state entry into the town of Brugge.

Curiously, following her marriage, Margaret spent little time with her new husband, and their marriage always remained childless. Charles's first marriage, to Catherine of France (who had been five years his senior and who had died at the age of eighteen) may never have been consummated simply because of the bridegroom's youth. But although Charles later succeeded in fathering one daughter, by his second wife, Isabelle of Bourbon, he seems to have shown very little interest in the opposite sex. In fact it has been suggested, both during his lifetime, and by more recent historians, that he may possibly have been homosexual.[5]

Nevertheless, Margaret, now Duchess of Burgundy, got on very well with her mother-in-law, Isabel of Portugal, and also with her stepdaughter, Marie. Margaret shared her own mother's deep religious devotion, and was a great patron of education and of religious foundations in her new homeland. She was also a great patron of the arts. Margaret also proved politically astute. She was an able diplomat, who succeeded in reconciling her brother George to Edward IV in 1471, and who also proved an able assistant to her husband as he struggled to fight off his cousin, the French King.

When Charles was killed at the Battle of Nancy (5 January 1477), Margaret did her best to aid and support her stepdaughter, Marie, whose territories were then being overrun by French forces. When her own brother George, Duke of Clarence was widowed in 1476, Margaret initially favoured the idea of a marriage between him and Marie. Later, however, she supported the more practical plan of a union between her stepdaughter and Maximilian of Habsburg, the King of the Romans.

When Marie and Maximilian were married, Margaret swore loyalty to her new stepson-in-law, and from then on the two of them generally worked as one. When young Marie died in an accident, in March 1481/82, Maximilian proved rather unpopular as regent for his son, Philip. Nevertheless, Margaret did her best to assist Maximilian, and it was she who was chiefly responsible for young Philip's education.

However, another set of problems began to confront Margaret in 1483. First, her brother Edward IV died unexpectedly. Then her nephew, Edward V was set aside as illegitimate, and her youngest brother became King Richard III. Finally, two years later, Richard was killed at Bosworth and Henry VII seized power in England.

Margaret refused to recognise the change of dynasty, and her dowager court at Mechelen quickly became a safe haven for Yorkist exiles. It was in the context of her court at Mechelen, as we shall see shortly, that Margaret subsequently received the Dublin King, recognised him as her nephew, and planned for his coronation.

8

The Earl of Kildare and the Irish Contingent

In Ireland, as in England, there were different reactions to the emergence of the Dublin King in opposition to Henry VII. Nicholas St Lawrence, Lord Howth seems to have favoured the Tudor monarch. Generally, however, among the Anglo-Irish nobility, opposition to Henry VII appears to have been quite widespread. Hence there was a good deal of support for 'Edward VI'. In fact the only major Irish family which supported Henry VII was the Butler family, earls of Ormonde. The Butlers had been declared traitors by King Edward IV, so they had no great love for the royal house of York.

As Hayden has noted, however, the Irish supporters of the Dublin King 'were not the real native *Hiberni*. In the long lists of those implicated in the plot we find but one certainly Celtic name'. 'It is to be noted that all the thirty-two names on the Dublin list of those pardoned are Anglo-Irish. On the Kinsale list there are thirty-nine names, of which one "Morys O'Kine" is certainly Celtic, while one "Denis Redyggan" is rather doubtful; the rest are Anglo-Irish. Nothing could more clearly show that Polydore Vergil and Bernard André are quite incorrect in stating that the native Irish supported Simnel'.[1]

The premier Anglo-Irish peer was Gerald the Great (Gearoid Mór FitzGerald), eighth Earl of Kildare. *An iarla mór* ('the great Earl') was said to be a man of exceptional charisma and impressive charm, although, rather like his friend and patron the Duke of Clarence, he has also been described as hot-tempered and unpredictable as a young man:

> Nothing is known of his early life, although Walter Hussey, in the Book of Howth, recalled in the 1540s that he was 'without great knowledge or learning, but rudely brought up according to the usage of his country'. He was, however, 'a mightie man of stature, full of honour and courage', 'a warrior incomparable', 'hardlie able to rule himself when he were moved to anger', but quickly appeased. … [although he was at home in the English language,] Kildare spoke and wrote in Gaelic, as occasion demanded, and his court included a Gaelic entourage, with a judge, physician, poets, and other captains, household servants, and receivers.[2]

By his second wife (a cousin of Henry VII) the Earl of Kildare later became an ancestor of the late Diana, Princess of Wales and thus also of her sons, the Duke of Cambridge and his younger brother.

In 1477, at the age of about 19, Gerald was appointed Lord Deputy to George, Duke of Clarence in succession to his late father, Thomas, seventh Earl of Kildare, who had been given that post by Clarence's father, Richard, Duke of York, in 1455. Following the execution of the Duke of Clarence, in February 1477/78, Gerald Fitzgerald was dismissed as Lord Deputy by Edward IV in favour of Lord Grey of Ruthin. However, Lord Grey proved incapable of asserting his authority in Ireland, and in 1479, faced by a rebellion of the Irish nobility, Edward IV found himself forced to restore the Earl of Kildare to his former post. Kildare then remained in office until 1494. Subsequently he was once again reappointed Lord Deputy in 1496, after which he retained the post until his death in September 1513.

Gerald's links with the house of York were strong. His mother, Jane Fitzgerald (a cousin of his father), was one of the daughters of James Fitzgerald, sixth Earl of Desmond, who had been one of the godfathers of George, Duke of Clarence at his baptism in Dublin in 1449. On his mother's side his uncle was Thomas, the seventh Earl of Desmond, who was put to death in 1468, reportedly at the instigation of Elizabeth Woodville – just like the Duke of Clarence, ten years later.[3] It would therefore have been in no way surprising if, in 1477, faced with the death of his wife and son – at the hands of the hated Elizabeth Woodville, as he apparently believed – the Duke of Clarence should have decided to entrust his surviving elder son and heir, Edward, Earl of Warwick, to the Earl of Kildare. As the nephew of another victim of Elizabeth Woodville, Gerald would have been very well able to understand Clarence's point of view. Thus there appears to be some evidence for believing that the Earl of Kildare may have received a 2-year-old boy from England into his household as his ward in late March or early April 1477. There is also some indication that the arrival of this little boy may have been preceded by a personal visit of the Duke of Clarence, with the intention of establishing the child's identity, and requesting Gerald's assistance in taking care of him.

Following the death of Richard III at Bosworth, and the accession of the unknown stranger as King Henry VII, Gerald was easily able to retain his post in Ireland, where, as yet, the new Tudor dynasty exerted very little control. However, the presence in his household of an English ward, whom he believed to be the true son of the Duke of Clarence would have given him a wonderful opportunity to oppose the new dynasty in a much more vigorous manner, by attempting to displace Henry VII from his newly acquired throne – upon which the new king's seat was still somewhat insecure. As we shall see, Gerald was obviously in contact both with Clarence's sister, Margaret, Duchess of Burgundy, in Mechelen, and also with Clarence's nephew John, Earl of Lincoln in England.

As a result, the young ward, whose presence in the Kildare household I have posited, was apparently shipped to the Low Countries to pay a visit to Margaret. There Lincoln and Lovell joined the two of them, and the plot to proclaim and crown the Dublin King was set in motion.

During the Dublin King's brief reign in Ireland, the Earl of Kildare effectively functioned as his Irish regent, or Lord Chancellor (see below). 'For the invasion of England … Kildare recruited 4000 Gaelic kerne commanded by his brother to reinforce the 2000 German mercenaries supplied by Margaret of Burgundy'.[4] However, in June 1487, when the boy-king and his supporters (including Kildare's younger brother, Thomas) crossed the sea to England, Kildare himself remained safely in Ireland.

There, the earl continued to rule in the name of the Dublin King. Indeed, the one surviving document in the Irish archives issued in the boy-king's name, and bearing the only surviving impression of his royal seal, is a letter issued by Kildare after the boy had left the country. Incidentally, the fact that Kildare used the great royal seal of 'Edward VI' on this letter proves that the seal was not taken to England with the Dublin King and his troops, and then lost at the Battle of Stoke. It remained in Ireland in the hands of the Earl of Kildare. In fact, Kildare retained, and used, the great seal even after 'Edward VI' had been defeated. What finally became of the seal matrix, and whether it still exists somewhere in Ireland, is unknown.

Thanks to his commanding position in his homeland, after the Dublin King's defeat at the Battle of Stoke the Earl of Kildare found himself pardoned by Henry VII, and retained in his post. Curiously, however, he subsequently proved wary of the second Yorkist claimant, generally known as Perkin Warbeck, and did not support the claims of that pretender. For Gerald, it therefore seems possible that the key factor behind his support of the Dublin King may have been the fact that the first pretender had been brought up in the earl's own household, as his ward, since the age of 2. As a result, he personally seems to have felt no doubts regarding this boy's authenticity as a royal prince. On the other hand, while many apparently believed that Perkin Warbeck was the younger son of Edward IV, Gerald Fitzgerald had no personal knowledge on that point. What is more, the younger son of Elizabeth Woodville – even if genuine – may have exerted little appeal to his loyalty.

The younger brother of the Earl of Kildare, who commanded the Irish contingent which accompanied the Dublin King to England, was Sir Thomas FitzGerald of Laccagh. Born in about 1458, Sir Thomas' base was at Laccagh in County Kildare. He had been appointed Lord Chancellor of Ireland in 1483. Yet, despite his service to Richard III, and the fact that, like much of the Irish nobility, Sir Thomas was known to favour the Yorkist cause, Henry VII (whose control over Ireland was questionable) had little option but to confirm him in this post after the Battle of Bosworth. His subsequent support for the Dublin King led ultimately to Sir Thomas' death at the Battle of Stoke. Nevertheless, his family subsequently managed to retain its tenure of his estate at Laccagh. Amongst the later descendants of Sir Thomas Fitzgerald was the first Duke of Wellington.

9

Henry VII and John Morton

The rival of 'Edward VI' for the crown and throne of England was Henry VII. He had been in possession of the crown since 22 August 1485, on the morning of which day, members of Henry's French and Welsh army had killed the last reigning Yorkist king, Richard III.

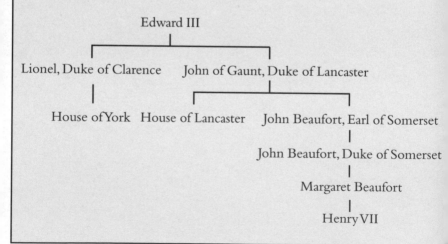

THE ENGLISH ROYAL DESCENT OF HENRY VII

Edward III

Lionel, Duke of Clarence   John of Gaunt, Duke of Lancaster

House of York   House of Lancaster   John Beaufort, Earl of Somerset

John Beaufort, Duke of Somerset

Margaret Beaufort

Henry VII

Born in 1457, Henry VII was the only child of Edmund, Earl of Richmond and his very young wife, Lady Margaret Beaufort. On his mother's side Henry was the 3x great grandson of King Edward III through the following line of descent:

On his father's side, Henry VII was the nephew of Henry VI. However, that paternal connection did not convey to him any claim to the English throne. His father and King Henry VI were half-brothers only because they shared the same mother. Thus Henry VII was not descended from any of the Lancastrian kings – though through his paternal grandmother he was quite closely related to the fifteenth-century Kings of France.

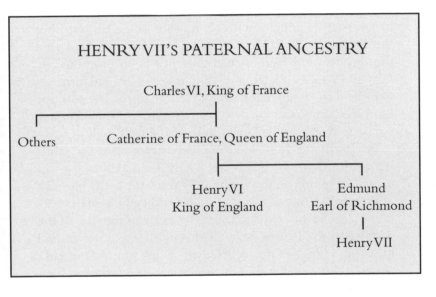

HENRY VII'S PATERNAL ANCESTRY

Charles VI, King of France

Others

Catherine of France, Queen of England

Henry VI
King of England

Edmund
Earl of Richmond

Henry VII

Henry VII's father is usually said to have been the son of Owen Tudor, and the surname Tudor is accordingly assigned to Henry VII's royal dynasty. However as this author and others have shown,[1] there is some evidence that Edmund, Earl of Richmond may have been the illegitimate son of Edmund Beaufort, Duke of Somerset – and thus the cousin of his wife, Margaret Beaufort. Although the evidence on this

point is not conclusive (and never will be, unless the royal
Tudor Y-chromosome can be established and matched to
the Y-chromosome of John of Gaunt), there is no doubt that
Richard III, in his proclamation against Henry VII, cast doubts
on the legitimacy of his descent. This point has often been
questioned, since the Beauforts, while originally born illegitimate, were subsequently legitimised. However, Richard III
may simply have had at the back of his mind his own and
his family's suspicions regarding the dubious paternity of
Henry VII's father.

Henry VII was actually born fatherless, at Pembroke Castle
on 28 January 1456/57, because the Earl of Richmond had
died three months earlier. What is more, the infant Henry also
had very little contact with his mother, since his wardship
was assigned to Lord Herbert by Edward IV when he seized
the throne. Lord Herbert had then just been promoted by
Edward IV to the Earldom of Pembroke, which had formerly
been held by Jasper Tudor, young Henry's uncle. It seems that
Lord Herbert – now the new Lord Pembroke – hoped in due
course to marry young Henry to his daughter, Cecily.

In 1469 the 12-year-old Henry had accompanied his guardian to the Battle of Edgecote, where Lord Pembroke was
naturally fighting on the Yorkist side. Since the battle proved a
Yorkist defeat, one of its sequels was Lord Pembroke's execution. Young Henry returned after the battle to the care of the
widowed Lady Pembroke, while his mother and her second
husband, Henry Stafford, tried to secure the young lad's
return to his own family. This aim was finally brought about
by the Lancastrian Readeption of 1470, as a result of which
young Henry found himself in the care of the other Earl of
Pembroke, his Uncle Jasper.

On 27 October 1470 the Lancastrian Readeption also
secured young Henry a meeting with his uncle, the restored
King Henry VI. At this meeting Henry VI was later reputed
to have prophesied his half-nephew's future accession to
the throne. About six months later, when Edward IV ousted

Henry VI and reclaimed the crown of England, Henry Tudor fled the country, escaping with his uncle Jasper into exile in the Duchy of Brittany.

Meanwhile Henry's mother, now married to Lord Stanley (later first Earl of Derby), was by no means an unacceptable figure at the court of her second cousin Edward IV.[2] As we have already seen, on grand occasions such as the marriage of Richard of Shrewsbury, Duke of York Lady Margaret fulfilled a public role as a significant figure within the Yorkist regime. Indeed, later, at the coronation of Richard III, she was the senior attendant of Richard's queen at their joint coronation. Apart from the fact that he was in the hands of his politically incorrect uncle, there was therefore no official reason why young Henry Tudor should have remained in exile. Indeed, his mother tried hard to secure his return.

Her plans changed, however, when Edward IV died, Edward V was declared illegitimate and Richard III was offered the crown. The Woodville family of Edward IV's bigamous queen now found themselves in a political no man's land, and Margaret Beaufort took advantage of this situation to court the former queen. Margaret seems to have proposed to Elizabeth Woodville a marriage between her son, Henry, and Elizabeth Woodville's eldest daughter, Elizabeth. In due course – possibly owing to the fact that the ex-child-king Edward V had died in the meantime, while his younger brother, Richard, Duke of York was out of the ex-queen's hands and inaccessible – the cunning Margaret developed this marriage plan into something much more ambitious: a plan to secure recognition for her son as the Lancastrian heir to the throne (which he certainly was not) and then to promote the young Henry as King of England – with Elizabeth of York at his side as his queen consort.

As part of the Duke of Buckingham's rebellion, Henry was first proclaimed king in Cornwall on 3 November 1483. But, Henry, who was still on the Continent, found himself delayed by bad weather and other setbacks. When at last he reached the

West Country from Brittany, he discovered that Richard III
was firmly in control of the situation. Therefore he simply
returned quietly to his place of exile.

Early in the following year Richard III attempted to have
Henry extradited from Brittany. Henry, however, was fore-
warned of this plan and fled from Brittany into France. There
the regents for Henry's cousin, the young King Charles VIII,
saw, in this new arrival, a wonderful potential weapon for them
to use against their hostile neighbour, King Richard III. As a
result, Henry Tudor suddenly found himself endowed with a
backing of French money, and with French ships and fighting
men at his disposal. This was the situation which led to his
invasion of England in 1485; the invasion which culminated in
the Battle of Bosworth, and which produced the unexpected
outcome of a new King of England and a new royal dynasty.

Although some of those who had supported the previous
regime fought on for a while, others, like Viscount Lovell, felt
obliged to flee into sanctuary. Yet others, such as the Earl of
Surrey, preferred to try to make peace with the new political reality in order to prevent the loss of all their property.
Henry VII's attempt to win over Yorkists was aided by his marriage to Elizabeth, eldest daughter of Edward IV and Elizabeth
Woodville, whose legitimacy he had urgently restored. The
couple married on 18 January 1485/86. The new queen was
soon pregnant, and the political publicity machine of the
new regime swung into action to proclaim that as a result the
conflict between York and Lancaster had finally been brought
to an end. But not everyone was convinced. Indeed, this was
the very context within which the most determined of the
Yorkists set out to ensure that Henry VII's reign would be of
short duration. Their plan was that in the longer term 'King
Edward VI' would be the real ruler of England.

One of Henry VII's chief advisors at the time of the Dublin
King's emergence was John Morton. Morton had probably
been born in about 1420, so that in 1486 he was about 66 years
of age.

Henry Stafford, 2nd Duke of Buckingham, redrawn from an eighteenth-century engraving.

John Morton was born in Dorset – possibly in Bere Regis, a village whose parish church he later rebuilt. However, his was not a West Country family in its origins: his father, Richard Morton, had come to Dorset from Nottinghamshire. John Morton's background was socially middling. One of his uncles served as an MP for the town of Shaftesbury on one occasion, and John's younger brother later became sheriff of Dorset and Somerset. John Morton himself entered the church, and received his higher education at the University of Oxford.

From 1452/53 John Morton was the Rector of Shellingford (Berkshire). At the same time he was emerging as a canon

Henry VII with John Islip,
Abbot of Westminster, and
the Benedictine monks of
Westminster Abbey.

lawyer in the Canterbury Court of Arches. Probably through
Archbishop Thomas Bourchier of Canterbury, Morton
began to become a prominent figure, being appointed chancellor to Edward of Westminster, Prince of Wales, the alleged
(though somewhat dubious) son of Henry VI. At the same
time he was accumulating other ecclesiastical appointments
in various dioceses.

Morton had grown up under the rule of the Lancastrian
dynasty, and had gradually been brought into the direct service
of that ruling house. This, together with his legal expertise,
probably accounts for the fact that in 1460 he was responsible for drafting the Bill of Attainder against Richard, Duke
of York (the father of the future Yorkist kings, Edward IV and
Richard III). That and other pro-Lancastrian actions on his
part led to Morton's subsequent exclusion from the pardons
issued by Edward IV when he seized the throne.

In fact, Morton was captured after the Battle of Towton,
and briefly imprisoned in the Tower of London, from which
he escaped. He then left his homeland and joined Henry VI's
queen, Margaret of Anjou, in exile in France. He became a
prominent figure at her exiled court, taking an active part
both in diplomacy and in Margaret's attempts to re-establish
herself in England in 1462–63. But since these attempts failed,
and since Morton himself had lost all his property in England,
he appeared to have settled down abroad, where he was soon
studying theology at the University of Louvain.

Morton was naturally involved in the Lancastrian
Readeption of 1470–71. Ultimately, however, when that failed,

he decided to come to some accommodation with the restored Yorkist King Edward IV. Thus he at last received a royal pardon, together with new government appointments. He served for seven years as Master of the Rolls, but also became increasingly involved in diplomacy. During the 1470s and the early 1480s he acted on several occasions as Edward IV's envoy in France and Burgundy. Meanwhile, in 1478 the Pope appointed him Bishop of Ely, with the full approval of Edward IV, who, by this time, had come to rely heavily on Morton's expertise.

But when Edward IV died, in 1483, Morton once again found himself on the wrong side politically. Following Bishop Stillington's revelation to the royal council of Edward IV's bigamy, and the division of opinion which that produced, Morton sided with Lord Hastings, expressing himself to be in favour of keeping quiet about the problem of Edward V's technical illegitimacy. As a result, when Hastings had his head cut off, Morton was arrested.

Unfortunately, and probably unwisely, Richard III placed Morton in the custody of the Duke of Buckingham. Bishop Morton was undoubtedly involved in Buckingham's subsequent rebellion, and when Buckingham fell, Morton was attainted. Once again, however, he fled abroad, where he involved himself in the faction surrounding Henry Tudor. Indeed, it was reportedly Morton who warned Henry of Richard III's attempt to extradite him from the Duchy of Brittany, where Henry was then living in exile.[3] As a result of this warning, Henry sought safety with his cousin, the King of France. The result of this was ultimately the offer of French support for Henry's campaign of 1485, which resulted in the death of Richard III and the establishment in England of a new ruling dynasty. Meanwhile, Bishop Morton had also secured Papal backing for the claims of Henry VII.

When Henry VII became king, Bishop Morton found himself re-established at the court in England, where in 1486 he succeeded the ancient Cardinal Bourchier as Archbishop of Canterbury. The Act of Attainder against him was reversed, and he became a member of the king's council. In March 1486/87, by which time the Dublin King's claim to the throne had already been made public, Bishop Morton found himself appointed Henry VII's Chancellor of England. Given his life history and his position in the new Tudor government, there was not a shred of doubt that Morton would now do all in his power to ensure that the Dublin King was defeated. He would also do whatever was needed to ensure that 'Edward VI' was reduced to a figure of no consequence.

PART 3

1486–1487

10

Evidence from England

According to Adrien de But's chronicle, on 5 October 1485, when John Morton, Bishop of Ely (who was then on his way back to England) reached Calais, he heard that the recently enthroned king, Henry VII (whom, however, Adrien de But prefers to call simply 'the Earl of Richmond'), had been killed – together with some of his barons – by a sudden outbreak of plague:

> Regarding the rightful successor of the new king, however, not a little controversy arose. Some acclaimed the son of the Duke of Clarence, as the true king – a distinguished youth, who had been rescued from slaughter carried out by his uncle, King Richard – though the present writer never heard anything of such [slaughter].[1]

In any case, in the end, no new English sovereign was proclaimed at this early date, since, as Adrien de But went on to say, no confirmation was ever received of the story of Henry VII's death.

Adrien de But's short report is very interesting in that it shows how rumours about affairs in England were rife at that time. With the benefit of hindsight, of course, we now know that, in reality, Henry VII had not died of plague within a mere two months of seizing the throne. As for Richard III, the question of whether or not he had engaged in slaughter is still very much a matter of hot dispute and debate! Even so, the evidence we have in no way suggests that Richard had ever contemplated slaughtering his nephew, the Earl of Warwick. As we saw earlier, Richard III had, in fact, promoted the little boy who was living under his protection to government posts.

At the same time it is important to recognise that Henry VII was a very new king, who had come to power as the result of an armed rebellion against his predecessor (who had been killed in the struggle). It is all too easy to assume that everyone knew that Henry would be king for a number of years. But in 1485 and 1486 there was no such certainty. In fact, many people, both in England and in other countries, were probably waiting with bated breath to see who would come forward to contest Henry VII's recent usurpation.

That this was indeed the case is made plain by the fact that in the course of the following year (1486) the Stafford brothers – Sir Humphrey, who had taken sanctuary after Bosworth at St John's Abbey in Colchester together with Viscount Lovell, and Humphrey's brother, Thomas Stafford, raised a rather hopeless and ill-fated rebellion in their native Worcestershire. The Staffords' attempt was a complete failure. However, at the same time 'it was noticed that a number of people in Ireland were embarking on a campaign to bring in a new king, the son of the Duke of Clarence (brother of the former kings, Edward and Richard), who by right of his mother was Duke [*sic*] of Warwick'.[2] Moreover, the Mechelen household accounts of Margaret of York, dowager Duchess of Burgundy include an interesting entry relating to the feast of the local martyr, St Rombout (Rumbold), on 24 June 1486. It appears that on the occasion of this significant local celebration Margaret paid for eight flagons of wine as a gift to 'the son of Clarence from England'.[3]

This very important surviving record in the dowager duch-ess's accounts makes it clear that, in the summer of 1486, a son of the Duke of Clarence – that is to say, one of Margaret's nephews – was understood to be staying with his aunt at her palace in Mechelen. Of course, the only known son of the Duke of Clarence who was alive in June 1486 was the Earl of Warwick, therefore unless this reference is to an otherwise completely unknown bastard son of the late Duke of Clarence, it seems that it was the Earl of Warwick who was believed to be visiting his aunt in Mechelen. Incidentally, a curious coinci-dence, in the present context, lies in the fact that St Rumbold was reputed to have been an Irish, early Christian missionary who had been martyred in Mechelen. The Irish link of the saint was potentially prophetic, for 'the son of Clarence' may also have come to Mechelen from Dublin. Moreover it was almost certainly the same reputed 'son of Clarence' who was crowned in Ireland less than a year later.

Unlike the documents from the Low Countries, most of the surviving evidence in England dating from 1486, and relat-ing to the existence of a Yorkist movement to remove the recently enthroned Henry VII, speaks of people other than the Earl of Warwick who were involved in the scheme. The two most important figures in the surviving English sources are the late Richard III's close friend Francis, Lord Lovell and the Earl of Warwick's older cousin, the Earl of Lincoln.

The lack of mention of the Earl of Warwick could possi-bly be due to chance regarding which writings have survived. However, the boy himself was very young. Thus the lead in planning a coup against Henry VII had necessarily to be taken by older and more experienced Yorkists – the very men who are mentioned in the surviving records. Even so, one passing English reference to Warwick does survive. It can be found in a letter written on 29 November 1486.

The letter confirms that Edward of Clarence, then aged 11 years and 9 months, and under normal circumstances probably potentially unlikely to figure in news from the English capital, had come to be seen as a figure of some importance. The pre-cise whereabouts of the Earl of Warwick at the time of writing are not absolutely clear from the surviving missive. However, the people mentioned in the letter were certainly not all in London. One cannot therefore simply assume that the ref-erence is to a prisoner in the Tower, or a person attending Henry VII's royal court (that is to say, Henry VII's official Earl of Warwick). The message may equally well relate to the alter-native earl – Margaret of York's summer guest in Mechelen – who was almost certainly still in Flanders in November 1486.

The letter in question was written by a priest called Thomas Betanson, 'to his worshipful master Sir Robart Plomton kt'. With his spelling and grammar slightly modernised, this priest, who was then serving the church of St Sepulchre-without-Newgate, wrote:

> Sir, as for tidings, here there are only a few. The king & queen are staying at Greenwich; the Lord Percy [son and heir of the fourth Earl of Northumberland] is at Winchester; the Earl of Oxford is in Essex; the Earl of Derby and his son are with the king. Also there is but little talk here of the Earl of Warwick now, but after Christmas they say there will be more talk of [him].[4] Also there are many enemies on the sea, & divers ships taken, & there are many of the kings house taken for thieves.'[5]

In fact this letter, which apparently links the Earl of Warwick with the enemies on the ships, and which expects to hear more of the earl after Christmas, seems inherently unlikely to refer to the boy who was either at Henry VII's court, or who was already a prisoner in the Tower of London. It is therefore probable that it refers to the *other* Earl of Warwick – the boy who was in Flanders at the time when the message was writ-ten. In other words, the implication would appear to be that the *real* Earl of Warwick was considered by Thomas Betanson to be the Mechelen 'son of Clarence'. And, as we have already seen, it is probable that the Mechelen 'son of Clarence' was that same child who, in the following year, was to be crowned as 'King Edward VI' – the Dublin King.

Much of the other evidence from England regarding the progress of the Yorkist movement during 1486 relates to Francis, Lord Lovell. Francis had an interesting background. As we have seen, he had been a close companion of Richard, Duke of Gloucester (the future Richard III) during his adolescence, when both of them had been under the guardianship of 'Warwick the Kingmaker'. Lord Lovell was also a connection of Eleanor Talbot. It had, of course, been the revelation of Eleanor's secret marriage to Edward IV which changed the order of succession in the summer of 1483, and brought Richard III to the throne.

Francis, Lord Lovell had remained a faithful servant of Richard III after the latter became king, and their connection had been lampooned in the famous couplet quoted earlier. In 1485, in the face of the threatened Tudor invasion, Francis Lovell had been sent by Richard III to guard the south coast. Possibly he fought with Richard at the Battle of Bosworth, as many historians have maintained. However, it is also possible that, based as he had been in the south of England, defending the coast, Lovell had found himself unable to rejoin his king in time to take part in his last battle. At all events, unlike the king, the Duke of Norfolk, and Richard Ratcliffe, he certainly survived the defeat of August 1485. Francis then took refuge at St John's Abbey in Colchester.

St John's Abbey Church, Colchester, redrawn by the author from BL, Cotton MS Nero D viii, f. 345.

This important Benedictine abbey, which stood just outside the walls of Colchester on the southern side of the
town, had been founded in 1095.[6] It possessed very powerful rights of sanctuary.[7] 'There were two types of sanctuary
in medieval England.' Any church could offer some degree
of protection, but 'some abbeys and minsters had special rites
of sanctuary … anyone who took refuge in such a sanctuary
could remain there with impunity for life'.[8] Colchester Abbey
had been granted such extraordinary rights of sanctuary in
1109.[9] However, these rights appear to have been contested
later, because in the mid fifteenth century Abbot Ardeley had
appealed to Henry VI to have them confirmed. The abbot's
request was submitted upon the grounds that during the king's
incapacity, the community at St John's had expended much
time and effort in praying for his recovery. As a result of Abbot
Ardeley's petition, on 13 May 1453 Henry VI had issued an
explicit formal confirmation of the sanctuary rights of St
John's Abbey.[10]

Francis Lovell was not originally from the Colchester
area, but from Oxfordshire. However, Colchester is close to
the Essex–Suffolk border and, as we have seen, Francis had
spent part of his youth in the neighbouring county of Suffolk.
Thus he was probably well aware of the possible advantages
of claiming sanctuary at St John's Abbey, partly thanks to his
brief period of residence in the vicinity, and also thanks to his
friendship with the late Duke of Norfolk. John Howard had
spent most of his life on the Suffolk–Essex border. The ancestral manor of his father's family was at Stoke-by-Nayland,
in Suffolk, but he had been Constable of Colchester Castle,
and owned a fine town house in Colchester (now the *Red
Lion* in Colchester's High Street). His role as Admiral of the
Northern Seas had also often taken him to the nearby ports of
Harwich and Dovercourt. Howard had himself taken sanctuary at St John's Abbey in Colchester during the Lancastrian
Readeption (1470–1), and the same abbot – Abbot Walter
Stansted – who had received Howard in 1470, was still in office

at the abbey in Colchester in 1485, when Viscount Lovell arrived at the impressive Abbey Gatehouse (which survives to this day – see plates 16 and 17) to ask for sanctuary.[11]

Francis Lovell remained at St John's Abbey for several months. But by the spring of 1486, he was on the move again. Just across the border in Suffolk, Lovell's former guardian – one of the late king's sisters – had her home and power-base. Elizabeth of York and her husband, John de la Pole, the Duke and Duchess of Suffolk, had their principal residence at Wingfield Castle. However, they also had connections with many other places in the county of Suffolk. The couple is, to this day, commemorated in the surviving fifteenth-century stained glass at the church of Stratford St Mary, a mere 5 or 6 miles to the north-east of Colchester. And, of course, the eldest son of the Duke and Duchess of Suffolk was the Earl of Lincoln. Although his father was trying to be politically correct in the eyes of Henry VII, Lincoln, Richard III's nephew, was already strongly opposed to the man who had defeated and killed his uncle. Lincoln would have had little difficulty in contacting – and possibly meeting – Francis Lovell while he was still safe in sanctuary at the abbey in Colchester.

Moreover, as we have seen, Francis was not the only Yorkist who had claimed sanctuary at St John's Abbey in the aftermath of Bosworth. While he was there he had with him an older companion. This was Sir Humphrey Stafford of Grafton in Worcestershire (*c.*1426–86). Sir Humphrey had inherited his manor in Worcestershire in 1449. He had proved an enthusiastic Yorkist, and he apparently fought with Richard III at Bosworth, after which he had fled to St John's Abbey in Colchester and claimed sanctuary. Incidentally the fact that Stafford had apparently come to Colchester Abbey from Bosworth Field raises the possibility that Viscount Lovell may also have fought at Bosworth, and that he and Sir Humphrey Stafford may then have escaped from the battlefield together and fled south to Colchester:

Lovell and his companion in sanctuary, Humphrey Stafford of Grafton (Worcestershire), sought to stir up rebellion against the new regime: Stafford in the west midlands and Lovell in Yorkshire. But the leading northern families failed to support the rising, and by the time Henry VII entered York on 20 April Lovell's forces had dispersed.[12]

A surviving letter from Warwick the Kingmaker's sister, Margaret (Neville), Countess of Oxford,[13] to John Paston III, written on 19 May 1486, tells us something of Lovell's subsequent movements. Written at the Earl of Oxford's estate at Lavenham in Suffolk, this letter warns that Francis Lovell is on the loose in the eastern counties, either seeking to regain sanctuary, or to find a ship to take him abroad. The Countess therefore orders John Paston in the king's name, and in his capacity as the Sheriff of Norfolk and Suffolk, to keep a good look-out and do all in his power to capture Lovell.[14]

Towards the end of 1486, the weather on the European mainland was inclement. 'In November and December there were many problems with wind, rain and frost ... and it was rumoured that the king of England would be deposed in favour of the true heir, the Duke of Clarence's son'.[15] Despite the inclement weather, and with Adrien de But's second point very firmly in his mind, by January 1486/87 either Lovell had already crossed the sea to Flanders, or he was about to do so.

At about this time, Lady Oxford's correspondent, John Paston III, wrote to the Earl of Oxford[16] with (as he thought) news of Lovell's departure, naming those whom he believed were accompanying the Viscount. However, it seems that the King and Lord Oxford thought they were better informed. On 24 January 1486/87 the Earl of Oxford replied to John Paston III as follows:

To my right trusty and wellbeloved counsellor John Paston, esquire.

This house was anciently the Rose & Crown Inn & here in 1483 Richard. Duke of Gloucester (Richard III) captured the uncrowned boy King Edward V. who was later murdered in the Tower of London

1 'Princes in the Tower' mythology: a plaque on the former Rose and Crown Inn at Stony Stratford (Milton Keynes), which purports to give 'facts' about the fate of Edward V. In reality there is no evidence to indicate that Edward V stayed at the Rose and Crown, or that he was 'captured', or that he was murdered. © Iris Day.

2 Warwick Castle, the birthplace of Edward of Clarence, Earl of Warwick.

3 The gatehouse of Tewkesbury Abbey, Gloucestershire. Edward, Earl of Warwick probably stayed with his parents at Tewkesbury Abbey in the autumn of 1476.

4 The ruins of Sheriff Hutton Castle, Yorkshire. Here, according to the authorised version of his history, Edward, Earl of Warwick lived with some of his cousins, including Elizabeth of York, during the reign of his uncle Richard III. © Tommaso Romero and Vanessa Roe.

5 According to one account Lambert Simnel's father lived close to Oxford Castle – shown here as it might have looked in about 1480.

Lambert Simnel's father said to have been a [mer]chant of the Augustinian [Ab]bey of Osney, Oxford. [The]ese are the abbey ruins [as] they were in about [15]00.

The Earl of Warwick's [off]icial guardian, [14]85–86: Margaret [Be]aufort, Countess of [Ric]hmond and Derby, the [mo]ther of Henry VII.

8 Elizabeth of York junior, daughter of Edward IV and Elizabeth Woodville, cousin of Edward, Earl of Warwick and consort of Henry VII.

9 Elizabeth of York senior, Duchess of Suffolk, a sister of Edward IV and Richard III, the mother of John de la Pole, Earl of Lincoln, and a possible aunt of the Dublin King (effigy circa 1500, from her tomb at Wingfield Church, Suffolk).

10 The seal of John de la Pole, Earl of Lincoln, nephew of Edward IV and Richard III; a possible cousin and key supporter of the Dublin King. Reproduced courtesy of Colchester and Ipswich Museums Service

11 Margaret of York, Duchess of Burgundy
(after her marriage portrait of c.1468).
Margaret was a key supporter of the
Dublin King.

12 Mechelen, Belgium, with the
tower and crossing of St Rombout
(Rumbold)'s Church (a cathedral since
1559). St Rombout's tower was under
construction in 1486, when 'Clarence's
son' was staying in Mechelen.

13 Margaret of York's palace in Mechelen, where she entertained 'Clarence's son' in
1486.

14 Monuments in Mechelen commemorating Margaret of York. *Above left:* a modern copy of her 1503 funeral inscription, commissioned by the author and the Richard III Society. *Above right:* arms and inscription over the entrance to her palace.

15 St John's Abbey gatehouse, Colchester. Through this entranc Francis, Viscount Lovell passed ir 1485, seeking sanctuary.

16 *Above:* Surviving remains of St John's Abbey, Colchester: archways and vaulting.

17 *Right:* The arms of the Duke of Clarence's Irish deputy, Gerald, Earl of Kildare, the effective ruler of most of Ireland. Kildare was a key supporter of the Dublin King, and possibly his guardian during his childhood.

18 Ruins of Maynooth Castle, County Kildare. This was the home of the Earl of Kildare, and it may have been where the Dublin King was brought up for part of his childhood.

19 A model of old St Paul's Cathedral, where Henry VII displayed the official Earl of Warwick in an attempt to undermine the claims of the Dublin King.

20 The surviving medieval tower of Dublin Castle. The castle was the official residence of the Dublin King during his reign in Ireland.

1 The surviving medieval north wall of the nave of Christ Church Cathedral, where the Dublin King was crowned.

2 The Dublin King is said to have been crowned with an open gold circlet borrowed from the image of the Blessed Virgin in the Church of Sainte Marie de la Dam (Our Lady of Dame-gate) on Cork Hill. Neither the image nor the crown have survived, but this gold open crown worn by the fifteenth-century image of Our Lady of Caversham may give some idea of the appearance of the crown used at the Dublin coronation.

23 Examples of the kind of items which might have been used in the Dublin coronation. *Left:* a medieval chrismatory for containing holy oils. *Right:* a typical verger's church staff.

24 *Left:* the fifteenth-century brass eagle lectern of Christ Chuch Cathedral, which probably figured in the coronation ceremony of 1487. *Right:* the sword of state presented to Dublin by Henry IV in 1404. This might possibly have been used at the coronation of 1487.

25 & 26 *Above left:* Copy of a nineteenth-century image of the post-coronation procession of the Dublin King. The boy is shown seated on the shoulders of William Darcy of Platten. However, this depiction is inaccurate in some respects, since the boy-king is not wearing royal robes or regalia. © Muhammad Hanif. *Above right:* The only surviving contemporary image of the Dublin King, 'Edward VI', crowned and enthroned, and holding the orb and sceptre, from the obverse of his great seal. Reproduced courtesy of the National Library of Ireland.

27 *Far left:* A modern image of the Dublin King in his coronation robes, based on the representation on his great seal. © Riikka Nikko.

28 *Left:* The royal arms of the Dublin King from the reverse of his great seal. Note the crown, which is ornamented only with fleurs-de-lis – like a French royal coronet. A fleur-de-lis also marks the start of the inscription. Reproduced courtesy of the National Library of Ireland.

29 Letter issued in 1487, in the name of 'King Edward VI', appointing Peter (Piers) Butler as Sheriff of Kilkenny. This letter bears the only surviving example of an impression of the Dublin King's great royal seal. Reproduced courtesy of the National Library of Ireland.

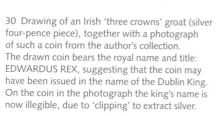

30 Drawing of an Irish 'three crowns' groat (silver four-pence piece), together with a photograph of such a coin from the author's collection. The drawn coin bears the royal name and title: EDWARDUS REX, suggesting that the coin may have been issued in the name of the Dublin King. On the coin in the photograph the king's name is now illegible, due to 'clipping' to extract silver.

31 A reconstruction by the author of the appearance of John Morton, Bishop of Ely, and later Cardinal Archbishop of Canterbury. There are only two surviving contemporary images of Morton: his damaged tomb effigy in Canterbury Cathedral, and his face on a roof boss at Bere Regis Church, Dorset. This reconstruction is based on the (inset) photograph of the Bere Regis face.

32 Morton's Tower – a building constructed by Cardinal Archbishop Morton at the entrance to Lambeth Palace. © Deidre O'Sullivan.

34 An eighteenth-century imaginary depiction of Lambert Simnel as a scullion in Henry VII's kitchens. Note that he appears to be about 17 years of age.

35 The official Earl of Warwick residence, 1486–99. A modern view of the Tower of London, seen from across the River Thames.

36 The former church of Bishan Priory, a house of Augustinian canons in Berkshire, redrawn from a medieval illustration. Nothing now remains of this church, where the official Earl of Warwick was interred in 1499.

37 The burial place of Perkin Warbeck/Richard of England. An eighteenth-century engraving of the north-western end of the nave of the Austin Friars Church, Old Broad Street, London, before its restoration in the nineteenth century.

38 An early twentieth-century photograph of the restored nave of the Austin Friars Church, Old Broad Street. Unfortunately this building no longer exists. It was destroyed by German bombing in 1940.

39 The nave of the Austin Friars Church, looking west, in its restored state, in 1865 (following the fire of 1862).

40 The nave and south aisle of the Austin Friars Church, looking east, prior to the final destruction of the building in 1940.

John Paston, I commend me to you. And as for such tidings
as you have sent hither, the King had knowledge thereof
more than a week ago; and as for such names as you have
sent, supposing them to be gone with the Lord Lovell, they
are yet in England, for he is departing with 14 persons and
no more. At the King's coming to London I would advise
you to see His Highness.

And Almighty God keep you.
Written at Windsor the 24th day of January.
Oxford.[17]

By February 1486/87, King Henry VII was well aware that
plots were afoot to oust him from the throne and replace
him with the Earl of Warwick. Probably he had also heard
that the 'son of Clarence' was in Mechelen, staying with
his putative aunt, a lady whom Henry called 'the diabolicall duches'. On the Feast of Candlemas (Friday, 2 February
1486/87) 'the king called a Council at Richmond … and,
acting on its advice, had the real [*sic*] Earl of Warwick taken
from the Tower and led through the streets of London to St
Paul's. Here the boy held a kind of audience in the church,
speaking particularly to persons who it was thought might be
likely to participate in the Simnel Plot (Polydore Virgil). That
little effect was produced on them is pretty evident from the
example of Lincoln, who, immediately after his interview
with the young Earl, fled from England and betook himself
to the Court of Burgundy'.[18]

And indeed our next surviving piece of English evidence
relates not to Lovell, but to the Earl of Lincoln. On 31 May 1487
an inhabitant of York, James Taite, was accused of having said
on 30 March of that same year 'that the Earl of Lincoln wold
give the King's grace a breakfast [give him what he deserved]
as it was enformed him by the servant of the said Earl's'.[19] In
response to the accusation levelled against him, Taite offered
a rather garbled statement about his meeting with servants of
the Earl of Lincoln. These servants were leading with them

Lincoln's horse – which, by chance, Taite recognised, because he had stabled that same horse during Lincoln's most recent visit to York, as part of the entourage of Henry VII.

What emerges from Taite's statement is that some of Lincoln's servants were definitely in the vicinity of York in March 1486/87 in charge of their master's horse. Moreover, it seems that they expected Lincoln himself to join them at some stage. They also knew that he was aiming to take revenge on those who had not (in his opinion) accorded him his due rights. In addition, Taite's statement reveals that the Earl of Northumberland was not thought to be committed to Lincoln's plans. However, some of the local gentry – and other local people – apparently were.

James Taite's statement, in its modernised form, reads:

I, James Tayte, rode to Retford [Nottinghamshire]. And last Lady Day [25 March 1486/87] when I was in Doncaster, on my way home, I met seven horses of strangers. Among them there was a white horse that was being led. And a merchant's servant pointed out to me that in that horse's saddle there was gold and silver.

When I heard that, I asked him where he came from, and he said, from London. Then another of the same merchant's men asked me whether there was any death [plague] within the City or not, and I said, no. Then I revealed to him that I should know one member of their company by his horse. He asked me how it came about that I recognised this horse. I answered that I had seen him in York the last time the King's good grace was there – for I thought that he was my Lorde of Lincoln's pony – for with me was he lodged.

When this man told him [the merchant?] what I had said, he came back to me and asked me how I was. And asked me how I knew this horse, and I said he was my Lord of Lincoln's, and he bade me speak the truth. I knew then by what he was saying to me that it really was my Lord of Lincoln's horse.

And then I asked him how my Lord of Lincoln was, and asked him where he was. And he told me that, to the best of his knowledge, he [Lincoln] had departed from the King's grace. And I asked him, whether he had gone to sea – for he has many friends on land. And I also showed him that my Lord had many good friendes in this country as far as I knew. I said all that in order to try to find out more about what he was telling me.

Then he revealed to me – though I shall also see it for myself very soon – that John of Lincoln shall pay back all those who show him no love nor favour.

I asked him whether my Lord of Northumberland and he [Lincoln] were of one mind. He replied that 'he [Northumberland] is not doing very much, therefore we don't place much trust in him. But as you shall see, there are very good gentlemen about who will support my Lord [Lincoln]. Can you tell me anything about how far I must go to reach Sir Thomas Mallevery's place? For we have a letter to give him or send to him'.

Then I asked him if he would be coming to York, and he said: 'No, I must go to Hull. But if I come to York I will call on you'.

Later I went to Wentbridge, to an inn, and looked for these merchants that were riding on to York. And the good man of the house told me that they were sleeping in their beds. I went back there twice to look for them, and I asked the inn-keeper to tell me where the man was that rode that pony [the Earl of Lincoln?]. 'Hasn't he been here', I said, 'I've been waiting for him for too long'. Then I left him.

After that, between Darlington and Wentbridge, I met a man that was born a servant of my Lord of Lincoln, that had been lying in his bed at Wentbridge. And I asked about that same man [Lincoln?] – since they were sometimes together in company. He said he had sent for him in great haste. He had sent a hired man to find him.

And I came straight to York.

Then these same merchants of London came to York, and
a servant of theirs told me that they would meet the Prior
of Tynmouthe at the sign of the Boar [the Blue Boar in
Castlegate] in York.

And I went to Master Karlill, to tell him all the things
I had heard, as I have already mentioned, for my own safety,
and in order to keep the oath that I swore to God and the
King, simply because he was one of the King's Chaplains.

This servant of my Lord of Lincoln that had revealed
everything to me on the journey, as I was coming from
Doncaster, is called Saunder[s?].

And I told Master Karlill that the last time the King
was here, two fellows that live near Middleham said 'Here
is good gate for us to Robin of Redesdall over the walls'.
This is what I said, and not a word more, I swear. And the
same two fellows used to hang about my Lord of Lincoln's
household, and went there for food and drink.[20]

Meanwhile, in the eastern counties it is not quite clear what
John Paston III had been doing, but it seems that his behaviour
had by now caused Oxford – and the king – to suspect him of
possible involvement in the Yorkist conspiracy. The following
letter was sent by T. Balkey to John Paston III,[21] probably on
29 April 1487:[22]

Right worshipful and my especial good master, I commend me unto your good mastership. Sir, it is so that
there hath been a great rumour and marvellous noise of
your departing from Yarmouth, for some said in a Spanish
ship and some said in your ship, and some said against
your will ye were departed; of which departing my lord
Steward had knowledge and commanded soon after your
old servant Richard FitzWater to ride to Norwich and so
to Yarmouth to know the truth. And at Norwich I spoke
with your said servant, and there he showed unto me that
my lord had sent another of his servants unto my lord of

Oxford to show unto his lordship of your departing, &c.
And furthermore he showed unto me privately that my
lord hath imagined and purposed many grievous things
against your mastership; for which cause he showed unto
me that in any wise your mastership should not come that
way. And I shall show your mastership much more at your
coming, with the grace of God, who ever preserve your
good mastership.

At Norwich the Sunday next after Saint Mark.
Your seruaunt T. Balkey[23]

Balkey was not the only person who thought that John Paston
may have been travelling by sea. Sir Edmond Bedyngfeld sent
another letter to John Paston III on 16 May 1487:[24]

Vn-to my right wurshypfull cosyn John Paston, eswquyer
for the body.

Bedyngfeld has received a sealed commission of array from
'my lorde' (The Earl of Oxford) in connection with the invasion of Ireland by supporters of the Dublin King, together
with a letter, of which he encloses a copy – see Davis, *Paston
Letters*, p. 453, no. 811A:

As for you, ye be sore taken in some place, saying that ye
intende such things as is like to follow great mischief. I said
I understood no such [thing] nor things like it. And it is
thought ye intende not to go forth this journey, nor no
gentleman in that quarter but Robert Brandon that hath
promised to go with them, as they say.[25]

The writer then goes on to give details of the movements of
Sir William Boleyn, Sir Harry Heydon, Hopton and Wysman.
Bedyngfeld is interested in 'what gentlemen intende to go …
and be assured to go to-gether':[26]

Furthermore, cousin, it is said that after my lord's[27] departing to the King ye were met at Barkwey, which is construed
that ye had been with the Lady Lovell; but rather said never
well. And in as much as we understand my lord's pleasure,
it is well done we deal wisely thereafter. And next to the
King I answered plainly I was bound to do him service and
to fulfil his commandment to the uttermost of my power,
by the grace of God, who ever preserve you to his pleasure.

    Written at Oxburgh the 16 day of May.

Your cousin E. Bedyngfeld[28]

John Paston III was obviously close to family members of
Viscount Lovell, whose mother-in-law, Alice, Lady Fitzhugh
later wrote him a letter in which she describes herself as 'you
living modir [mother]', and which talks about how her daughter was trying to find what had become of Lovell (23 February
1487/88).[29] Lovell 'diasappeared after the Battle of Stoke (at
which John Paston III was knighted), and is said to have been
drowned while trying to escape [*Complete Peerage*, viii 225].
According to Gairdner "another story" reported that he did
escape and lived in concealment for some time after. If this
were true it would account for the present letter's address to
John III as knight'.[30]

    The ultimate fate of Francis Lovell remains a mystery.
Meanwhile, however, the evidence from the Paston corre-
spondence shows very clearly how uncertain the situation was
in England in 1486, and how much gossip and rumour were
current. As for John Paston III, in 1486 it appears that, whatever his private sympathies and opinions, in the end he played
safe and remained loyal to the government in power.

    Nevertheless, both the Earl of Lincoln and Viscount Lovell
did take ships from England and made their way to Margaret
of York's palace at Mechelen. As we have already seen from the
evidence of the Paston letters, Viscount Lovell probably made
his trip to Flanders in January 1486/87. The Earl of Lincoln
departed slightly later; we know that on Friday, 2 February

1486/87, (the Feast of Candlemas) he was present at a meeting of Henry VII's royal council at the Palace of Sheen.[31]

At this meeting, the royal council received an embassy from the King of France. It probably also discussed the news from Flanders and Ireland about the activities of Margaret of York and the 'son of Clarence', and this was also the occasion on which Henry VII made the decision to publicly display his official Earl of Warwick in London:

> At that council was the Earl of Lincoln, which incontinently after the said council departed the land and went into Flanders to the lord Lovell and accompanied himself with the king's rebels and enemies, noising in that country that the Earl of Warwick should be in Ireland, which himself knew and daily spoke with him at Sheen before his departing.[32]

But, of course, the Earl of Warwick whom Lincoln had been seeing at Sheen was the offficial one – presumably the same one that Lincoln had known earlier, at Sheriff Hutton Castle, during the reign of Richard III, and also the one whom Henry VII would shortly put on show in London in order to prove his whereabouts.

Clearly Henry VII must have been aware of exactly what action Lincoln had taken by the third week of Lent (about 20 March 1486/87). At that time the king set off via Essex into Suffolk. That county was the heartland of the Earl of Lincoln's family, and Henry presumably felt that, among other things, he now needed to sort out where the rest of the de la Poles stood politically. At the same time he also needed to reassure himself that the county of Suffolk was safe.

Henry VII stayed briefly at Bury St Edmunds, and it is evident that he was preoccupied with the likely rising against him, because while there he ordered the arrest of his wife's half-brother, the Marquess of Dorset. The arrest of Dorset in the context of this particular political situation is of some interest, because of course, as we saw earlier, it was the Marquess of Dorset who had been the guardian of the official Earl of Warwick under Edward IV, following the execution of Warwick's father, the Duke of Clarence.

It surely cannot be coincidental that the official Earl of Warwick's former guardian was imprisoned at precisely this moment – at a time when one boy claiming to be the Earl of Warwick was about to invade England, while another boy, officially designated as the Earl of Warwick, was about to be displayed by Henry VII in London. Moreover, the idea that Dorset's arrest was somehow connected with the coming invasion – and also with Dorset's own links with the Earl of Warwick – is reinforced by the fact that immediately after the Battle of Stoke, when 'Edward VI' had been defeated, the Marquess of Dorset was set free again.[33]

Meanwhile Lincoln had joined Lovell at Mechelen, where he met with his aunt, the dowager Duchess of Burgundy. Presumably once Margaret herself had received her newly arrived nephew, she presented him to her other beguiling young guest, his putative cousin, the young 'son of Clarence'.

11

Burgundian Preparations

We have no surviving record of any of the discussions which took place in Margaret of York's Mechelen Palace between the dowager Duchess of Burgundy and her guests. However, there can be no doubt that meetings and discussions did take place there. In these meetings Margaret must have explored with her nephew, the Earl of Lincoln, and with Viscount Lovell, and others, what exactly they planned to do in order to promote the cause of the 'son of Clarence' and the future of the royal house of York.

The two royal candidates for the role of the Dublin King (in bold), with two of his key supporters (underlined).

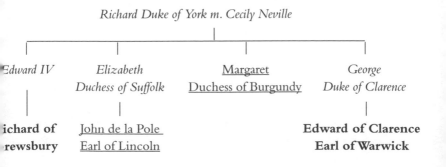

Richard Duke of York m. Cecily Neville

Edward IV	Elizabeth *Duchess of Suffolk*	<u>Margaret</u> <u>Duchess of Burgundy</u>	George *Duke of Clarence*
Richard of **Shrewsbury**	<u>John de la Pole</u> <u>Earl of Lincoln</u>		**Edward of Clarence** **Earl of Warwick**

The 'son of Clarence' himself had arrived in Mechelen some
months before Viscount Lovell and the Earl of Lincoln. We
know that this boy was in the Mechelen palace by Saturday,
24 June 1486 – the feast day of St Rumbold – since on that
day, as we have already noted, Margaret gave him a present of
some wine. Apparently it was Margaret herself who had sent
for him, but no precise record survives of how, or when, or
from where, the boy reached Mechelen.

When the 'son of Clarence' arrived at Mechelen, the official
Earl of Warwick was, of course, in England. At that time he may
still have been under the guardianship of Henry VII's mother,
Margaret Beaufort, Countess of Richmond and Derby. During
February 1486/87 this boy had been attending Henry's royal
court at the Palace of Sheen. Thus it is clear that the 'son of
Clarence' who was in Mechelen in June 1486 cannot possibly
have been identical with the official Earl. And, of course, no
one would have been in a better position to know and prove
this than the Earl of Lincoln himself, since he had been in
the company of the official Warwick at Sheen before he left
England to meet the 'son of Clarence' in Mechelen.

Actually, as we have already seen, Vergil later confused
the situation even further by reporting that there had been
rumours in London at about this time that the official Earl of
Warwick had died. He claimed that it was:

> When Simons learned this, [*that*] thinking the time had
> come for his intended crime, he changed the lad's name
> and called him Edward, the name of the Duke of Clarence's
> son, *who was of the same age*, so that neither was older than
> the other, and immediately took him and crossed over
> to Ireland.[1]

However, even if Vergil was correct in alleging that there
were rumours of Warwick's demise, in reality the official earl
had not died. Moreover, it seems highly unlikely that the boy
held by Henry VII as the Earl of Warwick ever left the king's

custody. That means that the 'son of Clarence' received by Margaret of York in Mechelen in the summer of 1486 must have come from somewhere else. Given the alternative life history of the young Earl of Warwick presented in Chapter 5, the most likely location would obviously be Ireland.

Bernard André implies that the Dublin King was in Ireland when the Earl of Lincoln endorsed him. Although the surviving evidence makes it quite clear that the 'son of Clarence' was already in Mechelen at the time when the Earl of Lincoln made the decision to *publicly* embrace the boy's cause, Lincoln had clearly been in touch with his aunt Margaret for some time. It is therefore conceivable that he had heard news about the 'son of Clarence' from the duchess before that boy left Ireland for Flanders, and had then shown interest in this candidate for the throne.

André then goes on to say that the boy made his trip to the Low Countries because he had received a letter from Margaret of York inviting him to come and visit her. André's implication is clearly that the 'son of Clarence' went to Mechelen *from Ireland*. Later André says that he returned from the Low Countries, backed by an army supplied by Margaret, and that he then travelled to England, with his army, to assert his claim there.[2]

Thus it seems that the 'son of Clarence' must have come to Mechelen from Ireland, in which case there are three possibilities regarding his true identity:

a) The boy was delivered to the Earl of Kildare in 1476/77 as the Earl of Warwick, and was then brought up under Kildare's guardianship at his Castle of Maynooth in County Kildare. Under the umbrella of this first basic theory there are two possible further interpretations.

i) The boy was the genuine Earl of Warwick, sent to Ireland by his father, the Duke of Clarence.

ii) The little boy was a substitute 'Earl of Warwick' created as part of Clarence's rather confusing plans regarding his son and heir.

b) He was a fraud: a boy trained to imitate the manners
of a prince by a scheming priest whose precise motivation
remains unknown; a boy who had been brought to Ireland
from Oxford only recently.

There is no way of knowing for certain which explanation of
the boy's origin and identity is correct. Nevertheless, whatever his true identity and origin, it appears certain that this
child, who had either been brought up in Ireland by the Earl
of Kildare, or taken to Ireland by a priest called Symonds/
Simons, was identical with the boy who was subsequently
crowned as 'King Edward VI' in Dublin in 1487.

But in that case we cannot ignore the fact that the Dublin
King also had the full support of Margaret, Duchess of
Burgundy – and of the troops she had sent to support his
claim. What is more, he also had the full backing of the Earl
of Lincoln and of Viscount Lovell. Therefore presumably the
boy who was crowned in Dublin's Christ Church Cathedral
must also have been one and the same person as the 'son of
Clarence' whose presence in Mechelen was recorded more or
less by accident in June 1486.

The picture that emerges is therefore that the boy crowned
in Dublin in 1487 had previously been the guest of Margaret
of York in her Mechelen Palace, but that earlier (i.e. before
June 1486) he had been living in Ireland. And it is absolutely
certain that the Dublin King cannot possibly have been the
official Earl of Warwick, since *he* had been at Henry VII's
court at Sheen in February 1486/87, at a time when the
'son of Clarence' (i.e. the future Dublin King) was already at
Margaret's palace in Mechelen.

How can we possibly clarify the true identity of this boy?
We have no precise record of how well Margaret of York knew
the official Earl of Warwick. She certainly could not have met
the official earl prior to her visit to England in 1480, for at the
time when she left England for her marriage with Charles the
Bold, Warwick had not yet been born. It is not even certain

that she met him during her 1480 visit – though the surviving accounts of Edward IV appear to suggest that plans were in place for such a meeting. What is more, even if the meeting actually happened, it perhaps occurred in the context of a large family gathering. Thus Margaret may not have paid a great deal of attention to one particular young nephew among all the various relatives who had come to greet her.

But the question of whether or not Margaret had met the official Earl of Warwick in 1480 seems, in any case, to be irrelevant. After all, the 'son of Clarence' whom she received in 1486 came to her from Ireland, at a time when the official Earl of Warwick was in or near London, with Henry VII. It is therefore obvious that Margaret could not possibly have recognised the 1486 'son of Clarence' as the boy she had (perhaps) met at the court of Edward IV in 1480 – because he was not the same person.

Thus it seems that in the early summer of 1486 Margaret of York received at Mechelen a boy she had never previously set eyes on, sent to her from Ireland by the Fitzgerald family as her nephew. Given the fact that the official Earl of Warwick was then known to be in Henry VII's custody, what on earth persuaded the dowager duchess to accept the identity of this boy from Ireland and endorse him as her nephew?

Even more surprising is the fact that the boy from Dublin was also accepted by the Earl of Lincoln as his cousin, even though Lincoln had spent about *two years* in the company of the official Earl of Warwick, when both of them had been resident at Sheriff Hutton Castle in Yorkshire.

There seem to be only two possible explanations for the extraordinary behaviour of Margaret of York and the Earl of Lincoln. The first explanation – a very simple one – is that neither of them had any interest in the truth. According to that scenario, even though the boy presented to them was an impostor to whom neither of them was related in any way, they merely wanted to oust Henry VII, and put the house of York back in control of things in England. However, the second possibility is that, for some reason, both Margaret and Lincoln were genuinely convinced that the boy from Ireland really was the 'son of Clarence'.

The first of these explanations raises very serious questions. Henry VII's wife, and the mother of the future royal line, was Elizabeth of York, the genuine niece of Margaret and the genuine first cousin of Lincoln. Why displace this *real* daughter of the house of York (together with all her future descendants) merely in order to replace her with an impostor? Of course Elizabeth, like all the children of Edward IV's Woodville marriage, had formally been declared illegitimate by Parliament in 1484. Nevertheless, Margaret later supported the claim to the throne of Perkin Warbeck, who said he was Elizabeth of York's younger brother, Richard, Duke of York. Thus, despite their dubious legitimacy, when the chips were down Margaret clearly considered Edward IV's Woodville children preferable to any non-Yorkist candidate for the English crown.

And even if the Yorkist line of Elizabeth seemed unacceptable to Margaret, when linked with the bloodline of Henry VII, her obvious solution would have been to replace Henry with an *authentic* Yorkist claimant. The most obvious contender would then have been the Earl of Lincoln himself. As we already know, this very obvious potential Yorkist solution was plainly evident, even to those contemporaries who believed that the Dublin King was a fake. Indeed it explains why King Henry VII himself found the plot hatched by Margaret and Lincoln utterly mystifying.

It therefore appears that both Margaret and Lincoln must have been convinced – or succeeded in convincing themselves – that the boy in Margaret's palace really was the 'son of Clarence'. Since not a shred of evidence exists to suggest that the Duke of Clarence ever fathered a bastard child, as far as is known, his only surviving son in 1486 was Edward, Earl of Warwick. This does not, of course, guarantee that Margaret and Lincoln got it right. In the last century, when a woman appeared claiming to be the Grand Duchess Anastasia

Nikolaevna of Russia, some members of the Imperial family accepted her and some rejected her. Likewise some of the imperial family's supporters recognised, and some rejected, the claimant. In the end it became apparent that the woman was an impostor – though she herself may have believed her own claim.

In the same way, a boy brought up by the Earl of Kildare in Ireland, and then sent to Mechelen, may well have believed in his own royal identity. If Kildare thought that his ward was the 'son of Clarence', obviously he would have brought him up under that name. This may have created a situation somewhat similar to an intriguing earlier episode in Russian history, when the son of 'False Dimitry II' (a pretender to the Russian throne) was brought up as an imperial prince, in spite of the fact that his father had been (and must have known himself to be) an impostor.[3]

It seems probable that in 1486 Margaret of York and her nephew, the Earl of Lincoln, were confronted, not only by a stranger who looked to be about 9 years old, and who was claiming to be the 'son of Clarence', but also by letters from the Earl of Kildare backing that claim. As we saw in Chapter 5, it is possible that the Duke of Clarence had sent his real son to Ireland in 1476/77. If Clarence did such a thing, then in the interests of the little boy's future, he might have felt obliged to ensure that he also left some proof of the child's identity. Perhaps Margaret of York and her nephew the Earl of Lincoln were therefore confronted, in 1486, by a claimant who was actually 11 years old (but looked younger), and who was backed not only by letters from the Earl of Kildare, but also by a document of some kind from Margaret's dearly loved brother, written and sealed by him before his death, nine years earlier. If so, that would have been a document which sought to provide some kind of proof that this boy really was the 'son of Clarence'.

Whatever it was that made Margaret of York and the Earl of Lincoln accept the claim of the boy from Ireland, once they had made this decision there were various sequels. First, Margaret had to employ armed forces who would back up the claim of the new Yorkist king. She therefore recruited an army for him under the command of an experienced German general called Martin Schwartz. Schwartz, who came originally from Augsburg in Germany, was a shoemaker's son by birth. He grew up to become a mercenary soldier, and then rose to a position of command. He was reportedly an able, if somewhat arrogant, officer, and he is first on record as having fought for Margaret of York's husband, Charles the Bold, Duke of Burgundy, at the siege of Neuss in 1475.

Nine years later, in 1486, Schwartz was recruited by Maximilian of Austria, the widowed husband of Margaret of York's stepdaughter, Marie of Burgundy, and the father of her son and heir, Philip of Austria. As regent for his young son, Maximilian needed Schwartz's help in driving the French out of Flanders. During the 1486 campaign, Martin Schwartz had found himself in command of 200 Swiss mercenaries.

As a result of his earlier service to her late husband, and his recent action on behalf of her stepson-in-law, Martin Schwartz's name and capabilities must already have been well known to Margaret and her advisors. Thus, in the spring of 1487, following her consultations with her nephew the Earl of Lincoln, with Francis Lovell, and others, Margaret sent for Martin and agreed a new military contract with him. Under the terms of this agreement Schwartz was to supply an army of 2,000 troops, under his own command, for the eventual invasion and conquest of England.[4] Obviously the decision was also taken that the forthcoming campaign would be centred initially on Ireland. After all, this was one part of the new king's realm which was accessible to them without any need for battle.

Once the decision had been made that 'Edward VI' would begin his reign in Ireland, it probably followed logically that a coronation for him should be celebrated there. In that way his kingship could be both ceremonially authenticated and divinely blessed, without any need for access to Westminster Abbey. But no previous coronation had ever taken place at Christ Church Cathedral in Dublin. How, then, would this Irish cathedral manage to carry out the planned ceremony, where would it obtain the necessary equipment, and what plans for the coronation needed to be made in Mechelen before the departure for Ireland?

Obviously the first requirement would have been an appropriate order of service. Although it seems highly unlikely that Dublin's medieval cathedral library would have held copies of the liturgy for a coronation, in itself this would not really have presented a problem. Of course an appropriate book could probably have been obtained by Margaret and dispatched by her from Mechelen. However, even this would not really have been necessary. The point is that the ritual of coronation is, and has always been, based upon the ceremony of consecration, or ordination, of a Catholic bishop – a church service with which the cathedral clergy would undoubtedly have been very familiar, and for which they would certainly have had copies of the Church's liturgy.[5]

Both the episcopal ordination ceremony and the royal coronation ceremony are set within the context of a celebration of high mass. The rite of ordination or consecration for a bishop begins after the first parts of a normal mass (the penitential rite and the liturgy of the word). Following the gospel reading, the consecration begins with the singing of the hymn *Veni, Creator Spiritus*. The bishop-elect is then presented to the congregation and makes his promises. Following the singing of the Litany of the Saints, the bishop is then anointed with chrism (holy oil). After this he is invested with a ring, his head is crowned with a mitre, and he is given his crozier, or pastoral staff. He is then formally seated on his bishop's chair or throne (*cathedra*). The normal rite of mass then resumes, but after the communion and the concluding prayers the solemn hymn of thanksgiving, *Te Deum laudamus*, is sung, before the liturgy concludes with a solemn blessing.[6]

The basic format of the coronation ceremony is identical with that of an episcopal ordination. The king is first presented to the congregation and takes his royal oath. He is then anointed with holy oil, receives a royal ring, the crown and a sceptre, and is finally enthroned. Actually, the usual coronation ceremonial in England and France had, by the fifteenth century, become somewhat more elaborate. After his anointing, the king was first given spurs and a sword. After receiving his crown he was given not just one sceptre, but two. In England he also then received an orb, though at French royal coronations, no orb was presented. But in Dublin, of course, none of the usual royal coronation equipment of England would have been available. So what ceremonial items would be used at the Dublin King's coronation?

While the English term 'coronation' focuses attention on the placing of a crown upon the sovereign's head, the French term for this ceremony is *sacre*, which focuses primarily on the act of anointing. Both aspects are essential parts of the ceremony, and require special equipment. The anointing comes first. Coronations at Westminster or Rheims used special containers (ampullas) of royal holy oil for the anointing ceremony of an English or French king. However, this special royal oil was not used undiluted. One drop of it was extracted from the ampulla and mixed with the church's own holy oil (chrism), which was consecrated annually by the local Ordinary on the Wednesday of Holy Week (the Wednesday before Easter). In Dublin, of course, no royal ampulla would be on hand to provide a drop of special royal oil for the consecration ceremony. Nevertheless, there would be no problem about accessing Christ Church Cathedral's own store of chrism for the year in question. Therefore the Dublin King could simply be anointed using the cathedral's supply of holy oil.

The next requirements were spurs and a sword. These could perhaps have been prepared in Mechelen, on Margaret of York's orders. However, such items would also have been very easy to find in fifteenth-century Dublin. The spurs and swords

The anointing of a medieval boy-king in preparation for his crowning.

used at modern English coronations are valuable specimens of the jeweller's art, but this was by no means an essential requirement. Ordinary spurs and an ordinary sword would have served the purpose equally well. In any case a sword of state had been presented to Dublin by King Henry IV in 1404.

The required coronation ring would also have been relatively easy to supply. In Mechelen, before the group set off for Ireland, and at the expense of Margaret of York, such a ring could easily have been ordered to fit the young royal hand. Alternatively a Dublin jeweller may have been asked to make the ring after the chosen king arrived there. As for the other items of regalia, finding a sceptre would not present too many difficulties. Metal staffs were used for various functions in medieval churches. The staff of a processional cross, or the ceremonial staff of a verger, could therefore be adapted for this purpose. Indeed, in 1804, when Napoleon I was planning his coronation as Emperor of the French, he found that much of the pre-Revolutionary regalia had been damaged or destroyed. He therefore used the staff of the Precentor of St Denis as the basis of one of his sceptres.[7]

The crown might present more of a problem. Both English and French coronation ritual usually required two crowns: a solemn holy crown for the act of coronation itself, together with a lesser (though often more heavily bejewelled and costly) 'state crown' to be worn during the celebrations after the church ceremony. In England the coronation crown was attributed to the canonised pre-Conquest king, Edward the Confessor. In France, no fewer than three sacred coronation crowns were available at this period. One was attributed to the canonised emperor Charlemagne, while two had belonged to King Louis IX (St Louis).[8]

Of course, Margaret of York could easily have found jewellers in Mechelen to produce a small state crown for the Dublin King-elect. This need not have been overly expensive, and she may well have commissioned such an artefact for him. However, surviving reports of the actual coronation ceremony tell us that the Dublin King was formally crowned with an open gold circlet borrowed from the votive statue of the Blessed Virgin which stood in the Church of Sainte Marie de la Dam (or Sainte Marie del Dame).[9] The earliest surviving source for this information about the crown used at the ceremony reports that:

> the crown that was used, they borrowed from the statue of the Blessed Virgin Mary, preserved in the church dedicated to her memory, near the gate of the city which is commonly called Dame-gate.[10]

In 1487 this church stood on Cork Hill, a short distance to the east of Christ Church Cathedral, and just outside Dublin Castle. Little survives today of medieval Dublin, and the gold crown, the image of the Blessed Virgin, and the Church of Our Lady of Dame-gate, have all long since been lost. The site of the church was reused in 1761 by the merchants of Dublin for the building of their Royal Exchange building, which was constructed between 1769 and 1779. In the 1850s the Royal Exchange was taken over for civic administration and became Dublin's City Hall. However, even today, the main road to the north of the City Hall is called Dame Street.

Why should the coronation crown of the Dublin King have been borrowed from the head of a cult image of the Blessed Virgin? Why not use a new crown made for him at his aunt's

expense in Mechelen? This arrangement has tended to be interpreted by previous writers as a sign that the Dublin coronation
was a very muddled affair, hastily concocted without proper
planning, and without any of the proper resources. As we have
already seen, however, no coronation ceremony would have
been possible without some prior planning. Thus the true explanation is probably quite different. Those who planned, and later
organised, the Dublin ritual must have been very well aware of
the fact that they would not have access to the traditional English
coronation crown – the Crown of St Edward the Confessor. This
holy crown had reputedly been removed from the saint's head
when his remains were moved into his shrine, in order that it
could be used for all future English coronations. Faced with the
absence of this – or indeed any other – saint's crown, what more
suitable head could the organisers have chosen, from which to
borrow a suitable holy crown for the Dublin King's coronation,
than the head of the Blessed Virgin Mary?

Finally, of course, a throne would be needed. Once again
that would probably have presented no problem. The word
'cathedral' is derived from the Latin term *cathedra*, meaning the
formal chair or throne of a bishop. All cathedrals would have
contained such a throne. Therefore it is probable that the ceremonial episcopal chair in Christ Church Cathedral was used
for the Dublin King's enthronement. But in any case, even at
a period when chairs were much less common items of fur-
niture than they are today, both the cathedral and its clergy
would undoubtedly have had access to such things.

In addition to the equipment needed in order to carry out
his coronation, one other item would have been an obvious essential requirement for the use of the Dublin King
and his government after the boy had been crowned. They
would need a royal seal. It is certain that a royal seal of 'King
Edward VI' was created – and was used. Indeed, one impression of the seal survives, and was recently rediscovered in the
Irish National Library. It is attached to a letter issued in the
name of 'Edward VI' by the Earl of Kildare.

merlin chantant baixe seruoit·· Et se epoit en ung toucquet·
Voyant que le diable escripuoit De deux comeres le cacquet·

A bishop's chair such as the one in this picture may have provided a suitable throne for the Dublin King's use at his coronation.

Sadly, the seal impression is damaged and has not survived intact. Thus, for example, the royal inscription which it originally bore, and which would have confirmed that the Dublin King bore the royal name of 'Edward VI', is now broken. As a result the royal name and numeral are lost. However, the obverse of the seal impression does preserve for posterity a unique image of the boy-king himself, seated on his throne.

As usual on such items, the reverse displays his royal arms (see plates 26 and 28).

Two interesting points emerge from these images. The crown worn by 'Edward VI' on the obverse, and the crown which surmounts his royal arms on the reverse of the seal, are both open crowns (i.e. without arches). This in itself is not remarkable. While it is true that arched crowns were coming into fashion in England in the fifteenth century – and are depicted, for example, on the royal seals of Edward IV and Richard III, and on coins of Henry VII – open crowns were also still very much in use.

However, one feature of the crowns depicted on the seal of the Dublin King is unusual. Both images comprise a circle surmounted by fleurs-de-lis. This was not the usual design for a fifteenth-century English king's crown. The usual design was similar to that found on the circle of the modern royal crown. That is to say the ornaments comprise alternating crosses pattée and fleurs-de-lis. It is true that contemporary English coins bore a representation of a king's head bearing a crown with fleurs de lis, but that image had been introduced by Edward I in 1279, and had remained unchanged ever since. It did not represent contemporary reality. Moreover, representations of royal crowns on the great seals of fifteenth-century English kings certainly did not show crowns adorned just with fleurs-de-lis. But while fifteenth-century *English* crowns were not of this design, the royal crown of *France* – together with the coronets used by French princes of the blood royal – did bear only fleurs-de-lis.

Of course the Dukes of Burgundy had been French princes of the blood, and they had used such coronets. Indeed, as the widow of the last duke, Margaret of York was still entitled to a French royal crown of this design in 1486 and 1487. Perhaps, therefore, the royal seal of 'King Edward VI' was made in Mechelen during the summer of 1486, on the instructions of Margaret of York. If so, the Mechelen metalworker who fashioned it would almost certainly never have seen an actual

English king's crown. However, he might well have seen the crowns depicted on English coins, and he was probably accustomed to the design of French-style crowns, as worn by the former dukes of Burgundy. Thus he depicted both the Dublin King and his royal coat of arms with just such a French-style crown. In other words, the surviving impression of the royal seal of 'Edward VI' constitutes one possible indication that preparations for the reign of the Dublin King were made in Mechelen, prior to his return to Ireland – presumably commissioned and paid for by the boy-king's self-acknowledged aunt, Margaret of York.

12

The Reign of the Dublin King

The Dublin King and his supporters probably remained in Mechelen with Margaret of York until after the celebration of the feast of Easter, which, in 1487, fell on Sunday, 15 April. Meanwhile Henry VII had ridden from Bury St Edmunds to Norfolk, where he celebrated Easter in Norwich, staying at the bishop's palace. It was in the hall of the episcopal palace that he fulfilled his royal obligation of feet washing on Maundy Thursday (12 April). He took the Earl of Lincoln's father, the Duke of Suffolk, with him to Norwich; probably he thought it wise to have the duke where he could see him – just in case. On Easter Monday, following the Sunday celebrations, the king briefly travelled north, towards the Norfolk coast, making a rapid pilgrimage to the Shrine of Our Lady of Walsingham.[1]

It seems that Henry was uncertain at this stage what his opponents in Flanders were planning to do. He knew that they 'then wer in Selande and Flawndres to the see warde and, as was reportede, [were] to lande in this realme, [but] in what parte it was no certeynte'.[2] But of course, the king was well aware that the Earl of Lincoln's homeland was in the eastern counties, and that this part of the country had also, until quite recently, been the Yorkist power-base of the late John Howard, Duke of Norfolk. Thus the king made arrangements to assemble a fleet at the port of Harwich, while on 7 April he had ordered the repair and manning of beacons along the coast. It therefore seems that he was at least half expecting that his enemies would take the shortest sea route from the ports of Flanders and land somewhere in Norfolk, Suffolk or Essex.

However, he also took a wider perspective. Having made due provision for the defence of the East Anglian coast, he then rode via Cambridge, Huntingdon and Northampton to Coventry. The Duke of Suffolk remained with him for the first part of the journey, but then the king sent the duke to Windsor, to act as his deputy at the annual Garter Feast of St George (Monday, 23 April). The king himself spent St George's Day in Coventry. It was some time in the course of about the next two weeks (from the end of April to the beginning of May) that Henry VII received the news that his enemies had sailed from the Low Countries and had crossed the Channel, to land in Ireland.[3]

Henry VII had also been in contact with the city of York. He wrote to the city from Huntingdon on Friday, 20 April. Two days later, on Sunday, 22 April 1487, the following royal letter was read to William Todd, the mayor, and to members of the city council:

> Trusty and welbeloved we grete you wele, and perceve wele the fast love and trouthe ye bere unto us accordingly to your dutie, and trust of your assured contynuaunce in the same, wherby ye shall cause us alwey to rest your favourable and gracious souverain lord. And for somoche peraventure as our rebelles and ther adherentes might by some crafty meanes and by espiell doo som reproche or vilany to our Citie there in case ye ne wer forseyng and advertised of the same, we therfor hertly pray you, and as ye tendre the welle of oure said Citie, and of yourself, exorte and desire you, that ye have yourself from hens-furth in such await that noon espies passe by you untaken, nor that any or rebelles or ther adherentes come amonges

you, but that ye kepe due watche and warde for the suretie therof, as well by day as by night, and from tyme to tyme as unto youre discreccions it shalbe thoght behovefull. And on this we shalbe with Godis leve be nere unto you alwey tassiste and relief you if the case require. Ye can not doo for us that we shall forget, but soo remember it hereafter, that ye shall have cause of reason to thinke youre dutie unto us for wel employed. Yeven undre oure signet at our Towne of Huntyngdon the xx day April.[4]

In this letter the king warned that supporters of the Dublin King might attempt to get into York and subvert the city's loyalty. However, he encouraged the city council to make sure that York remained loyal to the new royal dynasty.

Another letter from Henry VII was sent to York on Thursday, 3 May. This time the king – now based in Coventry – reported that his opponents had sailed from Flanders towards Ireland, therefore there appeared to be no immediate need to defend the city of York:

Trusty and welbeloved we grete you wele. And forsomoche us we have certain knowleige in sundry wise that our rebelles bene departid out of Flaundres, and goon westwardes, it is thoght by us and by oure Counsaill that ye shal not nede to have any strength or company of men of werre for this season to and by amonges you, and therfore we pray you that ye woll have sad regard to the good rule and sauf keping of oure Citie there, to the appesing of rumours and correcting of evel disposed folkes, with sending unto us youre newes from tyme to tyme. And assure yourself that for this true acquitail ye have beene of unto us, wherin we pray you to continewe, we shal be soo good and gracious souverain lord unto you as of reason ye shall have good cause to thinke the same for wel employed. Yevene undre our signet at our Citie of Coventre the iiij day of May.[5]

Five days later Henry VII wrote to the mayor again, to tell him that he did not now expect the enemy to come to York. However the king made it clear that he was keeping an eye on developments. If it seemed necessary he would contact the city again, or the Earl of Northumberland would take the necessary action:

> From the King to the Mayor, Aldermen, etc.
>
> Trusty and welbeloved we grete you wele, and have undrestand by manyfold reportes made unto us the effectuel devoir and grete besinesses that ye put you in, for the good provision and preparacion of vitaill and othre stuff for such men of wirship and theire retenues, as we late commaunded to goo thidder for the surtye and defense of our Citie ther, if oure rebelles had arrived nigh thoos parties, for the which as we for many othre causes have doon, we thanke you hertely, and thus by your truthes and good myndes daily to us contynued ye have assured the favour of our good grace unto you, like as ye shall fynd in effect in such poursutes as ye shall make unto us hereafter; lating you wit that seing our rebelles, as we be ascertayned, bee departid westwardes, we have licensid suche personnes as we comaunded to make ther repar thiddre, to depart thens for a season and to resort to you agene if the caas shall so require, and also our cousin the Erle of Northumberland entendeth hastily to be in the cuntrey nigh unto you, which we doubt not wol gladly assiste and strength you at all tymes if ye desire hym so to doo. Yeven undre our signet at our castell of Kenelworth the viijth day of May.[6]

Meanwhile, 'King Edward VI', together with his supposed cousin the Earl of Lincoln; Viscount Lovell; General Martin Schwartz and the troops recruited by Margaret of York had all landed in Dublin on Saturday, 5 May 1487. This date is confirmed by a surviving letter from Henry VII to the Earl of Ormond.[7] In Dublin they 'were joined by such troops as

Kildare had been able to enlist. These seem to have been Celtic Irish for the most part, and were evidently mere "bonnachts" or mercenaries, since no Irish chief led them and we do not hear to which clan or clans they belonged. Polydore Vergil says they were almost unarmed – doubtless their weapons seemed to the Germans and English somewhat primitive'.[8] Although some Irish cities, including Kinsale, Drogheda and probably Trim, backed the cause of the Dublin King, Waterford was openly opposed to him. John Butler, the Mayor of Waterford, 'even dispatched messengers charged with remonstrances to Dublin'.[9] But of course his surname suggests that the mayor was related to Henry VII's supporter, the Earl of Ormonde.

In the Irish capital, however, plans were going ahead to mark and bless the installation of the Dublin King on a grand scale. It was on the Feast of the Ascension (Thursday, 24 May 1487) that the most remarkable event of this entire story took place. On that Thursday 'Edward VI' was crowned in one of Dublin's two cathedrals – the Cathedral Priory of the Holy Trinity – commonly known at Christ Church. For the first (and only) time in its history this four-hundred-year-old church was to witness and host a royal anointing and crowning.

It was not, however, the first time that a king of England had been seen in the cathedral. In 1171 Henry II, the theoretical royal progenitor of the dynasty of 'Edward VI', had attended Christmas mass in the same church. Indeed, that was reported to be the first occasion after the murder of Archbishop Thomas Becket that the repentant Henry II – the first king of the house of Anjou – had been permitted to receive Holy Communion.

According to later accounts, the coronation mass of 1487 was well attended. Irish lords, led by the Earl of Kildare, members of the church hierarchy, and, of course, the Earl of Lincoln and Viscount Lovell were all present. Reportedly the Irish clergy were headed by the primate of Ireland, Dr Ottaviano Spinelli del Palacio (or Palatio), Archbishop of Armagh. However, in an attempt to avoid problems with Henry VII, Ottaviano himself later claimed that he had 'opposed the profane coronation'.[10] The Archbishop of Dublin, Walter FitzSimon(s), was certainly present. Thus it might possibly have been Archbishop FitzSimon (promoted to the archbishopric three years earlier, during the reign of Richard III) who carried out the anointing and crowning of the child-king 'Edward VI'. Despite this archbishop's tantalizing surname, there is no surviving evidence that he was in any way connected with priests or organ-makers based in Oxford. Other members of the church hierarchy who seem to have attended the Dublin coronation include John Payne, Bishop of Meath; William Roche, Bishop of Cloyne; and Edmund Lane, Bishop of Kildare. Reportedly it was the Bishop of Meath who preached the homily, in which he summarised the claim to the throne of 'King Edward VI'.[11]

The ceremony was apparently carried out with due propriety and solemnity. The little king was anointed with the chrism of the cathedral priory, crowned with the holy crown of the Blessed Virgin, Our Lady of Dame-gate, and duly enthroned, probably in Archbishop FitzSimon's own ceremonial *cathedra*. Evidently this unique occasion created great interest in the Irish capital, and crowds were waiting outside the cathedral to see the new king emerge. Unfortunately because of his rather small size, initially it was rather difficult for them to catch sight of him. He was therefore enthroned again, this time upon the shoulders of the young William Darcy of Platten, county Meath, cousin of Lord Darcy of Knayth, grandson of the late Baron Killeen, and a protégé of the Earl of Kildare.[12] '*Great Darcy of Platen*, [was] a man of very tall stature'.[13] Thus, seated upon Darcy's shoulders, 'Edward VI' was carried back from the cathedral priory to Dublin Castle. There the traditional post coronation banquet was held.

News of the Dublin coronation of 'King Edward VI' is said to have been subsequently conveyed to Henry VII either by Nicholas St Lawrence, fourth Baron Howth, or by a man called Thomas Butler – presumably another relative of the Earl of Ormonde.[14]

With 'Edward VI' duly enthroned as the Dublin King, the government of Ireland was now officially conducted in his name. One normal function of sovereigns has long been the issue of coinage. Indeed, it has not always been necessary to actually establish oneself as a universally accepted, fully recognised king in order to be able to issue coins. At various times mere claimants to thrones have had coins struck and circulated in their names. The usurper Carausius, who claimed the Roman imperial throne in the third century, issued coins in London and Colchester, even though he never actually became a true Roman emperor. More recently, coins were issued in the names of various ousted European kings. The Stuart princes issued coins at various times after James II had lost his British thrones. In nineteenth-century France and Spain, too, coins were issued in the names of unsuccessful or deprived claimants.

Thus, it would be in no way surprising if coins had been issued in 1486 and 1487 in the name of the Dublin King. While it has never been suggested that coins bearing his name and title circulated in England, it has certainly been asserted that coins were issued in Ireland in the name of 'Edward VI'. What is more, there does appear to be some evidence to support this contention. Unfortunately, however, owing to two particular characteristics of medieval coinage, which we shall see in a moment, the evidence is not – and can never be – absolutely conclusive.[15]

Many valuable studies relating to the 'coins' of the Yorkist pretenders have been published over approximately the last hundred and fifty years.[16] and it is useful to begin by outlining the general understanding of the coinage of the period.

Although in Ireland some copper coins were made and circulated in the fifteenth century, in England at that period only silver and gold coins existed. English coinage was based around the 'long cross' silver penny (1*d*), which had first been issued in this design by Edward I in 1279. This silver penny was subsequently reproduced by all the succeeding rulers up until

the year 1489, with its overall design and its royal 'portrait'
basically unchanged (as we have already noted in the context
of English crown designs).

In 1351 a silver four penny piece ('groat') and two penny
piece ('half groat') joined the penny.[17] At the same time
Edward III also introduced gold coins called the 'noble' (worth
80d), half noble (worth 40d) and quarter noble (worth 20d)
All of these coins continued to be issued, with their designs
virtually unchanged, during the reign of Richard II, and
throughout the Lancastrian period.

In 1464–65, however, Edward IV reformed the English
coinage.[18] This action seems to have been as contentious and
unpopular at that period as changes in currency are today.
Overall, Edward IV's modifications resulted in a reduction
of the bullion weight of all English coins.[19] The noble and its
subdivisions were abolished, and new gold coins were introduced to replace them. These were the 'ryal' (120d) together
with its half and quarter, and also the 'angel' (80d). During the
Readeption of Henry VI the 'angel' was joined by the 'angelet'
or half angel (40d). It was also Edward IV – the first monarch
of the house of York – who introduced the use of the rose
emblem for the first time on English coins, often accompanied
by the Yorkist sunburst.[20]

One very important fact which must be taken into account
relates to the inscriptions on coins at this period. Throughout
the fifteenth century all English coins bore the reigning monarch's name and titles in Latin. However, the king's regnal
number was never included in the coin inscriptions. Also no
fifteenth-century English coins ever bore a year date.[21]

As we have already noted, no coinage attributed to the
Dublin King was ever produced in England. But in Ireland,
coins which have been attributed to 'Edward VI' actually
circulated as currency. The Irish silver coinage of the late fifteenth century was basically similar to that of England in
terms of its denominations. Ireland, however, had no gold
coinage. The Irish coinage was also distinctive in other

respects. For example, although the Irish silver coins had similar face values to those issued in England, they differed from the English currency both in their bullion value and in their designs.

Actually, for over one hundred years (between 1340 and 1460) no Anglo-Irish coins were produced, except for one issue of pennies in 1425–26. This was because the earlier issues of coinage in Ireland had resulted in the export of silver to England and the Continent, adversely affecting the Irish economy. When Edward IV's government decided to reinstate the issue of Irish currency, one of its priorities was therefore to seek to avoid any repetition of such problems.[22]

To avoid the export of bullion from Ireland it was essential to try to ensure that the planned new Irish coinage would be unacceptable in England. One obvious way to achieve this was to make the Irish coins of lower real value than their English equivalents. The other obvious way of ensuring that Irish coins could not creep into England unnoticed was to ensure that they looked different from their English counterparts. In this way Irish coins would appear recognisably 'foreign'. One curious result of all this is that the Irish silver coins of the Yorkist period are a good deal more imaginative in their design than the rather boring contemporary English issues, whose appearance had remained unchanged for more than a century. However, Irish coins again became very similar in appearance to their English counterparts in the 1470s, with the result that, once more, they began to be exported to England. Indeed, English hoards reveal that Irish coins were imported into England in quite large numbers.

Our picture of the evolution of the Irish coinage under Edward IV is informed not only by the surviving examples of the coins themselves, but also by documentary evidence. During the period in question, the Irish Parliament produced detailed legislation on the subject of the Irish coinage, and fortunately this has been preserved and published.[23] However, the legislation conflicts at times with what appears actually to have been issued in terms of coinage, and we shall return to this important point later.

In 1461 an agreement was made with one Germyn Lynch to the effect that the latter should mint 1*d*, 2*d* and 4*d* coins, bearing an open crown on the obverse, and with a long cross and pellets on the reverse, together with the name of the mint. These coins were to be struck at Dublin, Trim, Waterford (Dondory), Limerick and Galway.[24] The result of the agreement was Edward IV's 'crown' coinage of 1461–63 – though the coins did not bear the king's name. In 1463 the Irish Parliament legislated that this anonymous 'crown in a tressure' coinage should henceforth bear on its obverse an abbreviated version of the inscription *Edwardus Dei Gratia Dominus Hibernie*.[25] At the same time legislation set the weight of the groat at 48 grains. However, it appears that on this and other occasions the legislation in respect of coin weights was probably not carried into effect.[26]

In 1465 new instructions were issued. The weights of the coins were again to be slightly reduced (groat = 42.1 grains),[27] and Lynch was henceforth instructed to produce ¼*d*, ½*d*, 1*d*, 2*d* and 4*d* pieces, bearing an English-style obverse design, which showed a symbolic crowned full-face head of the monarch, with the inscription *Edwardus Dei Gratia Dominus Hibernie*. However, it is not clear whether these instructions were immediately carried out. Thus some authorities assign a series depicting a cross on a rose (obverse) and a sunburst (reverse) as Edward IV's third Irish coinage, from 1465–67.[28]

In 1467, for what is known as Edward IV's fourth Irish coinage, the English style 'crowned full-face bust' obverse design was introduced, while the reverse was changed to a *rose-en-soleil* design. At the same time Drogheda and Carlingford were added to the list of authorised mints and the weight of the coins was slightly increased.[29] The weight of the Irish groat was now formally set at 45 grains – still lower than the contemporary English standard.

In 1470 the Irish coinage adopted an English-style reverse design. The weight went down again slightly (groat =

43.6 grains) and the obverse inscription was expanded to read *Edwardus Dei Gratia Rex Anglie & Dominus Hibernie.*[30] Officially the list of authorised mints was reduced to three: Dublin, Trim and Drogheda. However, surviving examples of this coinage show that in fact mints were still functioning at Limerick, Waterford, Cork and Galway. Coins of this type (which, with a minor change in weight, lasted from 1470 to 1478) are more widely preserved than those of the earlier series.

A statute of 1478 made provision for the issue of a new silver coinage comprising 1d, 2d and 3d coins, but it gave no details of either the design or the weight.[31] The coins actually issued at this period did not conform to the specifications of the statute in terms of their face value, for half groats and 3d pieces were not made, in spite of the legislation. Only groats (4d) and pennies were issued. These retained a crowned bust of the king on the obverse, but introduced a new reverse design, which consisted of a rose superimposed upon the centre of a long cross.[32] This coinage seems to have continued in production right up to the end of Edward IV's reign and beyond.[33]

In 1482/83 Edward IV was apparently planning to authorise a new standard for the Irish coinage. His surviving indenture on this subject is undated but was probably issued at about the same time as the appointment of Thomas Galmole as master of the Irish mints, that is to say on 7 March 1482/83.[34] The indenture made provision for the issue of pennies and halfpennies of the English standard weights. However, it is thought that no such coins were issued. No further changes seem to have taken place in the Irish coinage prior to Edward IV's demise.[35]

In Ireland, as in England, following the death of Edward IV, it seems to be completely impossible to distinguish coins which were minted during the brief reign of Edward V. The accession of Richard III can, however, be discerned, because of the change in the royal name. Richard III seems to have briefly continued in his own name the production of Edward IV's 'rose on cross' coinage. After a short time, however, he appears to have introduced a new groat and half groat, known as the 'three crowns issue'. This is the key Irish coinage in our present context, because 'three crowns' coins continued to be issued for some years – into the reign of Henry VII. Thus these were the Irish coins which were in production, and in use, in 1486 and 1487 – during the period of the Dublin King.

This new coinage was probably originally inspired by the plans made by Edward IV, shortly before his death. However, as actually issued by Richard III, it was not an exact implementation of Edward IV's indenture of March(?) 1482/83. That indenture had provided for the minting of new pennies and halfpennies. However, the actual 'three crowns' coinage consisted only of groats and half groats.[36]

Over the years, there were minor variations in the details of both the design and the inscription. In general, the 'three crowns' coinage bears the royal arms of France quartering England, together with the first half of the royal title, on the obverse. On the reverse are the three crowns which at this period comprised the arms of Ireland,[37] together with the end of the royal title – the part referring to Ireland itself. Coins of the 'three crowns' series survive from the mints at Dublin and at Waterford. The coins of the Waterford mint display both the shield bearing the royal arms on the obverse, and the three crowns on the reverse, within tressures (borders of curves, or arches). But such tressures are absent from the coins minted in Dublin.[38]

Four types of inscription can be identified on surviving examples of the 'three crowns' coins. Some bear the name RICARD., some carry the name HENRICVS (or occasionally HENRIC.), some are inscribed with the name EDWARDVS, and some are anonymous. Thus one example is simply inscribed between the arms of the long crosses front and back:

obverse: REX A / NGLIE / FRAN / CIE
reverse: :ET ✹ / REX: / HYB / ERNIE

The inclusion of a small rose in this reverse inscription pos-sibly suggests (but does not prove) a Yorkist context in the case of this specimen,[39] and in fact some of these anonymous coins are among those generally attributed to the Dublin King.[40] Interestingly, a subgroup of this anonymous coinage comprises specimens where the royal arms on the obverse are flanked by tiny shields bearing the cross saltire of the Fitzgerald coat of arms.

In terms of rarity, the most numerous 'three crowns' coins are the various HENRICVS issues, and the anonymous coins. RICARD. specimens are rarer. The rarest examples are those inscribed EDWARDVS.[41] Until the 1960s it had been generally assumed that the existence of 'three crowns' coins inscribed EDWARDVS proved that this coinage had actually been introduced at the end of the reign of Edward IV, and that it was therefore the new coinage referred to in Edward's indenture of 1483. The design and inscription specified in that indenture appeared to fit the 'three crowns' coins, for the indenture stipulated that the new coins should carry 'the king's arms on one side upon a cross trefoiled on every side and with this scripture *Rex Anglie & Francie*, and on the other side the arms of Ireland on a like cross with this scripture *Dns Hibernie*'.[42] The obverse of the 'three crowns' coins cer-tainly conforms to the description in the indenture, while the reverse design, bearing three crowns one above another, super-imposed over a trefoiled cross is one possible interpretation of the wording of the indenture (though the document itself might perhaps have intended that the three crowns would be disposed upon a shield, two above and one below, as on the Irish copper farthings of Edward IV).

However, Dolley and others have pointed out that the indenture of 1483 spoke of coins of different values to those actually minted. The indenture refers to pennies and halfpen-nies, whereas the actual 'three crowns' coinage comprises half groats and groats only. Dolley therefore concluded: 'All the documentary evidence in fact shows is that at the very end

of the reign [of Edward IV] there was being contemplated a
new coinage for Ireland, and that the type specified was one
very similar to, but not identical with, one eventually used
by Richard III, though with the important distinction that
Edward seems to have envisaged an "English standard" coinage of pence and halfpence, whereas Richard was content to
continue with new types an "Irish standard" coinage of groats,
half groats and pennies'.[43] In general, Dolley's conclusion in
respect of the documentary evidence is correct (though his
statement that the coinage type envisioned by the indenture
was 'not identical with' that introduced by Richard III contains an element of assumption on his part). Nevertheless the
discrepancies between the specifications of the indenture and
the coinage later issued by Richard III do not in themselves
disprove the notion that Richard was intending to imple-
ment Edward's indenture. We have previously noted other,
similar discrepancies between documentary evidence and
actual coinage.

While 'three crowns' groats and half groats which bear the
names RICARD. and HENRICVS are generally assumed
to belong to the reigns of Richard III and Henry VII respectively, once it had been decided that coins of this series bearing
the royal name EDWARDVS could not be attributed to
Edward IV it obviously became necessary to account for them
in some other way. It was therefore proposed that the explanation must lie in the events of 1487. In other words, coin
collectors and researchers concluded that the 'three crowns'
coins inscribed EDWARDVS must have been issued in the
name of the Dublin King.[44] Since it is now certain that the
Dublin King reigned as 'Edward VI', this conclusion seems
reasonable.

In addition to the named 'three crowns' coins, we noted
earlier the existence of anonymous specimens, bearing royal
titles only. We also noted the fact that some anonymous specimens bear small shields with a cross saltire to the left and right
of the royal arms on the obverse, just below the horizontal arm

of the long cross. The cross saltire was the main charge on the coat of arms of the Fitzgerald family (the earls of Kildare and their cousins, the earls of Desmond).[45] In this instance it has generally been assumed that the Geraldine arms on the coins refer to Gerald, Earl of Kildare and that therefore the anonymous coins were also issued for the Dublin King – possibly either before he returned to Ireland and was crowned, or after he had been defeated at the Battle of Stoke. This is certainly plausible, but the evidence in respect of the anonymous 'three crowns' coins is not, and probably never can be, conclusive.

In addition to the probable issue of coins in the name of Edward VI, documents were also issued in his name. Not many examples of such documents survive. However, the Ormond Papers in the Irish National Library contain what appears to be a letter issued in the name of 'Edward VI' by the Earl of Kildare, as governor of Ireland.[46] In translation, this reads:

> Edward, by the Grace of God, King of England, France and Ireland, to all to whom these presents may come, greeting. Know that we have granted to our dear Peter Buttyller 'gentilman', otherwise called Peter Buttiller, son of James Buttiller 'gentilman', the office of sheriff of our county of Kilkenny, to have and to hold the said office to the aforesaid Peter during our pleasure – saving to us the fines and amercements coming from the said county – receiving from us in that office the accustomed fee.
>
> In witness whereof, we have had these our letters patent made.
>
> Witness our very dear cousin, Gerald, Earl of Kildare, our Lieutenant of our kingdom of Ireland, at Dublin, on the 13th day of August in the first year of our reign.
>
> Dovedalle.
>
> By writ of Privy seal.
>
> August 13 [1487][47]

In his note referring to this letter, Curtis observed:

This curious and puzzling document cannot be of the reign
of Edward IV, because in the first year of his reign the Earl
of Kildare was not a Gerald. It cannot be of the reign of
EdwardVI, because before the first year of his reign Sir Piers
Butler (Peter Butler, son of James Butler) was dead. There
is moreover adequate reason to show that it cannot belong
to the reign of EdwardV. In the first place the document is
dated August 13, and EdwardV's brief reign lasted only from
April 9 to June 22, 1483. In the second place it describes
the earl of Kildare as Lieutenant, an honour which he
never held under any official King of England; and in the
third place it styles Ireland a kingdom and Edward, King of
England, France and Ireland, a style which was not adopted
by any monarch prior to HenryVIII; for up to that time the
Kings of England were merely Lords of Ireland.[48] The only
conclusion left is that the document belongs to the 'reign'
of Lambert Simnel whom the Great Earl had crowned as
King Edward, on May 24, 1487. The date of the document
(August 13, 1487) seems at first sight to upset this conclusion,
for the Battle of Stoke, at which Simnel was captured, was
fought on June 16, 1487. But the date is no real objection to
its authenticity as a Simnel relic, for as late as October 20,
1487, two months after the suggested date of the document,
HenryVII, writing to the citizens of Waterford, records that
'the said Earl with the supportation of the inhabitants of
our said city of Dublin, and others there ... will not yet
know their seditious opinions, but unto this day uphold and
maintain the same'.

Affixed to the document is a seal which appears to be the
Great Seal of England, bearing the effigy of a child king.
Possibly this was an authentic seal of EdwardV, which had
come into the possession of theYorkist party in Ireland.

Despite what Curtis says, the design of the seal is not consistent with the usual designs of the great seals of approximately
contemporary English sovereigns, such as Edward IV or

Richard III. Their great seals do not have a coat of arms on the reverse but an equestrian figure of the king. Moreover, as we have already noted, the very clear depiction of the crown above the royal arms on the reverse of the seal is not English in design. It is an open French crown – with a bordure of eight fleurs-de-lis and no crosses. It is, in fact, identical to the normal crown of a French prince of the blood – such as the Duke of Burgundy. In addition the starting point of the reverse inscription is marked not by a cross or a rose (as might usually be the case in England) but by a fleur-de-lis. The crown worn by the young sovereign on the obverse of the seal also appears to be adorned only with fleurs-de-lis – no crosses. The most likely place for the seal to have been made is therefore somewhere in France or the Flemish lands of the former Dukes of Burgundy. As suggested earlier, since one of the key supporters of the Dublin King was Margaret of York, Duchess of Burgundy, it may well have been Margaret who had the seal made.

13

The Battle of Stoke Field

In Ireland, following the Dublin King's coronation, the attention of the members of his entourage was focussed chiefly on plans for their invasion of England. Therefore ships were being prepared to transport Martin Schwartz's German mercenaries, and the Irish foot soldiers, across the Irish Sea. Meanwhile in England the news of the Dublin coronation had created some unrest. Henry VII first had Archbishop John Morton of Canterbury ceremonially pronounce in Coventry a papal excommunication against anyone who dared to contest his right to rule. After that, the king rode on to Kenilworth Castle, where he had arranged for his wife and his mother to join him.[1]

The ships from Dublin, bearing 'Edward VI' and his troops, landed on Foulney Island on Whit Monday, 4 June 1487. This tiny island was, in itself, an unpromising place in which to land. However, it gave the rebels access to strong Ricardian loyalist territory in Yorkshire. They were reportedly greeted on their arrival by Sir Thomas Broughton and members of his family. Broughton was a former retainer of Richard III, who had offered shelter to Lord Lovell at his home of Broughton Tower, some 10 miles further north, the previous year. Now Broughton not only greeted the little army from Ireland, he also arranged for supplies for the soldiers from the Cistercian Abbey of Furness.

Meanwhile, however, in an attempt to limit local support for the Dublin King, Henry VII had the Archbishop of York repeat in the north Archbishop Morton's public proclamation of the papal bulls supporting his tenure of the royal title, and condemning any who opposed his sovereignty. The Archbishop of York was Thomas Rotherham, who had been appointed to this post in 1480, during the reign of Edward IV. He had also served Edward IV as Lord Chancellor. When Edward IV died, Rotherham had been one of the celebrants of the king's funeral mass, which the Earl of Lincoln had attended as chief mourner. However, Rotherham had sided with Elizabeth Woodville, to whom he had handed over the great seal. As a result, Richard III dismissed him, replacing him as Lord Chancellor with Bishop John Russell. Russell held the post until a few weeks before the Battle of Bosworth, when Rotherham briefly regained the Chancellorship, only to lose it again when Henry VII seized the crown. In general, Rotherham seems to have been a Yorkist, and Henry VII did not place much trust in him, but in the simple matter of proclaiming papal bulls, the archbishop had little room for manoeuvre.

Tradition says that the army of the Dublin King spent the night of Monday, 4 June, at Ulverston. Bennet suggested that on Tuesday, 5 June, they probably slept at Cartmel, and on Wednesday, 6 June, they probably stayed at Hornby Castle. Meanwhile, as Henry VII had intimated earlier, the Earl of Northumberland was now responsible for the defence of York. On 6 June Northumberland himself wrote the following letter to the city:

> Whereas the King our souverain lordes rebelles bene landed in Fourneys [Furness], at the pile of Fowdray, upon monday last past, which God helping I entend to resist, and for the same intent wolbe in the citie of York toward them upon sonday next comyng; therfore I desire and pray you to

cause provision of vitaill to be redy ayenst that tyme for such people as shall come and be ther with me, also that ye incontinent after the sight herof woll provide for the sure keping and saufgard of the said Citie, and that suche persones as ye goodly may forbere, the Citie kept, if it woll pleas you, they may accompany me in ther best and moost defensible array to do the King service for the entent afforsaid. And I pray you to yeve credence unto my right trusty servaunt Richard Burgh, squire, concernyng the premisses.

Writyn in my Maynour of Lekingfeld the vj day of Juyn.

Your loving frend,

H. Northumberland.[2]

The York City Archives have preserved a copy of this letter. They then go on to note that it:

was oppynly red bifore the Maior, Aidremen and Commune Counsaille of the Citie of York; first in the Counsaill Chambre within the Guilhall, and after bifore all the Comons of the said Citie in the said Guilhall ther assembled, where and when as well the said Maier, Aldremen, Shereffs and Commune Counsaill forsaid as the said Commons was aggreed eithre to othre holding up ther hands that they wold kep this Citie with ther bodiez and goods to thuttermost of ther powerez to the behove of our soverain lord the King ayenst any his rebells entending to entre the same.[3]

By Friday, 8 June, 'King Edward VI' and his putative cousin Lincoln were at Masham. Meanwhile King Henry VII had left Kenilworth and was marching to meet them at the head of his forces. On Archbishop Morton's advice Henry had declared a kind of martial law. He made first for Leicester – a place full of recent memories for him. And in another curious repeat of August 1485, once again the Stanley family appeared to be hedging their bets and doing their best not to commit themselves to either side.

The city of York was also divided. Despite popular mythology on the subject the city was by no means unquestioningly committed to support for the royal house of York. In the past, some of its men had fought for Henry VI, and the city had declined to allow Edward IV to enter it as king when he returned from exile in 1471. In the summer of 1487 some of the citizens – most particularly the mayor and the city council – were definitely supporting not the Dublin King but Henry VII.

Acting, presumably, upon Lincoln's instructions, 'King Edward VI' nevertheless wrote a letter to the mayor of York from Masham, asking to be allowed entry to the city, and requesting its support for his cause. A copy of the letter survives, and provides the vital evidence, cited in Chapter 3, which proves that the official royal style of the Dublin King was 'Edward VI'. The text of the letter reads:

By the King.
To our trusty and weilbiloved the Maiour, his brethren and comunaltye of our Citie of York.

Trusty and wellbiloved we grete you wele, and for somoch as we beene comen within this oure realme, not oonlly, by goddes grace, to atteyne oure right of the same, but also for the relief and well of our said realme, you and all othre our true subgiettes, whiche hath bene gretely injurid and oppressid in default of nowne ministracon of good rules and justice, desire therfor, and in our right herty wise pray you that in this behalve ye woll shew unto us your good aides and favourez. And where we and such power as we have broght with us, by meane of travayle of the see and upon the land, beene gretely weryed and laboured, it woll like you that we may have relief and ease of logeing and vitailles within oure citie ther, and soo to depart and truly pay for that as we shall take. And in your soo dooing ye shall doo thing unto us of right acceptable pleaser, and for the same find us your good and souverain lord at all tymes herafter. And of your disposicions herein to acertain us by this bringer. Yevene undre our signet at Masham the viij day of Juyn.[4]

Copies of this letter were made in York and dispatched to various people, including Henry VII and the Earl of Northumberland.

The city council also ordered that the wardens of the city should be instructed to be on guard, and to keep watch to ensure that no one entered the city:

> bot such as bee true liegemen unto our soverain lord the King, Herry the sevent. And the said Maior incontinently by thadvise of his bretherne, Aldermen, Shereffs and Common Counsaill forsaid, sent in message unto the said lords of Lincoln and Lovell iij of the Chamberleyns, yeving theme in commaundement to shew unto the said lords that my lord the Mayre, my masters his bretherne, Aldremen, the Shereffs, Commune Counsaill with thool [the whole] Communaltye of the Citie of York beene finally deter-mynd that he which the said lords callid the King they nor none of ther retinew or company entending to approach this Citie shuld have any entrie into the same, bot to with-stand them with ther bodies and goods, if they wold atteyne [attempt] soo to doo.[5]

Thus, the request of 'Edward VI' was turned down.

On the same day – Friday, 8 June – another letter was addressed to the mayor of York. This one was from the Earl of Northumberland. The Earl thanked the city for its friendly disposition towards him and for the care being taken to pro-tect the interests of King Henry VII. He informed the city that he was hoping to reach Pocklington by the evening of the following day. However, he promised not to tarry there but to press on in the hope of reaching York that same night (Saturday, 9 June). But whatever happened he promised to be with them by Sunday, 10 June, at the latest.[6]

On Saturday, 9 June, the mayor and council were advised that 'Edward VI', Lincoln and Lovell, with their army, were not actually approaching York, but had moved more or less due south from Masham in the direction of Boroughbridge. It was therefore concluded that they represented no immediate threat to the city.[7] Meanwhile, Henry, Lord Clifford requested entry with his retinue, in order that he might help to defend the city for Henry VII if necessary, and the mayor granted his request. At the same time, orders were given for 500 armed men of York to station themselves at Micklegate. Clifford, together with 400 men at arms on foot and on horseback, joined them there four hours later.

Despite his promise, it was actually not until Trinity Sunday (10 June) that the Earl of Northumberland, accompanied by many knights and lords of the region, reached the city:

> The same day at afternoune the Lord Clifford toke his jour-
> ney towardes the Kinges ennemyes lyng upon Bramham
> More, and loged hymself that night at Tadcastre, but the
> same night the Kinges ennymes lying negh [nigh] to the
> same towne, cam upon the said Lord Clifford folkes and
> made a grete skrymisse ther, into so moch that he, with
> such folkes as he might get, retourned to the Citie again;
> and at that same skrymisse wer slayne and maymed diverse
> of the said toune, and thinhabitants ther wer spoled and
> robbed, and the gardewyans [travelling trunks] and trussing
> coffers [packing chests] of the Lord Clifford was taken of[f]
> the bri[d]g[e] by misfortune, and had unto the other partie.[8]

Thus it was Lord Clifford — a cousin of the royal house of York, and a nobleman who, ironically, had experienced a very similar upbringing to that claimed by 'Edward VI' — who made the first armed contact with the forces of the Dublin King. In this initial skirmish, the troops of 'King Edward VI' were victorious, and Clifford, defeated, fell back to the city of York. Following this initial victory, on Tuesday, 12 June, the two lords Scrope attacked York in the name of King Edward. Although their attack failed to break in to the city, one of its outcomes was that it prevented Northumberland from joining Henry VII. On hearing of the attack, the earl, together with Lord Clifford, returned to York, where he remained until Thursday, 14 June – the Feast of Corpus Christi. That day, when the earl once again left York, he set off in the opposite direction – retreating northwards. Apparently Northumberland had now decided that the wisest course might be to replicate the standard Stanley tactics: lying low and sitting on the fence.[9]

The Feast of Corpus Christi was normally celebrated in York in a very grand manner, with processions of the Blessed Sacrament and religious plays. On the evening of Wednesday, 13 June, however, the mayor had issued a proclamation to the effect that this year the usual celebrations would have to be postponed for a month. Initially he proposed that they would be rescheduled for the Sunday following the Feast of the Translation of St Thomas of Canterbury (which feast was due on Saturday, 7 July). In the event, however, the 1487 Corpus Christi celebrations were ultimately delayed yet again. That year, in York, they were not held until Sunday, 5 August.[10]

Meanwhile another victory for the Dublin King's army against Henry VII's royal cavalry, in Sherwood Forest, caused the city to change its mind about which side it was on. York now finally declared its support for 'King Edward VI'. Meanwhile rumours began to spread, to the effect that Henry VII had given up and run away. Superficially, things were looking good for the Yorkist boy-king and his army.

However, Henry VII had not, in fact, fled. On Thursday, 14 June, Henry VII appeared to his army and sought to restore confidence. His quite impressive forces had now assembled close to Nottingham, and he began to march along the south bank of the river Trent. Meanwhile 'Edward VI', the Earl of Lincoln and their army were manoeuvring on the northern side of the same river. Despite York's change of heart, overall the Dublin King appears to have gained less military support than had been hoped. But on Friday, 15 June, 'Edward VI' and Lincoln crossed the Trent and camped at the village of East Stoke.

According to the later account of Bernard André, Henry VII inspired his army with the following impressive (but improbable) pre-battle oration:

My most loyal lords and very stout companions in my battles, who have joined me in running so many risks by land and by sea, behold, we are unwillingly being put to the test in another war. For, as you know, the Earl of Lincoln, a treacherous man, is upholding this iniquitous cause directed against myself, although I have given him no occasion for so doing. Nor, as you see, does he do so by stealth, but rather most impudently, without any fear of God, not just to create difficulty for us, but also to oblige the desire of a light-headed, chattering little woman, who is not unaware that her blood-line ended with the death of her brother Richard. But, since he was always an enemy of our family, she has no care about the welfare of her niece, my right noble consort, but rather is striving to destroy ourselves and our issue. So you see how often we are provoked by her. But she will never go unavenged by us. I swear by God and His holy angels, while I consult days and nights for your common peace, our old enemy strives against me. But God, a just judge, strong and long-suffering, will furnish a remedy for this evil too. Meanwhile I urge and ahort [*sic* – exhort?] you that at this time the lawful succession must prove stronger than the lawless mischief-making of those people. Nor should you have any doubt but that God Himself, Who made us the victors in the previous war, will now allow us to triumph over our enemies. So let us attack them fearlessly, since God is our helper.

He made an ending, and, since the time was pressing, although the Earl of Oxford was ready to make a response he bid him hold his silence and have regard for the urgent situation. So, moving 'as headlong as doves in the face of a dark storm', they took up arms. And now the royal army was approaching the barbarian squadrons, and they awaited our men on the brow of a hill, drawn up and ready. But God, the Lord of vengeance, punished their wrath with a sudden gale which arose while they were engaged in fighting, just as when Constantine was fighting against the enemies of the Church, and our men, who thought themselves bested, finally overcame them. Then a sudden shout of 'King Henry' rose up to heaven, as trumpets blared on all sides, and filled the ears of them all with rejoicing. There that petty king of villains, who, as I have said, had been crowned in Ireland, was taken in battle. Interrogated about what boldness induced the rascal to dare such a great deed, [he] did not deny that he had been compelled by certain criminals of his own rank in life. Asked next about his family and parentage, he admitted that they were altogether low-down personages of mean professions unworthy of mention in this history. And the Earl of Lincoln suffered an end fitting for his actions. For he was killed on the battlefield, and likewise many others, whose commander and ruler was Martin Schwarz, a man well-versed in the arts of war, who fell while fighting bravely. When the day had been won by our king, by the grace of God Almighty, with little loss of life, he returned to London to offer thanksgiving to God, accompanied by his entire force.[11]

The account of the Battle of Stoke, as recorded by the city of York, reads as follows:

The Satterday next after the fest of Corpus Christi, the King lying with a grete powre divyded in three hostez beyond Newark, the wayward of the same in which th'erl of Oxford, the Lord Straunge, Sir John Chyney, th'erl of Shrewsbury, and many othre to the nombre of x Ml [10,000] met with the Lordes of Lincolne and Lovell with othre many noblez, as well of Ynglisshmen as Irisshmen, and othres to the nombre of xxMl [20,000], of the more beyond Newauk, and there was a soore batell, in the which th'erl of Lincolne and many othre, as well Ynglisshmen as Irissh, to the nombre of vMl [5,000] were slayne and murdred ; the Lord Lovell was discomfotid and fled, with Sir Thomas Broghton and many othre, and the child which they callid ther King was takyn and broght unto the Kinges grace, and many othre in grete nombre which was juged to deth at Lincolne and othre placs theraboute. And upon Sonday by iii of the clok in the mornyng, tidinges came to my lord Maier from the feld, howe Almighty God had sent the King victorye of his ennymes and rebelles, and therupon my Lord Maier, taking with hyme his brethre Aldremen, with thool Counsaill of this Citie, upon certaine knowlege of the victory forsaid shewed by the mouthe of a servaunt of Master Recordour comyng streught from the said feld, came to the Cathedrall Church of York, and there caused all the ministres of the same to make lovinges [Laudes, or praises] to our Saveour for the tryumphe and victory forsaid, singing solemplye in the high qwere of the said church the psalme of *Te Deum Laudamus* with othre suffragies.[12]

Actually it seems to have been King Henry VII himself who gave the instructions for *Te Deum Laudamus* to be sung at York Minster in thanksgiving for his victory:

Trusty and welbeloved we grete you wele. And forsomoche as it hath liked our blissed Saveour to graunte unto us of his benigne grace the triumphe and victorye of oure rebelles without deth of any noble or gentilman on oure part, we therfor desire and pray you, and sithin this said victorye procedeth of hyme, and concernyth not oonly the wele and hondour of us, but also of this our royme, nrthlesse charge you, that calling unto you in the moost solempne church of oure Citie ther, your brethern Thaldermen and othre,

> ye doo lovinges and praisinges to be yevene to oure said
> Salveour aftre the best of your powers. Yevene undre oure
> signet at oure Toune of Newarke xvj day of Juyn.[13]

The York city records of the Battle of Stoke report that the
Dublin King was captured, and the *Heralds' Memoir* account
tells us that the pretender to the throne was captured by
Robert Bellingham, and that the boy's real name was revealed
to be John. Interestingly, the published version of the *Heralds'
Memoir* claims that the Continental account of the conflict
written by Adrien de But stated that the Dublin King was
never captured. According to Cavell's printed edition of the
Memoir, De But claimed that as soon as it became apparent
that his army was likely to be defeated by that of Henry VII,
Edward VI was sent off the field by his supporters, and was
subsequently taken to Guines.[14]

In point of fact, however, Cavell's statement on this point
contains errors. What De But's original text actually says is that:

> the Earl of Lincoln and Martin Zwarte fell with about five
> thousand men. But the king, who acted in a kindly way
> towards foreigners, commanded that all the prisoners from
> Ireland should be strangled. The young Duke of Clarence
> [*sic*] was also captured, whom the Earl of Suffolk, carefully
> delivered, and he fell back with him to Guisnes.[15]

'Guizam' in the original Latin text refers to Guînes (Guisnes),
which, with its castle, at that period comprised part of the
English territory of Calais.

The Earl of Suffolk – though he did not yet hold that title in
1487 (which implies that De But's account was actually written a few years after the Battle of Stoke) – was the Earl of
Lincoln's younger brother, Edmund de la Pole. Edmund inherited his elder brother's excellent claim to the English throne
when Lincoln was killed at Stoke. A few years later, Edmund
also inherited his father's title of Duke of Suffolk. However,

he was then, rather insultingly, demoted from duke to earl by Henry VII. Nevertheless, Edmund, in his turn, became a prominent Yorkist pretender to the throne. Eventually, he escaped from the hostile environment of Henry VII's England to Flanders, but was subsequently extradited by Henry VII. Finally, Henry VIII had him executed in 1513.

In 1487 Edmund would have been 15 or 16 years of age. Whether he was actually in the vicinity of the Battle of Stoke when it was fought is not known. However, it is not necessary to assume that Adrien de But wished to imply that Edmund helped the Dublin King to escape immediately after the battle. De But may simply have meant that Edmund helped Edward VI to escape from England *later*, possibly even after he had been taken to London as a prisoner. It is certainly intriguing to find that one Flemish chronicle records that the Dublin King did not remain in the custody of Henry VII, but escaped to Flanders, aided by the Earl of Lincoln's younger brother. If true, De But's account would, of course, mean that the Lambert Simnel who later served in Henry VII's kitchens – but who may have looked somewhat older than the boy who had been crowned in Ireland – was not actually identical with 'King Edward VI'.

Meanwhile, in the aftermath of the battle, Henry VII, with his usual thoroughness, took the time to write a letter to the Pope from Kenilworth Castle. This letter, written on Thursday, 5 July 1487, aimed to ensure that those members of the Church hierarchy in Ireland who had crowned the Dublin King would be duly punished:

> Whereas some of the prelates of Ireland, the Archbishop of Dublin, the archbishop of Armagh and the bishops of Meath and Derry, in contempt both of our sovereignty and of ecclesiastical censureship, aided and helped our rebels and foes, and an illegitimate child, victory against whom we have in our hands, and their rebels and our enemies, inventing that boy of theirs to be a son of the late Duke of

Clarence, they crowned him King of England, to the serious prejudice of us and our whole realm, we most humbly beg and request your Holiness to subject the aforementioned prelates to his ecclesiastical charge of censureship, and to take legal action against them.[16]

PART 4

The Aftermath

14

Lambert Simnel, Scullion and Falconer

According to Vergil's account of the Battle of Stoke, following the defeat of the Yorkist army:

> Young Lambert the pretender was taken, together with his tutor Richard, but the lives of the both of them were spared, because the former was innocent and, thanks to his youth, had done no wrong, as being incapable of doing anything in his own right, and the latter was a priest. And yet, so that he might learn (as they say) that a rock hangs over the head of the man who has cast it aloft, he was remanded to perpetual darkness and chains. Lambert is still alive, made a falconer by the king after he had turned the spit for a while in the royal kitchen and performed other base tasks.[1]

The emphasis on the pretender's youth seems consistent with the official estimates of his age cited earlier. This is worth noting in the light of contradictory age evidence which will be examined presently.

We have already noted that if only one priest called Symonds/Simons acted as Lambert Simnel's mentor then the account of his capture given by Vergil contradicts the earlier evidence from the Convocation of the Province of Canterbury. It remains

A young falconer. © Muhammad Hanif.

possible that two priests (possibly related to one another) were involved, and that one of them was apprehended before the coronation of the Dublin King, whereas the second was only captured after the Battle of Stoke. If this was not the case, and if there was only one priest mentor, it would seem that Vergil or his source must have been in error, because the evidence from the Canterbury court regarding its interrogation of the priest in February 1486/87 seems incontrovertible.

However, the Book of Howth, a sixteenth-century Irish source, appears to confirm Vergil's account in respect of the priest, and also in respect of Lambert Simnel's subsequent employment by Henry VII. The Book of Howth account is brief and omits any specific reference to work in the royal kitchens, though it depicts Lambert Simnel acting as a wine waiter. It states that 'this feigned King and crafty priest his master was taken alive. This priest was commanded to perpetual prison and this innocent child became falconer to the King after'.[2]

The Book of Howth is a manuscript which belonged to Christopher St Lawrence, eighth Baron Howth (*c.*1510–89). It recounts at some length a unique story relating to Lambert Simnel, representing the pretender as serving wine at table on one important occasion in 1489. In the Book of Howth, no precise date is assigned to this incident, but the event obviously post-dates the Battle of Stoke. The fact that the story relates to a period when Henry VII had invited Irish peers to attend his court in England allows the year in question to be identified.

In Ireland after the Battle of Stoke, Kildare and his supporters continued to follow their own course. However, in June 1488 Henry VII sent Sir Richard Edgecombe to Ireland to try to establish his authority. Edgecombe waited in Dublin for several weeks, until eventually Kildare came to Dublin and on 20 July it was agreed that he and the Irish peers would take oaths of allegiance to Henry VII. Following this, the king invited the Irish lords to come to England. Thus the banquet described in the Book of Howth took place in 1489.[3]

The story recounted in the book of Howth runs as follows:

> After the King sent for all his Lords of Ireland being in England with the King. After long talk with them, the King said to the Lords, 'My Masters of Ireland, you will crown apes at length'. Those Lords being a procession appointed, with certain Lords of England to be their companions and fellows in that procession appointed, amongst all one Lord was and the Lord of Houthe together, which trembled with fear, and scarse could speak, and said 'Sir, there shall be no butchery done upon none of us this time, praise be to God, for the face of the axe is turned from us'. This axe was borne afore the procession, as is accustomed, and as he was speaking he could scarse speak with fear. Being asked by the Lord of Houthe the cause why he frayed said, that 'the Lord my father and grandfather was beheaded'. 'Well,' said the Lord of Houthe, 'follow my counsel; serve God with all

your heart, and fear your Prince and obey his laws to your power, and you need never doubt of any such thing'.

This same day at dinner, where as these Lords of Ireland was at Court, a gentleman came where as they was at dinner, and told them that their new King Lambarte Symenell brought them wine to drink, and drank to them all. None would have taken the cup out of his hands, but bade the great Devil of Hell him take before that ever they saw him. 'Bring me the cup if the wine be good', said the Lord of Houth, being a merry gentleman, 'and I shall drink it off for the wine's sake and mine own sake also; and for thee, as thou art, so I leave thee, a poor innocent'. After, the Lords being there a time longer than their purses could well bear, they were licensed to go to their country, and the King did give the Lord of Houthe the apparel that he ware that day, and 300l. In gold, with thanks; and so departed.

The Lord Howth who figures in this story, and who attended the dinner in question, was Nicholas St Lawrence, fourth Baron Howth (*c.*1460–1526) – the same man whom we met earlier as one of Henry VII's reported sources of information concerning the Dublin coronation of 'King Edward VI'. However, the manuscript that survives is not contemporary. It is known to have belonged to the eighth Lord Howth, one of the three brothers, all grandsons of the fourth Lord Howth, who succeeded to the Howth title in turn, following the demise of their father.[4] How the eighth Lord Howth obtained the manuscript is not recorded. The identity of the English peer with whom his grandfather had been paired in the procession of 1489 is unknown. Thus the reported reason for the English peer's fear – namely that both his father and his grandfather had been beheaded – while by no means incredible – is hard to substantiate. However, the key point of the story in connection with Lambert Simnel relates to his serving of the wine, and how he was received by the Irish lords.

It has sometimes been stated that the Irish nobles failed to recognise Lambert Simnel when he served them wine on this occasion. Smith, for example, suggested that 'the other Irish lords [apart from Howth] needed to be informed in advance that the serving boy would be Lambert, and such information seems to presuppose that they might not have realised that he had been the lad they had crowned in Dublin'.[5] This is possibly an overstatement. For while it does certainly appear that none of the Irish lords spontaneously recognised the boy who was serving them, that could simply have been because they didn't actually take any notice of him. After all he was merely a servant.

Nevertheless, it is clear that Henry VII deliberately had the wine served by Simnel on this occasion. This raises the possibility that the king's objective was to confirm the identity of his new servant. He may have been hoping that independent witnesses (the Irish lords) would spontaneously recognise his serving lad as their former Dublin King. This could possibly imply that Henry VII himself had some doubts about the servant's identity. The reason for this could perhaps have been related to the fact that while the Dublin King had been described as a boy of 10, the Lambert Simnel who was captured after the Battle of Stoke seems to have been nearer the age of 17. This conflicting age evidence will be examined in greater detail presently.

If Henry VII did have doubts as to whether his captive was, in fact, identical with the boy who had been crowned in Dublin; if he was seeking independent confirmation of his prisoner's identity, that would certainly explain his gratitude and generosity to Lord Howth following the latter's apparent recognition of the former pretender. Ironically, however, Howth was one of the very few Anglo-Irish lords who had not supported the Dublin King. Therefore he may never have seen the boy while he was the titular head of state in Dublin. Thus, in reality, Howth's apparent acknowledgement of the identity of the person who served him the wine was probably meaningless.

It is also interesting to note that, according to the version of the story which has survived (possibly a somewhat biased account), Lord Howth appears to have been the *only* Anglo-Irish peer who accorded recognition to the servant on this occasion. Since he was also possibly the only Anglo-Irish lord present who had never seen the Dublin King while the boy was on his throne, it seems that the failure of his companions to recognise Lambert Simnel as their former boy-king was probably more significant than Howth's pretence of recognition.

Another issue which concerned Smith and other writers relates to the age of the young person who was taken into Henry VII's service after the Battle of Stoke, firstly as a kitchen lad, and subsequently as a falconer. As we have already seen, in 1487 the Dublin King was thought to be 10 years of age by representatives of Henry VII's government who saw the boy in Ireland during his 'reign'. At that time the real Earl of Warwick would have been 12; Richard of Shrewsbury, Duke of York would have been 14, and Edward V would have been approaching 17. The age differences between them certainly appear, on the face of things, to be significant, though it has been noted that the Earl of Warwick might have shared with his father, the Duke of Clarence, a stature lower than average, so that at the age of 12 he might possibly have been mistaken for a boy of 10. On the other hand the Duke of York and Edward V had a father who was much taller than average. It therefore seems improbable that either of them would have been mistaken for a 10-year-old in 1487.

In this context, however, it is very curious to discover that Francis Bacon describes Lambert Simnel as 'of the age of some fifteen years, a comely youth and well favoured, not without some extraordinary dignity and grace of aspect'.[6] In this particular sentence, Bacon is clearly referring to Simnel in 1485–86, because he goes on to explain that the boy's promising appearance attracted the attention of the man who was to become his priestly mentor. It is therefore evident that the pretension had not yet started. Of course, Bacon was not a contemporary, but the ultimate source for this estimated age must presumably have been someone who had seen Lambert Simnel. However, Bacon's immediate source for his stated age of 15 may have been Vergil, who had erroneously given 15 as the age of the Earl of Warwick in 1485.[7]

Of course, no one at the Tudor court had set eyes on Lambert Simnel in 1485–86. Henry VII's writers only saw Simnel *after* he was captured. They must therefore have estimated the pretender's age in 1485–86 from the appearance of the youth detained by Henry VII from 1487 onwards. In other words Bacon's information would appear to suggest that, after the Battle of Stoke, the person who was said be the captured Dublin King, and who was subsequently employed in the service of Henry VII, had the appearance of a lad of about 17 at or shortly after the time when he was captured.[8]

In this connection, it is noteworthy that at some point Vergil changed his text, deleting his initial use of the word 'boy' and substituting the word 'lad'. This seems to imply that he too had found himself confronting, and having to deal with, conflicting information which spoke of a Dublin King aged 10 but a captured pretender aged 16 or 17.[9] This apparent age discrepancy has been interpreted by some writers as suggesting that the Lambert Simnel who was Henry VII's prisoner after the Battle of Stoke cannot have been identical with the much younger Dublin King. And as we have seen, it is possible that Henry VII also found himself wondering about this.

To confuse the situation still further, some historians have chosen to accept the non-official evidence which suggests that the pretender was in his middle to late teens even at the time of his coronation. Consequently they have rejected the official statements which ascribe to him an age of 10 years. In other words, they assume that the Dublin King was six or seven years older than the official statements suggested. It has also been noted that the age ascribed to the teenaged pretender would then have been perfectly compatible with the age of Edward V, if he was still alive in 1487.

But we have already noted that no contemporary fifteenth-century source suggests that the Dublin King was, or ever claimed to be, Edward V. Moreover, we have produced clear evidence that he used the royal style of 'Edward VI'. Therefore the notion that the Dublin King was older than reported by the official Tudor sources is almost certainly worthless. It is far more likely that the Lambert Simnel who served Henry VII from 1487 – and who indeed may then have been in his late teens – was a different person than the younger boy who had been crowned in Dublin.

Vergil's statement that 'Lambert is still alive' has been taken by Michael Bennett and others to mean that Lambert lived until 1534 – the year in which Vergil's text was first published.[10] This interpretation may be correct, but actually the point is by no means certain. The problem is that although the first edition of Vergil's history was *published* in 1534 – and Vergil had updated his text somewhat with that publication in mind – the original text had been completed in 1512–13. It is therefore possible that Vergil's statement merely implies that Lambert Simnel was still alive in about 1513.

Nevertheless, whatever the precise meaning of Vergil's text, an independent source provides incontestable evidence that Lambert Simnel lived until at least the twenty-sixth year of the reign of Henry VIII (1524). From that year, records survive relating to the 'expenses of the funeral of Sir Thomas Lovel, Knt. of the Garter, who died at his manor of Elsynges in Endfeld, Middlesex, 25 May Corpus Christi even at 7 pm 26 Hen. VIII 1524'.[11] These records show that livery cloth was issued to ninety-seven yeomen. The list of the yeomen in question ends with the following words: 'broche turners, scullions, housekeepers, labourers, carters, Lambert Symnell, the schoolmaster, and Jack the lad in the kitchen'.[12] This implies that up until the early summer of 1524 Lambert Simnel had been employed by Sir Thomas Lovell in a relatively menial capacity, probably at his manor of Elsyng at Enfield, Middlesex. Lovell had acquired this manor in 1492, through his wife,

The possible burial place of Lambert Simnel. St Andrew's Church, Enfield, in 1895.

Isabel de Ros. The manor house had probably been built by her uncle, John Tiptoft, Earl of Worcester (executed 1470).

We have no precise record, then, of when Lambert Simnel died. Nor do we know where he was buried. If he died at, or near, Elsyng House (which is by no means certain), the nearest church and graveyard would have been at St Andrew's Church, Enfield, and Lambert Simnel may have been buried there. Until the monastery's dissolution in 1538, St Andrew's Church belonged to the Benedictine Abbey of Walden (at Saffron Walden in Essex). One possible means of clarifying Lambert Simnel's true identity – if only his bones could be recovered – would be by means of DNA. Unfortunately, however, there is currently little prospect of undertaking such scientific research: the earliest surviving memorial stone in St Andrew's graveyard dates only from 1680.[13] There are earlier monuments within the church, but none of these commemorates Lambert Simnel.

Bennett suggested that, 'given the rarity of the surname in England, Richard Simnel, canon of St Osith's in Essex at the time of the dissolution in 1539, may have been [Lambert's] son'.[14] Canon Richard Simnel certainly existed. That is proved by surviving documentation relating to the dissolution of St Osyth's Priory in Essex, which lists among the canons of that religious house on 8 August 31 Henry VIII, 'Ric. Symnell, canon'.[15]

As we have seen, however, Bennett's assumptions concerning the origins of the Simnel surname, and the frequency of its occurrence, are not based on any real evidence. Still, Canon Richard Simnel may perhaps have been a relative of Lambert. The possibility has already been noted that Lambert may have had at least one relative called Richard who served as a priest in the church (see above). However, this falls far short of proving that Canon Richard Simnel of St Osyth's was a relation, and there is certainly no proof that the canon was Lambert's son. Further fascinating evidence of when and where the surname SIMNEL(L) is recorded, both in the UK, and in some of the former British colonies, is offered in Appendix 3.

15

'Richard of England'

The case of the second Yorkist pretender – the man who called himself Richard of England, who was recognised by many important people as Richard of Shrewsbury, Duke of York, the younger of Edward IV's sons, and who is now known to history as Perkin Warbeck – has received a good deal more attention from historians than the case of the Dublin King. Several books have been written about him – and the most recent one, by Anne Wroe, was very extensive.[1]

Perkin Warbeck is important to our story in two ways. First, in telling the story of the Dublin King, the second claimant's case, and the results of his attempt on the English throne, cannot be ignored. The actions of Richard of England had an effect both on the foreign policy of Henry VII, and on the hopes of Margaret of York. Moreover, they eventually produced a very significant impact on at least one of the people associated with the case of the Dublin King, namely the official Earl of Warwick. It was the actions of Perkin Warbeck which ultimately provided the excuse for Warwick's execution. Second, it is rather important – and also potentially instructive and informative – to compare the cases of the Dublin King and of Perkin.

Strangely, in the past the case of the Dublin King has tended to be easily dismissed as insignificant. The boy at the centre of the plot has been almost universally dismissed as a fake. Perkin Warbeck, on the other hand, seems to have been taken seriously by foreign courts during the early stages of his campaign, and while some historians have dismissed him as a false claimant, others have at least speculated about the possibility that maybe his claim should be taken seriously.

Yet in the case of Perkin Warbeck one is dealing with a situation which, in the final analysis, is either black or white. Either Richard of England really was Richard, Duke of York, the younger son of Edward IV, or he was not. On the other hand the case of the Dublin King is a much more complex picture, in shades of grey. One cannot, for example, simply say that the Dublin King either was, or was not, the Earl of Warwick.

This is because there may have been more than one Earl of Warwick in existence in the 1470s and 1480s. Thus the Dublin King may have been the genuine biological son of the Duke and Duchess of Clarence, delivered by his father to Ireland when he was a very small child, and subsequently brought up there. On the other hand he may have been a child who somehow became involved at a very early age in the substitution plot of the Duke of Clarence. A boy who was not, perhaps, the biological son of the Duke of Clarence, but who may have been brought up for most of his young life *believing* that he was the Earl of Warwick. A third possibility is that the boy could have been a simple impostor, who was himself very well aware of the falseness of his claim.

What is more, not one of these possible scenarios is necessarily inconsistent with the official Tudor account which tells us that at some stage he bore the name of Simnel (or one of its variants). Thus, in every respect, the story of the Dublin King (which has for so many years been treated as a very simple tale) is actually far more complex than the story of Perkin Warbeck.

It was in 1493 that the city of York became aware that a second Yorkist claimant to the English throne was in prospect.

On 13 May of that year the city archives recorded that:

> the Maier shewed that the publike noyse and rumour was
> that the Kyngs enimys and rebelles beyng byond the sea
> with the lady Margaret, duches of Burgon, and en especiall
> oon callyng hym self Richard, duke of York and secund son
> to the Kyng Edward the iiijth, late Kyng of this realme, with
> other his adherents, entendeth in right short tyme to entre
> this the Kyngs realme; wherfor my said lord the Maier on
> the Kyngs byhalve, and as they wald answer unto the Kyngs
> highnes at theyr jouperty and perill, charges all the said
> presence and every of theym that they in there wards shuld
> prepare and make redy all suche ordinauncez and abiliments
> of warre as they had in theyr wards, and as well gunnes,
> gonne stones, gonne powder as portculez and other; also
> that every wardeyn to se almaner of reseants within theyr
> wards have theyr harnas redy as jake, salet, bowez, arowez
> and other weappyns as they wold answer for.[2]

Like the Dublin King, the new claimant was backed, morally
and financially, by his putative aunt, Margaret of York. He was
also well received by the crowned heads of Europe, beginning
with Margaret's relatives-in-law, the Habsburg family. Through
the Habsburg connection he also came to the attention of
Ferdinand and Isabel, the King and Queen of Spain, who, for
a complex mixture of reasons, also supported his claims. This
Spanish support may later have led to rather serious consequences for the claimant, as we shall see.

Eventually Richard of England found himself in Scotland,
where he was married to a relative of the Scottish king. Of
course, if the claimant really was Richard of Shrewsbury – or
as he now usually described himself, Richard of England –
Lady Catherine Gordon was his second wife, the first having
been little Anne Mowbray.

With the aid of his new relative by marriage, King James IV
of Scotland, Richard of England invaded the land he claimed

as his own. Yet, as in the earlier case of the Dublin King, his contest for the crown of England was ultimately unsuccessful. Local support failed to materialise, and he penetrated only a few miles into the kingdom he was seeking to win. Later, from Ireland, he made a second attempt, based on an invasion of Cornwall.

In the case of the first Yorkist claimant, as we have seen, reportedly the Dublin King was eventually captured by Henry VII and was later employed in a menial capacity in his household. However, we also have also learned that another version of the story exists, which states that 'Edward VI' escaped after the Battle of Stoke, and that the subsequent kitchen servant of Henry VII was, in reality, a different person, of a different age.

In the case of the second claimant, when all of Richard of England's attempts on the English throne had failed, he too was eventually captured by Henry VII — and that capture has never been disputed. Subsequently, however, Perkin Warbeck was treated in a totally different manner from Lambert Simnel. Eventually he was placed in prison in the Tower of London, and in 1499 Henry VII had him put to death.

No such fate ever overtook Lambert Simnel. Instead Lambert Simnel was completely and utterly discredited as a Yorkist claimant to the throne of England. The Tudor government therefore had

'Richard of England', also known as 'Perkin Warbeck', redrawn from the contemporary sketch at Arras.

nothing more to fear from him. History would remember him merely as a fake and an impostor. There was no reason to kill him.

Perkin Warbeck, on the other hand, was still seen in 1499 as an enigma. Despite the government's publication of his official identity as a native of Tournai, not everyone was convinced by this account, either at the time, or subsequently. While there has certainly never been universal agreement that he really was Richard of Shrewsbury, he seems to have closely resembled his putative father, King Edward IV. Thus, even if he was not precisely who he claimed to be, the possibility remains that he may have been a son of Edward IV – though perhaps a more blatantly illegitimate offspring than the so-called 'princes in the Tower'.

Whatever the true identity of Perkin Warbeck, it was precisely because Henry VII and his advisors had not succeeded in completely discrediting him that he needed first to be forced to make a public confession to the effect that he was an impostor, and then put to death. That way, even if he was a child of Edward IV, and a descendant of the royal house of York, he would no longer represent a threat to Henry VII and his dynasty.

16

'A Newe Maumet'

Most readers of this book probably had some previous knowledge of Lambert Simnel and Perkin Warbeck – though the present study has hopefully offered a wealth of new information regarding the case of Lambert Simnel. But probably many people imagine that Simnel and Warbeck were the only two genuine or fake Yorkist princes who contested the Tudor dynasty's right to its throne. In fact the true picture is very different. There were further Yorkist claimants to the throne from the de la Pole family in the early sixteenth century, one of whom ultimately became the fourth 'prince in the Tower'. Their story, which is not directly connected with that of the Dublin King, has been told by Desmond Seward in his book, *The Last White Rose.*[1] But the *first* of the other pretenders was not a de la Pole, and he emerged in 1498/99, at a time when Lambert Simnel, Perkin Warbeck and the third 'prince in the Tower' – the young man imprisoned by Henry VII under the title of the Earl of Warwick – were all still alive.

Not a great deal is known about the 1498/99 pretender. It is also hard to find any real evidence about the supporters of his cause (if there were any), or about the motivation behind his claims. However, we do have a name for him. The young man is reported to have been called Ralph Wilford. It is very important to include this little-known Yorkist pretender in our story because, whatever his personal motivation and true background, like Richard of England and Perkin Warbeck, he too had a highly significant effect on other people in our story. Indeed, Ralph Wilford's appearance on the scene may have been one of the key factors which ultimately led to the executions, not only of himself, but also of the claimant known as Perkin Warbeck, and of the third 'prince in the Tower' – the young man imprisoned under the title of the Earl of Warwick.

Polydore Vergil introduces Ralph as follows – but without recording his name:

> There was [a] certain Augustinian monk named Patrick, who, I suppose, *for the purpose of making the earl* [of Warwick] *unpopular*, began to suborn a disciple of his (whose name, as far as I know, is not recorded) and drum into his ears that he could easily gain the throne, if he would agree to follow his advice. The student not only did not refuse, but asked [*sic*] again and again asked him to be quick in putting his design in to practice. For what man is there who fears the law or danger to the extent that he refuses to do or suffer anything in the world for the sake of gaining a crown? Therefore the monk shared his plan and both of them went boldly to Kent, a county on other occasions not deaf to innovations. There the young man first revealed to some the secret that he was Edward of Warwick, lately escaped from the Tower of London by Patrick's help and art. Then he openly proclaimed this and begged all men's help. But the sedition lost its leadership before they could bring it to fruition, when teacher and pupil were both enchained, the latter put to death, and the former consigned to eternal darkness of prison because he was a monk. For among the English the clergy are held in such respect that a priest condemned of treason, like ordained priests guilty of other crimes, is spared his life.[2]

Vergil uses the words 'monk' and 'monastery' incorrectly on occasions. There were no Augustinian monks in existence. However, the orders of the Church include(d) Augustinian canons regular, and Augustinian friars. It is not clear to which of these two orders Patrick belonged. Since members of both orders would have moved about in the secular world outside their community, Patrick could have belonged to either.

It was Francis Bacon, writing about a hundred years after the events, who recorded that the new pretender's name was Ralph Wilford. Bacon also reported that this young man was the son of a cordwainer.[3] His father's profession is confirmed by the contemporary section of the *Great Chronicle of London* (written in the late fifteenth century or early in the sixteenth century). This later source also offers more precise dating, for it tells us that Ralph Wilford appeared on the scene between 8 and 24 February of year 14 of the reign of Henry VII (1498–99):

> In this passing of tyme In the bordurs of Norffolk and Suffolk was a newe maumet [*puppet*] arerid which namyd hym sylf to be the fforenamid earle of warwyk, The which by sly & coverty meanys essayed to wyn to hym soom adherentis, But all In vayn, In conclusion he was browgth before therle of Oxynfford, To whom at length he confessed that he was born In london, and that he was sone unto a Cordyner dwelling at the blak Bulle In Bysshoppsgate street, afftir which confession he was sent up the the kyng & ffrom hym to prison, and upon that areygnyd & convict of treason, and ffynally upon shrove tuysday [12 February 1498/9] hangid at Seynt Thomas watering[4] In his shirt, where he soo hyng styll tyll the Satyrday ffoluyng [16 February], and then ffor noyaunce of the way passers he was takyn doun & buried, being of the age of xix yeris or xxti.[5]

One rather intriguing point arises from *The Great Chronicle*'s account. This is the fact that Ralph Wilford's father is said to have resided at the Black Bull in Bishopsgate. This point is

The 'Black Bull of Clarence'. A livery badge of George, Duke of Clarence.

of interest because the Black Bull of Clarence had been one of the principal badges of George, Duke of Clarence, father of the genuine Earl of Warwick. Could it be that the Duke of Clarence had owned, or been patron of, the Black Bull in Bishopsgate? If so, might the cordwainer who was the father of this latest pretender have spent the earlier years of his life in Clarence's service?

Wilford appears to be a surname which originated as a toponym, from the village of Wilford in Nottinghamshire (which now forms part of the city of Nottingham). However, there were undoubtedly men named Wilford living in London at about the right period. In the year 1500–01 one of the two sheriffs of London was James Wilforde.[6] There were Wilfords living in the parish of St Mildred Poultry, in the 1540s, in the parish of St Lawrence Jewry in the 1560s, and in the parishes of St Stephen Walbrook and St Mary Woolnoth in the 1590s.[7] All these parishes were close to Bishopsgate. There are records of a Bull Inn on the north side of Leadenhall Street, at number 152 (adjacent to the junction with Bishopsgate, at the crossroads with Cornhill and Gracechurch Street) from the seventeenth to the nineteenth centuries.[8] However, perhaps more significant are Samuel Pepys' records of a Bull Inn, formerly called the Black Bull Inn, just off Bishopsgate Street, on the outskirts of the city of London:

> The Bull Inn was located where Tower 42 (previously known as the National Westminster Tower) now is, and was a recognised starting/finishing point on the main north road out of London. The Bull was one of many similar inns along Bishopsgate, and according to one writer "each had its approach through a low archway into a cobble-stone yard with galleries on three sides fenced by wooden balustrades, behind which were rows of bed chambers". It would probably have resembled the George Inn, 77 Borough High Street, near Borough Market, which is London's only surviving galleried coaching inn. It is claimed that the first playhouse under a patent of Queen Elizabeth 1st was put up in the Bull yard under James Burbage and Richard Tarleton, in which case it must have been of substantial size and just outside the city wall.[9]

So how does the unfortunate Ralph Wilford fit into our overall picture? It appears that he was simply a false Earl of Warwick. But if his father had been in the service of George, Duke of Clarence his family may have known – or thought they knew – something about the history of the genuine Earl of Warwick which suggested that Henry VII's third 'prince in the Tower' was not really the person claimed by the king. Were the Wilfords aware of the substitution project planned by the Duke of Clarence in 1476/7? Could this have been the inspiration behind Ralph's pretension?

Unfortunately, it is very hard to grasp what exactly the young man was hoping to achieve. Unlike the Dublin King and Richard of England Ralph Wilford apparently had no key

Yorkist backing for his cause, and lacked the support of the 'Diabolicall Duches', who seems never to have heard of him. Under such circumstances, could Ralph really have expected to make himself King of England? This seems hard to believe. If that was his aim, surely he was living in a fantasy world and had very little grasp of the true situation. After all, both the Dublin King and Richard of England had already made much stronger bids for the throne, and failed.

However, if the story that the de la Pole family had rescued the Dublin King after the Battle of Stoke, was true, and they had spirited him off to the Continent, the claim of Ralph Wilford might, perhaps, have been intended as a way of allowing the now 24-year-old 'King Edward VI' to make a comeback. Vergil, on the other hand, suggests that the young man's aim – or that of Friar (or Canon) Patrick – or of those unnamed instigators who were behind the plot – was to render unpopular the official Earl of Warwick, who lay imprisoned in the Tower of London.

Superficially, Vergil's suggestion may appear an odd one. Nevertheless, something significant may lie behind his words. Could those who wished to bring about the death of the official Earl of Warwick have perceived that introducing yet another pretender might make it easier for them to persuade the king? Moreover, by staging a public execution of his prisoner, the king could hopefully put a firm end to any further possibility of 'Earl of Warwick' pretenders. Such action would therefore make his position – and that of his dynasty – much safer.

In the final analysis, then, it is even possible that the inspiration behind the pretension of Ralph Wilford secretly came from Henry VII himself, or from his own government. This kind of motivation for Ralph's claim may seem more plausible when one takes into account the fact that there were reportedly other people around in the late 1490s who felt that they too had a vested interest in making the rule of the Tudor dynasty more secure.

17

Catherine of Aragon and the Spanish Interest

As we have seen, on Wednesday, 20 September 1486, 'the son of Clarence' was in Mechelen with his putative aunt. There, plans were being made for his coronation in Dublin the following year. But on that very same day, in Winchester, the little boy's 20-year-old putative cousin, Elizabeth of York, eldest daughter of Edward IV and Elizabeth Woodville, and now Queen Consort of England, had given birth to her first child by Henry VII. The baby proved to be a son. Because his blood claim to the English throne was so weak, Henry VII had recently commissioned research to prove that he was descended from the legendary ancient British King, Arthur. Now, in order to commemorate that rather dubious ancestral link, the king chose to have his new son and heir baptised as Arthur.

Nine months earlier, at about the time of Arthur's conception, another baby had been born. That birth took place at the bishop's palace at Alcalá de Henares, just outside the city of Madrid. The baby was a girl. Born an infanta of Spain, descended on both her father's and her mother's side from the ancient royal house of Trastámara, this little princess was the youngest daughter of Isabel the Catholic, Queen of Castile, and her husband and cousin, King Ferdinand V of Aragon. The Spanish royal couple were known to their

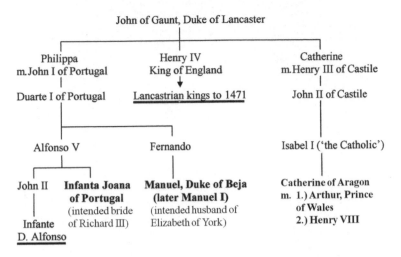

Heirs of the house of Lancaster.

contemporaries, and are remembered by later generations, as 'the Catholic Monarchs'.[1]

The infanta was born on 16 December 1485 and was baptised Catherine, in honour of her great-grandmother, Catherine of Lancaster, Queen of Castile. In fact, both Catherine of Lancaster and her half-sister, Philippa of Lancaster, Queen of Portugal, figured among the baby's ancestors. As a result of her undoubted descent from those two Lancastrian princesses (daughters of John of Gaunt, and sisters of King Henry IV), the baby Catalina de Castilia y Aragón inherited a strong Lancastrian claim to the English throne. It was a much stronger Lancastrian claim than that of King Henry VII.[2]

Given that Henry VII had already used his own marriage with a Yorkist heiress to improve his very mediocre blood claim to the English throne, this little Spanish infanta, so close in age to his son Arthur, was a very attractive proposition to him for the next generation of royal marriage in his family. As a result of such a marriage, his son would be given the opportunity to add genuine Lancastrian royal blood to the Tudor line.

Catherine of Aragon.

In fact, negotiations for an English royal marriage with a Trastámara infanta – with a similar aim of uniting his own Yorkist blood with the Lancastrian line – had briefly been explored by Richard III in 1485, following the death in 1485 of his first wife, Anne of Warwick. However, Richard would really have preferred a Portuguese princess as his second wife, since the royal house of Portugal were the most senior living Lancastrian descendants. In any case, in the end, lack of time and the course of events which overtook him put an end to Richard III's Lancastrian marriage negotiations.

But Henry VII now embraced the same idea with great enthusiasm, on behalf of his son. And unlike Richard III, Henry proved to have sufficient time to bring the Spanish marriage negotiations to a successful conclusion. Time was certainly needed, however, because the process did not prove simple. The marriage diplomacy between the English and Spanish courts turned out to be long and somewhat complex.

There were a number of reasons for the delays, and not all of them concern us. One thing, however, which seems to have preoccupied Catherine of Aragon's parents was their uncertainty in respect of the future of Henry VII's dynasty. Ferdinand and Isabel were only too aware of the long conflict for the English crown between the Lancastrian and Yorkist lines. Henry VII had not inherited the throne, but had seized it in battle. What is more, that had occurred very recently – in 1485 – just a few years before the marriage negotiations commenced.

Even more serious was the fact that after 1485 Henry VII's position was apparently still not really secure. Since his proclamation as king, he had been forced to face up to two competitors: first the Dublin King, and later Richard of England – a contender who had been supported at one stage by the Spanish monarchs themselves. If anything similar were to happen again, the future of Henry's son, and therefore of Arthur's royal consort, might well be in jeopardy.

It is therefore easy to see what outcome the Spanish monarchs now desired in England, in order for them to be willing to agree to dispatch their daughter, Catherine, across the Channel. They wished to have all contenders for the throne eliminated. In fact, a letter survives, written after the outcome they desired had been put into effect, which makes the Spanish point of view very plain.

The letter in question was sent by their ambassador at Henry VII's court, Dr Rodrigo Gonzalez de Puebla, to King Ferdinand and Queen Isabel on 11 January 1499/1500, when the decision to send Catherine to England had finally been taken. The letter is very instructive. De Puebla, who had been responsible for all the marriage negotiations in England informed his sovereigns that:

> this kingdom is at present so situated as has not been seen for the last five hundred years till now … because there were always brambles and thorns of such a kind that the English had occasion not to remain peacefully in obedience to their king, there being divers heirs of the kingdom and of such a quality that the matter could be disputed between the two sides. Now it has pleased God that all should be thoroughly and duly purged and cleansed, so that not a doubtful drop of royal blood remains in this kingdom, except the true blood of the king and queen, and above all that of the lord prince Arthur. And since of this fact and of the execution which was done on Perkin and on the son of the duke of Clarence, I have written to your highnesses by various ways, I do not wish to trouble you with lengthy writing.[3]

This letter makes it clear that the Spanish sovereigns had, for some time, been hoping for the executions of Richard of England and of the official Earl of Warwick. For Ferdinand and Isabel, these deaths were a necessarily prerequisite if they were to dispatch their daughter, Catherine, to England, to marry Prince Arthur. Only if these two important rivals were dead could the Spanish sovereigns feel sure that their daughter's future in England would be secure.

In the end, of course, their view of things proved to be mistaken in several respects. Their daughter was to encounter unforeseen problems of her own in England. These arose from the death of her first husband, Prince Authur, and from Catherine's failure to bear a living son by her second husband,

Arthur's brother, Henry VIII. What is more, the execution of Richard of England and of the official Earl of Warwick failed to remove all the possible Yorkist claimants to the English throne. Edmund de la Pole, the younger brother of the late Earl of Lincoln, was still a potential threat. The Earl of Warwick's elder sister was also living and had a number of children. But apparently the Spanish monarchs did not feel anxious about these Yorkist survivors. Nor do they seem to have been the least bit preoccupied concerning the continued existence of Lambert Simnel.

18

The Third 'Prince in the Tower'

In August 1485, following the death of Richard III, the official Earl of Warwick found himself one of the obvious Yorkist claimants to the throne. Indeed, if Richard himself had made some statement about the succession prior to the battle, Warwick may have been the next rightful Yorkist king. What is more, as we saw in Chapter 4, Warwick may also have been the most valid *Lancastrian* claimant to the English throne. It is not surprising, therefore, that, as we have seen, Henry VII acted quickly to remove the official Earl of Warwick from Sheriff Hutton to London. There the official Warwick remained for the rest of his life. And except for his brief public appearance at St Paul's in 1487 – which was designed to expose the alleged fraudulence of the Dublin King – Warwick was rarely seen by outsiders.

A second Warwick plot had followed: Ralph Wilford – 'the new maumet'. Thus, attention was clearly focussed on Warwick as one of the main Yorkist rivals to Henry VII. However, it has been suggested that, despite his very promising lineage, the official Warwick may have been personally unsuitable for the role of sovereign:

A number of historians have claimed that Warwick was mentally retarded. As Hazel Pierce points out, however, this

The Tower of London in the fifteenth century. Here the alleged Earl of Warwick spent the greater part of his life.

surmise is based entirely on a statement by the chronicler Edward Hall that Warwick had been kept imprisoned for so long "out of all company of men, and sight of beasts, in so much that he could not discern a Goose from a Capon." It seems likely that Hall simply meant that long imprisonment had made Warwick naive and unworldly.[1]

At all events, matters came to a head in 1499, when the Yorkist pretender known as Perkin Warbeck (who had also been imprisoned in the Tower in 1498), was accused of having plotted to free both himself and Warwick. As for the latter, he was also alleged to have conspired to depose Henry VII. As a result, in November 1499 both young prisoners were tried and executed. The official Earl of Warwick met his death at Tower Hill on Thursday, 28 November 1499. Robert Fabyan described the event as follows:

1499
In thys yere, the xvi. day of Nouember [Saturday], was areyned in the Whyte Halle at Westmynster, the forenamed Parkyn [Perkin], &. iii. other; the whych Parkyn and one Iohn Awatyr, were put shortly after in execucion at Tyborne. And soone after was the erle of Warwyke put to deth at the Towre Hylle, & one Blewet & Astwood at Tyborne.[2]

On Thursday, 21 November 1499, John Pullein wrote to Sir Robert Plumpton:

Sir, so it was þat Parkin Warbek & other iij were areyned Satterday next before the making herof [Saturday, 16 November] in þe Whitehall at Westmynster for ther offences, afore Sir John Sygly [sic, Sely], knight marshall, & Sir John Trobilfeild [sic, Turbervile], and ther they all were attended, & judgement given þat they shold be drawn on hirdills from þe Tower, thowout London to þe Tyburne, & ther to be hanged & cut down quicke, & ther bowels to be taken out & burned; ther heads to be stricke of, & [burned deleted] quartred, ther heads and quarters to be disposed at the kings pleasure; & on Munday next after [Monday, 18 November] at þe Gildalle in London, wher þe iudges & many other knights commysioners to inquer and determayn all offences and trespasses: & theder from the Tower was brought viij persones which were indited, & parte of

them confessed themselfe gyltie, & other parte were arrey-
ned, & as yet they be not iuged.³ I thinke the shall haue
iudgement this next Fryday [Friday, 22 November]. Sir, this
present day [Thursday, 21 November] was new barresses
made in Westmynster Hall, & thether was brought therle of
Warwik & arrened afore therle of Oxford, being the kings
greate comyssioner, & afore other lords, bycause he is a pere
of the realme ... & ther therle of Warwek confessed then-
ditments that were layd to his charge, and like iudgment
was given of him as is afore rehersed'.⁴

On 23 November 1499, Perkin Warbeck was drawn on a
hurdle from the Tower to Tyburn. There he read out a confession and was hanged. The Earl of Warwick was executed
by beheading on Tower Hill five days later, on Thursday,
28 November 1499.

A more detailed account of the executions – and also of
the fate of the two dead bodies – is preserved in the *Great
Chronicle of London*. This reports:

Upon the Thursday next ensuing [21 November 1499] was
In The Grete halle of westmynstir areygnyd the fforenamyd
Erle of warwyk being of the age of xxiiij yerys or there-
abowth, upon whom satt ffor Juge Therle of Oxynford
undyr a cloth of astate, where wtouth any processe of the
lawe The said Erle of warwyke for Tresons by hym there
confessed & doon, submyttid hym unto the kyngis grace
& mercy whereafftyr he was there adjugid to be drawyn
hangid & quartered, and afftir coveyed again to the Towyr.

And upon Satirdaye ffoluyng being the day of seynt
Clement & the xxiij day of Novembre was drawn from the
Tower unto Tybourn with oon John a watyr soom tyme
mayer of Corff as before is said, at which place of execution
was ordeynyd a small Scaffold whereupon þe said perkyn
being [&] standing, shewid there unto the people being of
an huge multitude, the specialte of his former confession,

and took It there upon his deth that he nevyr was the poer-
soon which he was namyd nor any thing of that blood, But
a stranger born lyke wyse as beforn he had shewid, and that
he namyd hym sylf to be the second sone of kyng Edward
was by the meane of þe said John a watyr there present &
other as before tyme he had trwly sheyd, afftyr which confession & fforegyffnesse axid of the kyngis grace & all other
that he had offendyd unto, he there upon the Galowis took
hid deth paciently, and with hym also the said John a watyr,
whoos bodyes were afftyr smyttyn doun and theyr hedis
there strykyn of & carried to london bridge & there pygth
upon two polys, and theyr bodyes afftyr conveyed unto the
ffrere augustynys & there buryed.

And upon the Thursday ffoluyng or the xxviij day of
November was the fforenamyd Erle of warwyk browgth
owth of the Towyr betwene ij servauntis of the marshall of
that place, and at the uttyr [outer] Gate delyverd unto the
Shyrevys, by whoos officers he was ffrom thens ladd unto
the scaffold & there byhedid, afftyr which excecucion doon
the Corps of hym with the hede was layd In to a Coffyn
& then born again Into the Towyr, which excecucion was
doon abowth iij of the clok at afftyr noune upon whoos
sawle & all Crysten Jhesu have mercy, The which Corps
& hede was upon the day ffoluyng conveyed by watyr
unto Byrsam beside wyndyssore and there eneterid with
his auncetours.[5]

As we have seen, the execution of Perkin Warbeck and of the
official Earl of Warwick may have been part of Henry VII's
process of clearing the ground for the royal marriage of
Prince Arthur to Catherine of Aragon; a marriage which was
finally solemnised in 1501. The remains of the official Earl
of Warwick were interred at Bisham Priory Church.[6] This
had been the traditional burial place of the Montagu earls of
Salisbury, from whom Warwick was descended, via his mother,
Isabel, Duchess of Clarence. At that time, Bisham Priory was

CHURCH OF THE AUSTIN FRIARS

NOW THE DUTCH CHURCH OF JESUS TEMPLE.

MID *14TH CENTURY* 16*TH CENTURY*. *MODERN.*

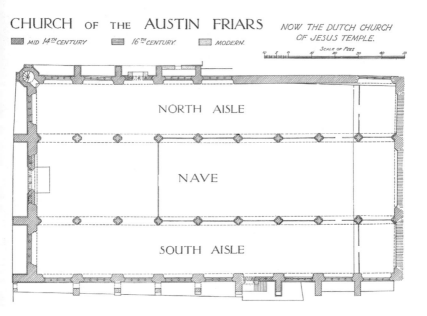

Plan of the Austin Friars' nave as it was prior to its destruction in 1940.

a house of Augustinian Canons, which had been founded in 1337 by the first Earl of Salisbury:[7]

> Within the walls of this convent were interred William, Earl of Salisbury, son of the founder, who distinguished himself at the battle of Poitiers; John, Earl of Salisbury, who, confederating against King Henry IV, was slain at Cirencester in 1401; Thomas, Earl of Salisbury, the famous hero of Henry V's reign, who lost his life at the Siege of Orleans in 1428; Richard Neville, Earl of Salisbury, who was beheaded at Pontefract in 1460, for his adherence to the House of York; Richard Neville, the great Earl of Warwick & Salisbury, and his brother John, Marquis of Montague, who both fell at the Battle of Barnet in 1470; and the unfortunate Prince Edward, Earl of Warwick, son of the Duke of Clarence, who, bred from his cradle in prison, was beheaded

in 1499 for attempting to taste the sweets of liberty. Most
of the above-mentioned illustrious characters had splendid
monuments in the conventual church; but these were all
destroyed after the dissolution of the abbey, without regard
to the rank or famed exploits of the deceased – not even
excepting the tomb of Salisbury, "the mirror of all martial
men, who in thirteen battles overcame and first trained
Henry V to the wars."[8]

As we have seen, it was in 1499, following his execution on
Tower Hill, that the body of the young man who – in theory
at least – was the last living male descendant of all those noble
lords, was brought to Bisham Priory to join the bones of his
forebears. His funeral was paid for by the king. The Privy Purse
Expenses of Henry VII record, for 8 December 1499, 'Payd for
the buriell of therle of Warwic by iiij bills, £12. 18s. 2d.'[9]

Sadly, nothing now remains of Bisham Priory Church.
There is therefore no immediate prospect of recovering the
remains of the official Edward, Earl of Warwick. This is a
pity. My earlier research established the mitochondrial DNA
sequence of Richard III and his siblings in 2004, and also
offered evidence of where that king's remains might be found.
It was as a direct result of that research that the excavation of
the Leicester Greyfriars site took place in 2012, resulting in
the recovery of Richard III's remains, and in their subsequent
identification using the mtDNA evidence.[10] Perhaps one day
similar archaeology may recover the remains of the official Earl
of Warwick. If his bones could be found, it could be possible
to compare his DNA – and particularly his Y-chromosome –
with that of the genuine Earl of Warwick's uncle, Richard III.

Such a study could potentially prove – or disprove – whether
the official Earl of Warwick really was the son of Richard III's
brother George, Duke of Clarence. Since we have no precise
information concerning the burial place of the remains of
Lambert Simnel, testing the DNA of the remains of the official Earl of Warwick, executed in 1499 by Henry VII, would

probably be the only direct way in which 'dead' DNA research might shed new light on the mystery surrounding the identity of the Dublin King. However, there are also theoretically some possibilities for 'live' DNA research, and these will be summarised in the final chapter.

As for the victim known as Perkin Warbeck, his head was displayed on London Bridge, and eventually it probably fell into the Thames. But, as reported in the *Great Chronicle of London* his headless corpse joined that of many other executed individuals, for it was buried somewhere in the Church of the Austin Friars in Old Broad Street – most probably in the nave. Despite Henry VIII's subsequent dissolution of England's religious houses, the nave of the Austin Friars Church in London survived intact for another 440 years. For most of that time it was known as the capital's 'Dutch Church'. Unfortunately, however, in 1940 the building was destroyed by German bombing. As a result there is now little or no prospect of recovering the remains of Richard of England, or of testing his DNA in an attempt to clarify the real identity of Perkin Warbeck.

Conclusions

In one respect there is now no doubt whatever about the identity of the person at the centre of this story: he was the Dublin King. This boy, who appeared to be about 10 years of age in 1487, was crowned King of England and France and Lord of Ireland at Christ Church Cathedral in Dublin on 24 May 1487, in the presence of at least one and possibly two archbishops, several bishops, a number of Anglo-Irish lords, and a small group of English nobles and gentry, led by his putative cousin the Earl of Lincoln, and by Viscount Lovell. After his proclamation as king, he bore the royal title of King Edward VI.

Nevertheless, problems exist on two levels. First, there is the question of the origin of the Dublin King. Where did he come from? What was his name before he became King Edward VI? Who were his parents? What was his family background? Where, and by whom was he brought up? Second, there is the question of what became of him when his brief sovereignty ended. Where did he live? What did he do? When did he die? Because his identity, both before and after his short nominal reign, is in doubt, this also raises questions about other historical characters, and his relationship with them.

We began by exploring the five possible stories of his childhood. From that careful examination, certain facts emerged. The Dublin King was definitely not Edward V, the elder son of Edward IV and Elizabeth Woodville. Nor was he Edward V's younger brother, Richard of Shrewsbury, Duke of York and Norfolk. What is more, there is no evidence that he ever claimed to be either of these so-called 'princes in the Tower', despite the subsequent allegations of two Tudor historians that at one point he assumed the identity of Richard of Shrewsbury.

There is now no doubt whatever that the royal identity claimed by the Dublin King was that of Edward of Clarence, Earl of Warwick. But while some contemporary sources stated that he really was the Earl of Warwick, others stated equally firmly that he was an impostor. The sources for both versions of the story are probably partisan in their different ways. Hence, any claim to say for certain which of the accounts is correct would simply be arrogant. The truth is that we do not know.

One further point which has emerged from this present reinvestigation of the story is that the king crowned in Dublin in 1487 seems to have been identical with the 'son of Clarence' who had been staying in Mechelen with Margaret of York in 1486. However, this Dublin King/'son of Clarence' could not possibly have been identical with the official Earl of Warwick, who had been in the custody of Henry VII since August 1485.

At the same time it seems probable that the official Earl of Warwick held by Henry VII between 1485 and 1487 was identical with the earlier official Earl of Warwick who had lived with other Yorkist princelings at Sheriff Hutton Castle from 1483 to 1485. He in turn was probably identical with the official Earl of Wawick who had been the ward of the Marquess of Dorset from 1478 until 1483. Thus this official Earl of Warwick was presumably the little boy, aged about 3, who had been delivered to messengers of King Edward IV by servants of the Clarence household at Warwick Castle following the execution of George, Duke of Clarence in February 1477/78.

But, as Edward IV knew, the problem is that the previous year the Duke of Clarence had attempted to send his real son, the 2-year-old Edward, Earl of Warwick out of England to either Flanders or Ireland, at the same time replacing him in the Clarence nursery with a substitute child. The great difficulty is that we do not know whether Clarence succeeded in carrying out this plan – or parts of it. Clearly, the official view of Edward IV's government was that Clarence had not succeeded. However, the wording of the Act of Attainder against Clarence leaves some doubts about how far the scheme had progressed.

At the same time there is evidence from both Irish and Flemish sources which suggests that the Dublin King/'son of Clarence' travelled to Mechelen from Ireland, where he had been resident for some time. When this is coupled with the later story that the Duke of Clarence had visited Ireland in 1476/77, the serious possibility emerges that George may have made arrangements for the housing and bringing up in Ireland of the Dublin King/'son of Clarence', as a result of which the little boy had subsequently lived there, under the care of Clarence's friend the Earl of Kildare.

Of course, there is no absolute proof that this is what took place. But if things did happen in that way, then it is highly probable that the Earl of Kildare believed that the child left in his care was the genuine Earl of Warwick. The logical consequence of that would have been that Kildare brought the child up under the name of Edward, Earl of Warwick. The little boy himself would therefore have grown up believing that he was a prince of the house of York, and the son of the Duke of Clarence.

Even then, however, the problem remains that we have no way of knowing whether a little boy sent to the Earl of Kildare by the Duke of Clarence some months before his arrest would have been the *real* Earl of Warwick, or a substitute child. Thus, although the Dublin King and the Mechelen 'son of Clarence' were probably one and the same person, the suggestion that he had been brought up by the Earl of Kildare contains an element of guesswork. And even if he had grown up under Kildare's guardianship, that fact by itself would not absolutely prove that he was the genuine Earl of Warwick.

There also remains yet another possibility. The boy might only have been brought to Ireland in about 1485 or 1486 – by a priest with a surname something like Simons, who had deliberately created a pseudo-royal impostor. However, we cannot overlook the fact that the official Tudor government evidence in favour of this last notion has proved to be flawed, and contains a number of contradictions.

We also need to take account of the fact that two genuine members of the royal house of York (one of whom had an excellent claim to the English throne in his own right) both accepted the Dublin King as the Earl of Warwick, and promoted him as King Edward VI. Significantly, these two Yorkist royals were the most independent members of their family in 1486 and 1487. They were therefore the ones who enjoyed the greatest freedom, and who had the best possible opportunity to say what they truly believed. Of course, they may, nevertheless, have been lying. However, their motivation would then be very hard to understand. Alternatively they may have been deceiving themselves, or allowing themselves to be deceived. However, the third possibility is that Margaret of York and the Earl of Lincoln may both have got it right.

We also have to confront the question of what happened to the Dublin King after the Battle of Stoke. Apparently a captive was handed over to Henry VII, who initially imprisoned him and then later employed him in a menial capacity. But because Henry VII had never previously set eyes on the Dublin King, he would have had no personal ability to recognise or identify his prisoner/kitchen boy. Interestingly, however, there is some evidence that those Anglo-Irish lords who had attended the Dublin King's coronation did not subsequently recognise him when they were confronted with Henry VII's kitchen boy. At the same time we also have one (possibly partisan) report that the Dublin King did not remain in the hands of Henry VII after the Battle of Stoke Field, but was taken away and concealed abroad by his supporters and surviving members of the house of York. In connection with these reports one also has to take account of the fact that Henry VII's prisoner and servant appears to have been about five years older than the individual who had been crowned as King Edward VI in Christ Church Cathedral.

At the same time there are certain question marks over what became of the official Earl of Warwick after 1487. The lad who had been in Henry VII's custody since 1485 is not reported to have had learning difficulties. Certainly he cannot have been obviously backward before 1485, since Richard III had promoted him in various ways. However, after 1487, there is a suggestion that the official Earl of Warwick may have been intellectually impaired. This story is problematic, and may merely be the result of a misinterpretation. Certainly, as far as we know, nothing had happened to him which would explain such a change. Nevertheless, there may be some question as to whether the official Earl of Warwick who was executed in 1499 and buried at Bisham Priory was indeed identical with the official Earl of Warwick prior to 1487.

In the end, none of the evidence is cut and dried, and readers must make their own decision as to which view they wish to take. The only way to make the picture clearer would be to seek the remains of some of the chief characters in the story and use scientific (DNA) testing to try to clarify who they really were.

This approach could possibly be used in the case of the official Earl of Warwick. If the chance ever arises for excavation on the site of the church of Bisham Priory, it would certainly be worth trying to find and identify his bones. The body should hopefully be recognisable, even if the coffin purchased for him by Henry VII is not labelled with his name and title, since we know that he was approximately 24 years old at the time of his death. An additional aid to identification would, of course, be the fact that his head was cut off.

There is also room for a future scientific examination of the remains found at the Tower of London in 1674. But if the evidence presented earlier in respect of Edward IV's sons was correct, those remains would probably tell us little or nothing about the true identity of the Dublin King. Unfortunately, as we have seen, thanks to the bombing of London in the Second World War, there is now very little prospect of finding or examining the remains of Edward IV's intriguing putative son Perkin Warbeck.

There may, however, be some possibilities for DNA research using living individuals. First, it would be very useful to hear from any living male residents of England, Wales or former British colonies who bear the surname Simnel(l). If living men who have this surname were willing to participate in DNA testing, it would then be possible to establish details of their Y-chromosome. Comparison of results from different individuals whose recent lines of descent are not closely connected could indicate whether there is a common (or, at least, a predominant) Y-chromosome sequence for that particular – and rather unusual – surname. It would also be interesting to compare the results with the Y-chromosome of Richard III.

What would be the point of this? Simply, if the Lambert Simnel who worked for Henry VII – and who may have living descendants today – was identical with the Dublin King, and if he was really a son of the royal house of York, he should have carried that family's Y-chromosome. Thus such testing could potentially reveal whether there is any living male with the surname Simnel who appears to be related to the house of York. To a lesser extent, it might also be interesting and possibly informative to carry out similar testing of living males who have the surname Wilford.

In the final analysis, maybe we need to bear in mind the fact that every known story about a mysteriously surviving claimant of a royal identity seems to have turned out, in the end, to be false. Thus, those young men who, in the early nineteenth century, claimed to be King Louis XVII of France all proved to be impostors. Likewise those who, in the twentieth century, claimed to be surviving Romanov children were not telling the truth.

Yet we must not lose sight of the fact that the story of the Dublin King has one unique twist to it, which may set it apart from all the other stories of miraculously rescued royal children. That key point, which makes the case of the Dublin

King unique, concerns the very strange scheme concocted by George, Duke of Clarence to send his son abroad and replace him in the Clarence nursery with a substitute child. In the final analysis we cannot be sure what the Duke of Clarence really did with his son in 1477. But the fact that he unquestionably had a plan to replace his son and heir with a human changeling, and to send his real son out of the country, cannot be overlooked or ignored. When coupled with the other surviving evidence, this raises a serious question mark over the official Tudor version of the Dublin King's story which has been told and retold with little real thought or enquiry for more than five hundred years.

Appendix 1

Timeline

1464	Secret (and ?bigamous) marriage of Edward IV and Elizabeth Woodville.
1469	Marriage of George and Isabel, Duke and Duchess of Clarence.
1470	2 November, birth of Edward, Prince of Wales (Edward V).
1473	17 August, birth of Richard of Shrewsbury (Duke of York and Norfolk).
1474/75	25 February, birth of Edward of Clarence, Earl of Warwick.
1476	22 December, death of Isabel, Duchess of Clarence.
1476/7	?Birth of Lambert (?or perhaps John), ?son of Thomas Simnel of ?Oxford.
	The widowed Duke of Clarence made plans to smuggle his son and heir, Edward, Earl of Warwick – aged about 2 – to either Ireland or Flanders, and replace him with a substitute child.
1477/8	18 February, execution of George, Duke of Clarence;
	?Edward, Earl of Warwick, aged about 3, was placed under the guardianship of the Marquess of Dorset, then aged about 25, married to his second wife, Cecily, and probably resident at the Tower of London.
1480	?Edward, Earl of Warwick, was given a selection of new leather footwear by Edward IV, just before the summer visit to England of his aunt, Margaret, whom the young Earl may have met. He was then aged 5.

1483	Death of Edward IV.
	Richard III assumed guardianship of Edward V (aged 12½, and Richard of Shrewsbury, approaching 10 years of age), and placed these two 'princes' at the Tower of London (whence they may later have been abducted by the Duke of Buckingham). Richard III also assumed guardianship of ?Edward, Earl of Warwick (aged 8) and placed him at Sheriff Hutton Castle together with other royal children. Richard gave ?Edward, Earl of Warwick appointments, so presumably the child did not then show any signs of learning difficulties.
1485	Henry VII took control of ?Edward, Earl of Warwick, then aged 10, and placed him initially under the guardianship of his own mother, Margaret Beaufort, Countess of Richmond and Stanley. Later Henry accommodated him at the Tower of London.
1486	'The son of Clarence' (then aged 11), was with his aunt Margaret of York in Flanders.
1487	'The son of Clarence' (aged 12), or Lambert (?John) Simnel (?aged 10), was crowned king in Dublin.
	?Edward, Earl of Warwick, was brought out of the Tower of London by Henry VII and displayed at St Paul's Cathedral in the hope that people would recognise him .
	'The son of Clarence' (aged 12), or Lambert (?John) Simnel (?aged 10), was captured at the Battle of Stoke and either subsequently employed by Henry VII, or shipped to the Continent by Edmund de la Pole.
1489	Henry VII entertained Irish lords in England and showed them Lambert Simnel (then aged 12?) their alleged former 'Dublin King'. All but one of the Irish Lords failed to recognise him.
1499	?Edward, Earl of Warwick, then aged 24 (and possibly intellectually impaired) was executed by Henry VII for allegedly attempting to escape from the Tower of London with Perkin Warbeck. His body and head were buried at Bisham Priory.

1525	Issue of robes to Lambert Simnel (then aged about 48?) for the funeral of Sir Thomas Lovell,[1] courtier and counsellor of Henry VII.
?	Some time after 1525 (and possibly after 1534) Lambert Simnel died.

Appendix 2

Contemporary and Near-Contemporary Records of the Dublin King's Identity

This summary restricts itself to sources written within twenty-five years of the coronation of the Dublin King. Ten sources are included. Of these:

> four state that he was the Earl of Warwick/King Edward
> *three* ascribe *no name* to the Dublin King
> *two* give his name as *Lambert Simnel*
> *one* gives his name as *John*.

In terms of statistics, these figures might perhaps be interpreted as suggesting that there is a 60 per cent chance that the Dublin King was a false claimant (though if so, his real name remains uncertain). At the same time, however, there seems to be a 40 per cent chance that he was the genuine Earl of Warwick. Apparently there would only be a 20 per cent chance that his real name was Lambert Simnel.

Restricting this analysis to include only the most closely contemporaneous sources would produce a result fractionally more favourable to the suggestion that the Dublin King really was the Earl of Warwick (approximately 43 per cent), with only a 10 per cent chance that his real name was Lambert Simnel.

The most obvious outcome of such analyses is that, despite the general tendency of historians to accept the official Tudor line, in fact the truth about the identity of the Dublin King remains very unclear.

SOURCE	THE IDENTITY OF THE PRETENDER
Closely contemporary sources	
Canterbury Convocation, Feb. 1486/87	[no name]
Herald's account, 1487	John
York City Archives, 1487	King Edward VI
Henry VII's letter to the Pope, 1487	spurium quemdam pueram
Kildare's Letter, Aug. 1487	King Edward
Parliament, Lincoln Attainder, Nov. 1487	Lambert Simnel (son of Thomas)
A. De But, Chronicle, c. 1490	Duke (*sic*) of Warwick/Duke of Clarence)/son of Duke of Clarence
+ about 13 years	
B. Andre, *Historia H. VII*, c. 1500	Unamed fake who claimed to be Richard, Duke of York
J. Molinet, *Chronique*, c. 1500	the genuine Earl of Warwick/King Edward
+ about 25 years	
Vergil, Anglica Historia, c. 1512	Lambert Simnel

Appendix 3

Frequency of the Occurrence of the Surname Simnel in the UK circa 1500–2000

Below is a provisional list of reported occurrences of the surname Simnel(l) in England and Wales over approximately the last five hundred years, based on internet sources.[1] So far, 102 entries have been found. However, entries which are close together in name, date and location may refer to various events in the life of a single individual. Thus the total number of Simnel(l) s represented by the list is almost certainly less than 100. Probably about ninety separate individuals are represented.

However, it is obvious that the list, as it stands at present, does not constitute a complete record of Simnel(l)s over approximately the past five hundred years. For example, an Edward T. Simnell was married in 1944, but there appears to be no record of his birth. Nor is there any record of his death. Possibly he was an American serviceman who married in the UK during the Second World War, but who had been born in the USA. However, Edward T. Simnell is by no means the only example of incompleteness in the list as it stands at present.

No Simnel(l) entries have so far been found in the current (2013–14) BT online phonebook – but of course if there are living Simnel(l)s, they may not have landline telephones, or they might have chosen to be ex-directory. Reportedly no entries, under either spelling of this surname, figure in the UK voters registers for the period 2002–14. That would appear to suggest that no adult UK citizens now bear the surname

Simnel(l). Nevertheless, in January 2014 there were several examples of the surname on Facebook – though an attempt at investigation subsequently showed that at least one of these was a pseudonym. (No answer was received in respect of the other Facebook enquiries.)

It is worth noting that there is also a record of at least one male Simnell emigrating from the United Kingdom to the United States of America, in 1912. Thus, it would be useful to conduct a search for living Simnels in the USA – and also in other parts of the English-speaking world. However, although the surname appears forty-seven times in Australian and New Zealand records dating from the nineteenth and twenti-eth centuries, the current situation in Australasia appears to be similar to that in the UK – there seem to be no living Simnel(l)s.[2]

The UK list below – incomplete though it appears to be – certainly indicates that during the past five hundred years the surname Simnel(l) was never common in England. But it was by no means unknown. To offer a statistical comparison, similar searches over the same time period were conducted, relating to three of the rarer surnames which figure in my own ancestry. These produced the following figures:

SEVIL   approximately 470 entries.[3]
BAULSOM approximately 280 entries.[4]
MINEVEH only 16 entries.[5] (However, Mineveh is very rare because it is a rather idiosyncratic variant of the slightly less rarified surname Minifie.)

There certainly are living individuals in the UK bearing the surnames Sevil and Baulsom. Therefore it is not completely impossible that living Simnel(l)s also still exist somewhere.

If there are any living males who bear the hereditary sur-name Simnel(l), I should be delighted to hear from them. It would be interesting to explore whether there is an identifiable Simnel(l) Y-chromosome. In other words do/

did the bearers of this surname represent a single family?
It would also be very interesting to be able to compare the
Simnel(l) Y-chromosome(s) with the Y-chromosome of King
Richard III!

Simnell, ?	buried 1645, Hampton, Middx
Simnell, unnamed male	d. 1869, Burton-upon-Trent, Staffs
Simnell, Abigail	buried 1695, St Ives, Huntingdonshire
Simnell, Agnes	buried 1641, Ramsey, Huntingdonshire
Simnell, Alce	married 1570, Boxsted, Essex
Simnell, Alce	buried 1630, St Ives, Huntingdonshire
Simnell, Alce	married 1639, St Ives, Huntingdonshire
Simnell, Alce	married 1797, Manchester, Lancs
Simnell, Alece	buried 1588, Bradwell-on-Sea, Essex
Simnell, Ann	bapt. 1633, Hayes, Middx.
Simnell, Ann	buried 1685, Holy Trinity, Cambridge
Simnel, Anna	married 1645, Hurworth, Durham
Simnell, Anne	married 1632, St Benet, Paul's Wharf, London
Simnell, Anne	living London, 1661
Simnell, Anne	living London, 1676
Simnel, Anne	buried 1749, Burslem, Staffs
Simnell, Audrey T.	married 1944, Lichfield, Staffs
Simnel, Clement	buried 1735, St Ives, Huntingdonshire
Simnell, Dorothy	married 1635, St Martin, Ludgate, London
Simnell, Edward T.	married 1944, Wenlock, Shropshire
Simnel, Eliza	b. 1854, Stafford – still living 1871
Simnel, Eliza Jane	bapt. 1861, Eastchurch, Kent
Simnell, Elizabeth	buried 1615, Ipswich, Suffolk
Simnell, Elizabeth	bapt. 1631, Hayes, Middx.

Simnell, Elizabeth	buried 1631, St Ives, Huntingdonshire
Simnell, Elizabeth	buried 1643, Acton Middx.
Simnell, Elizabeth	buried 1682, St Ives, Huntingdonshire
Simnel, Elizabeth	bapt. 1737, Mold, Flintshire
Simnel, Elizabeth	buried 1739, St Ives, Huntingdonshire
Simnel, Elizth Hanh	bapt. 1820, Plymouth, Devon
Simnel, Elizabeth	b. 1830 – buried 1831, Wolstanton, Staffs
Simnell, Elizabeth	d. 1895, Bangor, Caernarvonshire
Simnell, Elizth	b. 1877, living 1881, Cannock, Staffs
Simnell, Elz	married 1603, Westminster, Middx
Simnell, Elz	married 1626, St Giles in the Fields, Holborn, London
Simnell, Emily	b. 1856, living 1881, Nottingham, Notts
Simnell, George Charles	married 1886, Burton-upon-Trent, Staffs
Simnell, Hannah	married 1869, Burton-upon-Trent, Staffs
Simnell, Henry	buried 1641, Ramsey, Huntingdonshire
Simnell, Hernicus [sic]	buried 1626, St Ives, Huntingdonshire
Simnel, Henry	married 1899, Burton-upon-Trent, Staffs
Simnell, James	buried 1641, St Ives, Huntingdonshire
Simnell, Jane	married 1666, St Aug. & St Faith, London
Simnel, Jane	b. 1860 – still living 1881 London St Giles
Simnel, Joan	married 1594, St Margaret, Westminster
Simnel, Joan	married 1615, St Clement, Ipswich, Suffolk
Simnell, Joan(e)	married 1624, St Margaret, Westminster
Simnell, Johannes	buried 1635, St Ives, Huntingdonshire
Simnel, John	married 1576, St Margaret, Westminster
Simnell, John	bapt. 1577, St Margaret, Westminster
Simnell, John	married 1598, Westminster, Middx

Simnell, John	married 1610, St Margaret, Westminster
Simnell, John	buried 1612, St Margaret, Westminster
Simnel, John	buried 1613, Westminster, Middx
Simnell, John	b. 1857, living 1881, Derby, Derbyshire
Simnell, Joseph	b. 1835, living 1881, Derby, Derbyshire
Simnell, Joseph	married 1883, Burton-upon-Trent, Staffs
Simnell, J. H. (male)	b. 1887, left Liverpoool for Boston, USA, 1912
Simnel, M.	bapt. 1759, Neston, Cheshire
Simnel, Margaret	married 1613, St Clement, Ipswich, Suffolk
Simnell, Mary	married 1657, St Ives, Huntingdonshire
Simnell, Mary	buried 1667, St Ives, Huntingdonshire
Simnel, Mary	buried 1739, Maidstone, Kent
Simnell, Mary	b. 1809, living 1881, Liverpool, Lancs
Simnell, Mary	b. 1811, living 1901, Worcester, Worcs
Simnell, Mary	b. 1823, living 1851, Shoreditch, Middx
Simnell, Maureen	d. 1993, Ogwr, Glamorganshire
Simnel, Michael	married 1589, St Margaret, Westminster
Simnell, Micheall [sic],	buried 1593, St Margaret, Westminster
Simnel, Michael	buried 1594, Westminster, Middx
Simnell, Nancy	b. 1773, living 1851, Newington, Surrey
Simnel, Philip Stephen	b. 1966, East Ham, Essex
Simnell, Phoebe	b. 1833, living 1881, Derby, Derbyshire
Simnell, Richard	married 1567, Chelmsford, Essex
Simnel, Richard	buried 1630, St Ives, Huntingdonshire
Simnell, Richard	married 1642, St Bartholomew the Great, London
Simnell, Richard	buried 1667, St Ives, Huntingdonshire
Simnel, Richard	b. 1826, Stafford – still living 1871

Simnell, Rose	married 1698, Holywell-cum-Needingworth, Huntingdonshire
Simnell, Samuel	bapt. 1855, Bebington, Cheshire
Simnell, Samuel Thomas	b. 1901, Loughborough, Leics
Simnell, Sara	buried 1626, St Ives, Huntingdonshire
Simnel, Sara	buried 1638, St Ives, Huntingdonshire
Simnell, Sarah	b. 1691, buried 1776, London
Simnel, Thomas	buried 1620, Westminster, Middx
Simnel, Thomas	married 1629, Heston, Middx
Simnell, Thomas	buried 1630, St Ives, Huntingdonshire
Simnel, Thomas	married 1632, London
Simnel(l), Thomas	married 1645, Hurworth, Durham
Simnell, Thomas	buried 1666, Somersham, Huntingdonshire
Simnel, Thomas	bapt. 1722, St Clement Danes, Middx
Simnel, Thomas	buried 1723, St Clement Danes, Middx
Simnel, Thomas	bapt. 1723, St Clement Danes, Middx
Simnell, Thomas Frederick	b. 1858, Wolverhampton, Staffs.
Simnel, William	married 1588, Bures B T, Suffolk
Simnell, William	married 1590, Bradwell-on-Sea, Essex
Simnell, William	married 1643, St Peter, Cambridge, Cambs
Simnell, William	married 1686, Whittlesford, Cambs
Simnel, William	married 1695, St Ives, Huntingdonshire
Simnel, William	buried 1757, Neston, Cheshire
Simnel, William	bapt. 1759, Neston, Cheshire
Simnell, William	b. 1838, living 1911, Birmingham, Warks

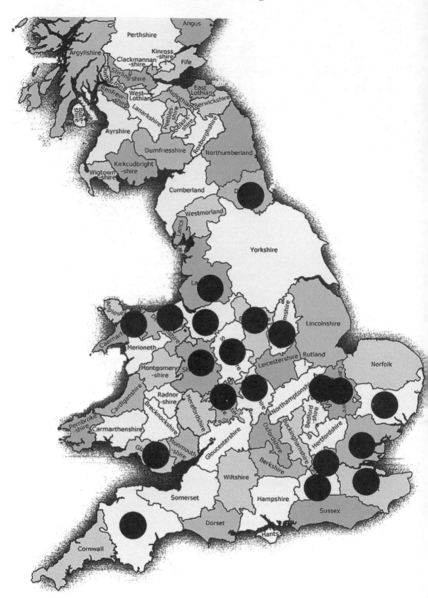

Map showing locations in England and Wales in which occurrences of the surname
SIMNEL have been documented over the last 500 years.

Notes

Abbreviations

CPR	Calendar of Patent Rolls
ODNB	Oxford Dictionary of National Biography
PROME	The Parliament Rolls of Medieval England

Introduction

1. An impostor appeared at the Carmelite friary in Oxford in 1318, claiming to be a son of Edward I, but no one seems to have believed him and he was quickly arrested and executed (A. Crossley & C. R. Elrington (eds), VCH, *A History of Oxford*, vol. 4, *The City of Oxford* (1979), pp. 3–73. http://www.british-history.ac.uk/report.aspx?compid=22803, accessed 28 August 2013.) In October 1399, after Henry IV had imprisoned Richard II, the deposed king's chaplain, Richard Maudeleyn, who reportedly resembled him, plotted to impersonate him briefly as part of a plan aimed at reversing the situation – but of course, had it succeeded, the real Richard II, not Maudeleyn, would have resumed the crown. The fifteenth-century case of Ralph Wilford is considered below – but seems not to have been a very serious attempt upon the throne. (VCH, *A History of Oxford*, pp. 3–73. Accessed 28 August 2013.)
   The author does not accept that the royal family known as 'Tudor' really bore this surname (see Ashdown-Hill J, *Royal Marriage Secrets*, Stroud 2013, p. 70 *et seq.*). Nevertheless, for convenience, the appelation *Tudor* is used throughout this book without further comment.
2. See Chapter 2, p. XX.
3. As the son and heir of the Duke of Clarence, Warwick's *Yorkist* claim was technically invalidated by the 1478 Act of Attainder of Edward IV against his father. However, as we shall see later, there was also another possible way of looking at his situation.
4. In some Continental countries new years did begin on 1 January, and throughout Europe (including in England) gifts called 'New Year's Day' presents were commonly exchanged on 1 January. But in medieval England 1 January had no practical significance in terms of the numbering of the year.

The Historical Background

1. For the evidence relating to this case, see Ashdown-Hill J, *Eleanor the Secret Queen*, Stroud 2009, and Ashdown-Hill, *Royal Marriage Secrets*, Chapter 9.
2. M.T. Hayden, 'Lambert Simnel in Ireland', *Studies: An Irish Quarterly Review*, 4 (1915), p. 625.

Part 1 – Possible Childhoods Of The Dublin King

1. Richard, Duke of York

1. Blank – but for the probable identity of the individual in question, see below.
2. D.F. Sutton, ed., Bernard André, *De Vita atque Gestis Henrici Septimi Historia*, on-line 2010, section 54.
3. E. Cavell, ed., *The Heralds' Memoir 1486–1490*, Richard III & Yorkist History Trust 2009, p. 59. Also http://en.wikipedia.org/wiki/John_Writhe, accessed September 2013.
4. For extensive consideration of this question see Ashdown-Hill, *Eleanor*, and Ashdown-Hill, *Royal Marriage Secrets*.
5. For year dates of this kind, see the author's note in the Introduction.
6. F. Sandford, *Genealogical History of England*, London 1707, [page number??].
7. For details of the Mowbray marriage and its context see J. Ashdown-Hill, 'Norfolk Requiem: The passing of the House of Mowbray', *Ricardian* 12 March 2001, 198–217.
8. In fact the Crowland Chronicle gives two different versions of the time of Buckingham's arrival. See J. Ashdown-Hill, *Richard III's 'Beloved Cousyn': John Howard and the House of York*, Stroud 2009, pp. 86–7.
9. N. Pronay & J. Cox, eds, The Crowland Chronicle Continuations 1459–1486, London 1986, pp. 156–7.
10. For details of the council meeting, see Ashdown-Hill, *'Beloved Cousyn'*, p. 93.
11. Reportedly, Elizabeth Woodville herself had been anxious about the validity of her marriage in 1477. C.A.J. Armstrong, ed., D. Mancini, *The Usurpation of Richard III*, Gloucester 1989, pp. 62–3. See also J. Ashdown-Hill, *The Third Plantagenet, George, Duke of Clarence, Richard III's Brother*, Stroud 2014.
12. See Ashdown-Hill, *'Beloved Cousyn'*, p. 98 *et seq.*
13. Based upon the handwriting.
14. Armstrong, *Usurpation of Richard III*, p. 128, n. 91.
15. A. Hanham, ed., *The Cely Letters 1472–1488*, London 1975, pp. 184–5, 285–6. Also A. Hanham, *The Celys and their World*, Cambridge 1985, p. 287.
16. Bishop William Grey of Ely died on 4 August 1478.
17. Hanham, *Celys and their World*, p. 287, recognises that 'most of these flying rumours were untrue'.
18. A. Crawford, ed., The Household Books of John Howard, Duke of Norfolk, 1462–71, 1481–83, Stroud 1992, Part 2, p. 348.

19. N.H. Nicolas, ed., Privy Purse Expenses of Elizabeth of York: Wardrobe accounts of Edward the Fourth, London 1830, pp. 155–6, 160–1.

20. For example, in C.F. Richmond, 'The Death of Edward V', *Northern History*, 25 (1989), pp. 278–80, Richmond argued from the date of 22 June 1483, given for Edward V's death in the Anlaby cartulary, in an entry written after 1509 (see below). In fact the significance of the grant of the title 'Duke of Norfolk' to John Howard remains debatable. Richard of Shrewsbury was given the dukedom of Norfolk in 1477 in preparation for his marriage to the Mowbray heiress, Anne. The marriage followed in 1478. Anne Mowbray's subsequent death, together with the fact that Lord Howard was the senior Mowbray coheir, are factors which may have influenced Richard III.

21. *CPR, 1485–1494*, pp. 307–8.

22. Petition of Elizabeth Talbot, dowager Duchess of Norfolk, to Henry VII, dated 27 November 1489, CPR 1485–1494, pp. 307–8.

23. He is often referred to as Richard IV but there is no contemporary evidence for this, or indeed for any royal numeral.

24. PROME, 1487 Parliament, Lincoln attainder [November 1487].

25. http://www.fpnotebook.com/endo/exam/hghtmsrmntinchldrn.htm, accessed August 2013. There appears to be little difference between medieval and modern heights – see Ashdown-Hill, *Third Plantagenet*, p. 61 and note 28.

26. The heights of Edward IV and his brothers, George and Richard, varied, probably because their father was tall but their mother was short (Ashdown-Hill, *Third Plantagenet*, p. 62). In the case of Richard of Shrewsbury we have no information regarding the height of his mother, but his father was certainly of above-average height.

27. Dr Jean Ross's claim is quoted in R. Drewett and M. Redhead, *The Trial of Richard III*, Gloucester 1984, p. 66.

28. Ashdown-Hill, *Eleanor*, pp. 181–85.

29. Ashdown-Hill, *Third Plantagenet*.

2. Edward V – and the Wider Problems of the Fate of the 'Princes'

1. A. Raine, ed., *York Civic Records,* vol. 2, Yorkshire Archaeological Society 1941, pp. 20–1 (original records, Book 6, fol. 97).

2. M. Bennett, *Lambert Simnel and the Battle of Stoke*, New York 1987, p. 121.

3. See, for example, J. Gairdner, ed., Letters and Papers Illustrative of the Reigns of Richard III and Henry VII, vol. 1, London 1861, p. 16.

4. G. Smith, 'Lambert Simnel and the King from Dublin', *Ricardian*, 10, no. 135, December 1996, p. 509.

5. Smith, 'Lambert Simnel and the King from Dublin', p. 517.

6. Smith, 'Lambert Simnel and the King from Dublin', p. 520.

7. Armstrong, *Usurpation of Richard III*, p. 105. Domenico Mancini (*c.*1434–1500) was from a Roman family of unremarkable origin, members of which subsequently attained noble status in France through their relationship with Cardinal Mazarin, first minister during the youth of Louis XIV.

8. Armstrong, *Usurpation of Richard III*, pp. 92–3.

9. See also A. Carson, *Richard III the Maligned King*, Stroud 2013, p. 169 (or p. 145 of earlier editions).

10. 'quo ultimo ex suis regulus usus fuit'. Armstrong / Armstrong, Usurpation of Richard III, pp. 92–3.

11. '*quod mortem sibi instare putaret*'. Author's translation.

12. J.-A. Buchon, ed., *Chroniques de Jean Molinet*, vol. 2, Paris 1828, p. 402. Molinet thought the elder son was called Peter and the younger, George.

13. C.L. Kingsford, ed., *The Stonor Letters and Papers*, vol. 2, Camden third series, XXX, London 1919, p. 161.

14. Richmond, 'The Death of Edward V', pp. 278–80.

15. Described in detail in R.H. Britnell, 'The Oath Book of Colchester and the Borough Constitution, 1372–1404', *Essex Archaeology and History*, 14 (1982), pp. 94–101. The evidence which follows was originally published as J. Ashdown-Hill, 'The Death of Edward V – new evidence from Colchester', *Essex Archaeology & History*, 35 (2004), pp. 226–30.

16. J. Ashdown-Hill, 'The client network, connections and patronage of Sir John Howard (Lord Howard, first Duke of Norfolk) in north-east Essex and south Suffolk', PhD thesis, University of Essex 2008, p. 226, section 4.15.4.

17. The actual accession dates were 9 April (Edward V) and 26 June (Richard III). It may be that 20 June 1483 was the date on which news of the prior marriage of Edward IV and Eleanor, and the consequent illegitimacy of Edward's Woodville offspring, first reached Colchester.

18. The Bailiffs were elected on the Monday following 8 September (Feast of the Nativity of the Blessed Virgin Mary) and assumed office on the Monday following 29 September (Michaelmas Day). (Britnell, 'Oath Book' p. 96.) In 1482 the election took place on Monday, 9 September, and the bailiffs took office on Monday, 30 September.

19. Occasionally one or two additions have been made, in different ink, at the end of a year's record, but before the start of the following year.

20. Britnell describes Benham's published version as 'edited in translation', but recognises that it fails to 'adequately represent the detail of the manuscripts'. Britnell, 'Oath Book', pp. 94; 99, n. 2.

21. W.G. Benham, ed., *The Oath Book, or Red Parchment Book of Colchester*, Colchester 1907, p. 134.

22. At this point there has been a subsequent and very heavy erasure of probably two words. From the surviving traces, the erased words may originally have read '*Regis spurii*' [illegitimate King] (see reconstructed image). Such a phrase used with reference to Edward V probably would have been erased after the accession of Henry VII.

23. Colchester *Oath Book* f. 107r (modern foliation – old page no. 156). Britnell notes ('Oath Book', p. 94) that the present binding of the Oath Book is late seventeenth century. Fols 85–144 contain fifteenth and sixteenth century material, but have no contemporary page or folio enumeration. The 'old' page numbering noted here presumably dates from the seventeenth century, when this material was gathered together and bound. The folio enumeration is in pencil, and is modern.

24. It is difficult to find a different English translation for *nuper*. 'Former' would sound odd in this context. However, the Latin word does not necessarily imply that Edward V was dead.

25. John Bisshop and Thomas Cristemesse were prominent Colcestrians of the time. John Bisshop had served as bailiff on several previous occasions. Thomas Cristemesse had not held this office before, but he was to hold it again later, and interestingly he was also subsequently elected to represent Colchester in the first Parliament of Henry VII.

26. By 'deposing' I mean removing a king from his throne, but without denying that he had been king up until that point. By 'excluding', on the other hand, I mean declaring that someone had never legally been king at all.

27. The destruction of all copies of the Act of 1484 was specifically commanded by Henry VII. The repeal and destruction of this Act was important to Henry because he planned to marry the eldest daughter of Edward IV and Elizabeth Woodville, and to represent her to the nation as the Yorkist heiress. It was therefore imperative for him to re-establish the legitimacy of Edward IV's children by Elizabeth Woodville. By so doing, however, he in effect reinstated Edward V as the rightful king. Henry VII's action in repealing the act of 1484 thus implies that Edward was already dead. Indeed had either 'prince' been living when the Act was repealed, Elizabeth of York's heiress status would have been questionable.

28. W.G. Benham, ed., *The Red Paper Book of Colchester*, Colchester 1902, p. 60 & *passim*.

29. The erasure could possibly date from slightly later, but it seems certain to have been made before Henry VII visited the town in 1487.

30. His second year of office ended on Monday, 3 October 1485 (being the Monday following Michaelmas Day).

31. It could perhaps be argued that the town clerk meant to imply that Edward V (reference to whose name could not entirely be avoided, since documents existed dated to the first year of his reign) was *legally* – but not necessarily physically – dead. However, this is not the obvious interpretation of the words used.

32. Hicks' assertion that 'by autumn [1483] they [Edward V and Richard of Shrewsbury] were generally assumed to be dead' (M. Hicks, *Richard III*, Stroud, 2000, p. 242) must be rejected in the light of the subsequent response to Perkin Warbeck.

33. C.S.L. Davies, 'A Requiem for King Edward', *Ricardian*, vol. 9, no. 114, September 1991, pp 102–05 (p. 102).

34. Ashdown-Hill, *Eleanor*, pp. 207 & 241.

35. Ashdown-Hill, 'Beloved Cousyn', p. 84, citing Crawford, Howard Household Books, part 2, p. 385.

36. Ashdown-Hill, 'Beloved Cousyn', p. 85, citing Crawford, Howard Household Books, part 2, p. 389.

37. Davies, 'A Requiem for King Edward', p. 103.

38. See, for example, D. Baldwin, *The Lost Prince , the Survival of Richard of York*, Stroud 2007.

39. Postscript from Richard III's letter to his Chancellor, 12 October 1483, quoted in P.M. Kendall, *Richard the Third*, London, 1956, p. 269.

3. Edward, Earl of Warwick – Authorised Version

1. 'ung rainceau extraict d'estoc de royale géniture, s'estoit nourri entre les fertils et seigneurieux arbrisseaux d'Irlande … ce très noble rainceau est Edouard, fils du duc de Clarence, lequel, par le conseil et meure délibération des nobles d'Irlande, et en

faveur de plusiers barons d'Angleterre, ses bienveuillans, fut délibéré de soi couron-
ner roy, et d'expulser de son royal trosne le comte de Richemont, qui lors occupoit
la couronne d'Angleterre.' J.-A. Buchon, ed., Chroniques de Jean Molinet, vol. 3,
Paris 1828, p. 152, author's translation.

2. D.F. Sutton, ed., Polydore Vergil, *Anglica Historia* (1555 version), online 2005, 2010 –
my emphasis.
3. PROME, 1487 Parliament, Lincoln attainder [November 1487].
4. Bodleian Library, MS. Top. Glouc. d.2, Founders' and benefectors' book of
Tewkesbury Abbey, fol. 39r.
5. See 'Edward, styled Earl of Warwick', *ODNB*.
6. Nicolas, *Privy Purse Expenses*, p. 157.
7. Nicolas, *Privy Purse Expenses*, pp. 158–9.
8. W. Grainge, *The Castles and Abbeys of Yorkshire*, York and London 1855, p. 238.
9. Grainge, *Castles and Abbeys*, pp. 238–9.
10. Grainge, *Castles and Abbeys*, p. 240, citing Leland.
11. Grainge, *Castles and Abbeys*, pp. 241–2.
12. 'John de la Pole, Earl of Lincoln', *ODNB*.
13. Ibid.
14. J. Ashdown-Hill, *The Last Days of Richard III*, Stroud 2010, 2013, Chapter 2.
15. See, for example, A.R. Myers, ed., G. Buck, *The History of the Life and Reigne of
Richard the Third* (1646), Wakefield 1973, p. 44.
16. See Ashdown-Hill, *Last Days of Richard III*, Chapter 7.
17. R. Horrox, ed., *British Library Harleian Manuscript 433*, vol. 4, London 1983, p. 66.
18. 'John de la Pole, Earl of Lincoln', *ODNB*.
19. Confirmed by the York city register, 13 May 1485, 'when it was determyned that
a letter should be consaved to be direct to the lordes of Warwik and Lincoln and
othre of the counsail at Sheriff Hoton ffrome the maire and his bretherne': L.C.
Attreed, ed., *York House Books 1461–1490*, vol. 1, Stroud 1991, p. 361.
20. M.K. Jones and M.G. Underwood, *The King's Mother, Lady Margaret Beaufort,
Countess of Richmond and Derby*, Cambridge 1992, 1995, p. 67, citing Campbell.
21. Edward Stafford, third Duke of Buckingham, born 1478, and restored to the title of
his executed father following the battle of Bosworth.
22. ? Probably he means Ralph, Lord Neville, the son and heir of Ralph Neville, third
Earl of Westmorland (c.1456–6 February 1498/99). Ralph (the son), born in about
1474, had been given into Henry VII's custody after Bosworth. However he did not
hold the title of Earl of Westmorland in 1486, as his father was still living.
23. SB no. 166, published in W. Campbell, ed., *Materials for a History of the Reign of Henry
VII*, vol. 1, London 1873, p. 311.
24. Sutton, *Anglica Historia*. See Chapter 4.

4. Edward, Earl of Warwick – Alternative Version

1. *Annals of Ulster*, vol. 3, (1379–1541) Dublin 1895, p. 315. Also cited in part in Hayden,
'Lambert Simnel', p. 631.
2. The Dublin King was crowned on the Feast of the Ascension (24 May), not the
Feast of Pentecost (3 June).

3. For the full text of the Act of Attainder, see Ashdown-Hill, *Third Plantagenet*, pp. 150–6.
4. He was abbot until 1481, but it is not known precisely in which year he succeeded John de Abingdon (abbot 1442 ?).
5. 'Abbot Strensham was godfather to Clarence's son, Edward', M. Hicks, Chapter 2, p. 29 in R.K. Morris and R Shoesmith (eds), *Tewkesbury Abbey: History, art and architecture*, Hereford 2003, 2012.
6. He was reappointed for a further twenty years in 1472. C. Ross, *Edward IV*, London 1974, 1991, p. 187, note 3. For fuller details of the life history of the Duke of Clarence see Ashdown-Hill, *Third Plantagenet*.
7. Joseph Strutt, 1773, quoted in A. Sutton & L.Visser-Fuchs, 'Richard III and the Knave of Cards: An illuminator's model in manuscript and print, 1440s to 1990s, *The Antiquaries Journal*, vol. 79 (1999), p. 257.
8. For full details of the evidence on this point see Ashdown-Hill, *Third Plantagenet*.
9. Traditionally in English histories his surname has tended to be spelt Waurin. However, the name is a toponym, and the modern spelling of the town name in northern France from which it is derived is Wavrin. Therefore, that is the spelling which will be used here.
10. '*le roy Edouard avoit deux jennes frères, lun eagie de neuf ans et lautre de huit ans*', W. Hardy and E.L.C.P Hardy, eds., J. de Wavrin, Recueil des Chroniques et Anchienne Istories de la Grant Bretaigne, à Present Nommé Engleterre, col. 5, 1891, reprinted Cambridge 2012, p. 357. Another observer thought George was 12 and Richard 11 (Calendar of State Papers – Milan, p. 73). This also suggests that the two boys were of very similar height despite their age difference.
11. Ashdown Hill, *Third Plantagenet*, citing http://www.fpnotebook.com/endo/exam/hghtmsrmntinchldrn.htm, accessed February 2013.
12. Based upon the modern average height of 5' 0" (152.40 cms) for boys of twelve.

5. Lambert Simnel

1. Cavell, *Heralds' Memoir*, pp. 116–17.
2. Parliament Rolls of Medieval England, 1487 Parliament, Lincoln attainder [November 1487].
3. In citing the father's profession as a baker, could André or his informants have been thinking of 'Simnel cake'?
4. Productus fuit quidam dominus Willielmus Symonds, presbyter, xxviii annorum aetatis, ut asseruit, qui ibidem in praesentia dictorum dominorum ac praelatorum et cleri, necnon majoris, aldermannorum, et vicecomitum civitatis London. Publice fatebatur et confessus est, quod ipse filium cujusdam _[blank] Orgininakes universitatis Oxon ad partes Hiberniae abduxit et transvexit Qui quidem filius pro comitate Warwici ibidem reputabatur, et quod ipse postea erat cum domino Lovell in Fuvnefotts, et istis et aliis ibidem per eum confessatis, praefatus reverendissimus in Christo pater rogavit praefatum majorem et vicecomites, ut praefatum dominum Will Symonds ad turrim London adducerent, ibidem custodiendum pro eo, quod idem reverendissimus pater habuit alium de comitava dicti domini Willielmi, et non habuit nisi unun personam in manerio suo de Lambeth. D. Wilkins, Concilia Magnae Britanniae et Hiberniae, vol. 3, London 1737, p. 618.

5. See Chapter 3.
6. Sutton, *Anglica Historia*.
7. Sutton, *Anglica Historia*. See Chapter 4.
8. 'Lambert Simnel', *ODNB*. http://www.oxforddnb.com/view/article/25569?docPos=1, accessed December 2013.
9. See for example J. Ashdown-Hill, 'Thomas Marshall or John Beche? Who was the last Abbot of Colchester?', *Essex Archaeology & History*, 4th series, vol. 4 (2013), pp. 228–32
10. http://www.surnamedb.com/Surname/Simnel, accessed August 2013; my emphases.
11. A.B. Emden, A Biographical Register of the University of Oxford to A.D. 1500, vol. 3, Oxford 1959; my emphasis.
12. The manuscript note is cited in Hayden, 'Lambert Simnel', p. 624.
13. 'The 12th century mother church of west Oxford, under the patronage of St Thomas Becket, Archbishop of Canterbury, martyred in 1170' http://www.achurch-nearyou.com/oxford-st-thomas-the-martyr/, accessed August 2013. See also http://en.wikipedia.org/wiki/St_Thomas_the_Martyr's_Church,_Oxford, accessed August 2013.
14. South of the modern Botley Road, http://en.wikipedia.org/wiki/Osney_Abbey, August 2013.
15. 'Lambert Simnel', *ODNB* – but no source is cited for this information.
16. 'Medieval Oxford', VCH, *History of Oxford*, pp. 3–73. http://www.british-history.ac.uk/report.aspx?compid=22803, accessed 28 August 2013.
17. 'Medieval Oxford', VCH, *History of Oxford*, pp. 3–73. http://www.british-history.ac.uk/report.aspx?compid=22803, accessed 28 August 2013.

Part 2 – Supporters And Enemies

6. Lincoln, Lovell and Yorkists in England

1. There were two fifteenth-century Elizabeths of York. This is the senior of the two. The junior Elizabeth was her niece, the eldest daughter of Edward IV and wife of Henry VII.
2. 'John de la Pole, Earl of Lincoln', *ODNB*.
3. 9 April 1484.
4. Horrox, *British Library Harleian Manuscript 433*, p. 66.
5. See, for example, Myers, *History of the Life and Reigne*, p. 44.
6. See, for example, Ashdown-Hill, *Last Days of Richard III*, Chapter 2.
7. Parliament Rolls of Medieval England, 1484 Parliament, Act of *Titulus Regius*, citing the petition of the Three Estates of the Realm of 1483; my emphasis.
8. J. Brown and E. Brown, 'The de la Poles, Earls and Dukes of Suffolk', Wingfield 2000, p. 6.
9. 'John de la Pole, second Duke of Suffolk', *ODNB*. http://www.oxforddnb.com/view/article/22450, accessed December 2013).
10. She must have conceived Prince Arthur in about December 1485.
11. Brown, 'The de la Poles, Earls and Dukes of Suffolk', p. 7.

12. He was certainly dead by 20 May 1492, 'John de la Pole, second Duke of Suffolk', *ODNB*.
13. *CPR*, 1467–1477, pp. 261, 312.
14. Eleanor's first husband, Sir Thomas Butler, was Lord Sudeley's son.
15. Horrox *British Library Harleian Manuscript 433*, pp. 3–4.
16. A.H. Thomas & I.D. Thornley, eds, *Great Chronicle of London*, London 1938, p. 236. There are several slightly different published versions of this rhyme.
17. Ashdown-Hill, *Eleanor*, p. 37.
18. M. Bennett, *The Battle of Bosworth*, Stroud 1993, p. 155.
19. Hayden, 'Lambert Simnel', p. 628.
20. Hayden, 'Lambert Simnel', p. 628.
21. www.girders.net/Bo/Bodrugan,%20Sir%20Henry,%20(d.1489).doc, accessed December 2013, citing *CPR 1461–67* pp. 539–40.
22. Hayden, 'Lambert Simnel', p. 631.
23. C. Weightman, *Margaret of York, Duchess of Burgundy, 1446–1503*, Gloucester 1989, pp. 168–9; http://en.wikipedia.org/wiki/High_Sheriff_of_Berkshire, accessed December 2013.
24. See Weightman, *Margaret of York*, pp. 156–7.
25. Thomas Howard was certainly imprisoned initially in the Tower of London. But though he remained in confinement for several years it is not certain that he spent all this time at the Tower. M.J. Tucker, *The Life of Thomas Howard Earl of Surrey and Second Duke of Norfolk 1443-1524*, London 1964, p. 49.
26. M.J. Tucker, *The Life of Thomas Howard Earl of Surrey and Second Duke of Norfolk 1443–1524*, London 1964, p. 49 and note 58. However, Tucker is dubious about this report.
27. Tucker, *Thomas Howard*, p. 49.

7. The 'Diabolicall Duches'

1. Hayden, 'Lambert Simnel', p. 623.
2. Weightman, *Margaret of York*, p. 150.
3. There was only one younger daughter, Ursula, who was born in 1455 – but died very young.
4. T. Hearne, *Liber Niger Scaccarii nec non Wilhelmi Worcestrii Annales Rerum Anglicarum*, vol. 2, London 1774, pp. 525–6. Later versions of Worcester's list, possibly confusing Margaret with her brother, William, incorrectly state that Margaret was born at Fotheringhay.
5. R. Vaughan, Charles the Bold, the Last Valois Duke of Burgundy, Woodbridge 2002, p. 159.

8. The Earl of Kildare and the Irish Contingent

1. Hayden, 'Lambert Simnel', pp. 626, 637.
2. 'Gerald Fitzgerald, eighth Earl of Kildare', *ODNB*.
3. For a detailed analysis of the execution of the Earl of Desmond, see J. Ashdown-Hill and A. Carson, 'The Execution of the Earl of Desmond', *Ricardian*, 15 (2005), pp. 70–93.
4. 'Gerald Fitzgerald, eighth Earl of Kildare', *ODNB*.

9. Henry VII and John Morton

1. See, for example, Ashdown-Hill, *Royal Marriage Secrets*, pp. 70–3.
2. Edward IV's maternal grandmother, Joan Beaufort, Countess of Westmorland, was the sister of Margaret Beaufort's grandfather.
3. 'Morton, John', *ODNB*.

Part 3 – 1486–1487

10. Evidence from England

1. 'Vta octobris, reverendus in Christo pater episcopus Heliensis, referendarius sanctissimi nostri papae Innocentii Octavi, per Dunensem monasterium iter ad Angliam faciens, dum Calisiam ingressus esset, mortem audivit comitis de richemont, nuper instituti regis cum nonnullis baronibus subito pestifera confectione sublatis, aliis contrarium asserentibus. De successore vero novi regis non parva contentio suborta est acclamantibus nonnullis esse verum regem filium ducis Clarentiae, juvenem egregium internecioni quae a Richardo rege avunculo suo exercebatur subtractum : sed quicquam actum sit scriptor hujusmodi necdum de morte novi regis audivit.' Baron Kervyn de Lettenhove, ed., Chroniques relatives à l'histoire de la Belgique sous la domination des Ducs de Bourgogne, vol. 1, Bruxelles 1870, Adrien de But, Chroniques, p. 649.
2. 'inire simultates cum nonnullis ad novum regem instituendum, filium ducis Clarentiae, fratris quondam regum Edwardii atque Richardi, qui quidem filius ex parte matris dux Verwecii in Yrlandia observabatur.' de But, Chroniques, p. 665.
3. 'Sone van Clarentie uit Ingelant', Weightman, Margaret of York, p. 158; A. Wroe, Perkin A Story of Deception, London 2003, p. 81.
4. This sentence, as written, appears to be incomplete.
5. The original version of the text reads: 'Sir, as for tidings, here is but few. The king & queen lyeth at Grenwyche; the Lord Perce is at Wynchester; the earle of Oxford is in Essex; the earle of Darby and his son be with the king. Also here is but little speche [of the *deleted*] of þe earle of Warwyke now, but after Christenmas they say ther wylbe more speech of. Also ther be mayny enimies on the see, & dyvers schippes take, & ther be many take of the kynges house for theves.' J. Kirby, ed, *The Plumton Letters and Papers*, Camden fifth series, vol. 8, Cambridge 1996, p. 67, no. 46.
6. J. Ashdown-Hill, *Mediaeval Colchester's Lost Landmarks*, Derby 2009, p. 28.
7. 'The important Benedictine Abbey of St John's was a mitred abbey with impressive rights of chartered sanctuary, identical to those enjoyed by Westminster Abbey', Ashdown-Hill, *'Beloved Cousyn'*, pp. 42, 151.
8. R.F. Hunnisett, *The Medieval Coroner*, Cambridge 1961; reprinted Florida 1986, p. 37.
9. J.C. Cox, The Sanctuaries and Sanctuary Seekers of Mediaeval England, London 1911, p. 197.
10. *CPR 1452–1461*, p. 80.
11. Richard III's mother, Cecily Neville, dowager Duchess of York, later remembered the Colchester abbey with gratitude and affection, providing for a bequest in her will. Ashdown-Hill, *Mediaeval Colchester's Lost Landmarks*, p. 45.

12. 'Francis Lovell', *ODNB*.
13. Margaret Neville, daughter of Richard Neville, fifth Earl of Salisbury, and the sister of Richard Neville, sixteenth Earl of Warwick, 'the Kingmaker'. She was thus the great aunt of Edward of Clarence, Earl of Warwick. She died between 20 November 1506 and 14 January 1507.
14. 'To my right trusti and welbeloued John Paston, shrieve of Norffolk and Suffolk. Right trusti and welbiloued, I recommaund me vnto you. And for as moche as I ame credebby enfourmed that Fraunceis, late Lorde Lovell, is now of late resorted into the Yle of Ely to the entente, by alle lykelyhod, to find the waies and meanes to gete him shipping and passage in your costes [*coasts*], or ellis to resorte ageyn to seintuary if he can or maie, I therfor hertily desire and praie you, and neuerthelesse in the Kinges name streitly chargie you, that ye in all goodly haste endevoire yourself that suche wetche [*watch*] or other meanes be vsed and hadde in the poortes, crekes, and othre places wher ye thinke nescessary by your discrecion to the letting of his seid purpose; and that ye also vse all the waies ye can or maie by your wisedom to the taking of the same late Lord Lovell. And what pleasur ye maie doo to the Kinges grace in this matier I am sure is not to you vnknowen. And God kepe you. Wreten at Lauenham the xix day of Maij. Margaret Oxynford'. N. Davis, ed., *Paston Letters and Papers of the Fifteenth Century*, part 2, Oxford 1976, pp. 447–8, no. 805.
15. 'Mensibus novembri et decembri superabundabant vix, ventrus, pluvial, gelu, … rumorque factus est de rege Angliae deponendo et filio ducis Clarentiae introducendo tanquam vero herede.' de But, Chroniques, p. 666.
16. John de Vere, thirteenth Earl of Oxford, born 8 September 1442, died 10 March 1512/13.
17. 'To my right trusty and welbelouyd councellour John Paston, esquire. John Paston, I comaund me to you. And as for such tithyngys as ye haue sent hider, the Kyng had knowlech therof more than a sevynnyght passed; and as for such names as ye haue sent, supposyng theym to be gone with the Lord Lovell, they be yitt in England, for he is departyng with xiiij personys and no moo. At the Kyngys coming to London I wold advise you to see his Highnes. And Almyghty God kepe you. Writen at Wyndesore the xxiiijth day of January. Oxynford'. Davis, *Paston Letters*, pp. 448–9, no. 807.
18. Hayden, 'Lambert Simnel', p. 627.
19. 'that therle of Lincoln wold giff the Kings grace a breakfast as it was enfourmed hyme by the servaunt of the said Erls'. Raine, *York Civic Records*, p. 3.
20. 'I James Tayte rade to Retford, and upon our Lady day last past as I come homeward in Doncastre, I hit with vij horsez of straungers, and there was amongs them a white horse led, shewing me by a merchaunt servaunt that it was that in saddell of that horse gold and silver; than I herd that said soo, and askid hyme fro whynce he come, and he said, froo London; than another of the same merchaunt menaskid me, wheder ther was any deth within the Citie or not, and I said, nay; than I shewed unto hyme that I shuld knowe oone of the company by his horse; he asking me where and howe I shuld knowe this horse, and I said agane that I knewe hyme in York the last tyme the Kynges good grace was ther, for I trowe that he was my Lorde of Lincolne hobye, for with me was he loged; than this man shewyng to hyme my saying, he com bak unto me and asakid me howe I fore, and askid me where I knewethis horse, and I said he was my Lord of Lincolnes, and he bad me say the truthe; and I wist well than that by the same watch word he was my Lord of

Lincone horssen, and tha, I asked hyme, howe my Lord of Lincoln fore, and askid hyme where he was, and he told me as far furth as he culd understand that he was departed from the Kinges grace; and I askid hyme, wheder to the see for he hath frendes enogh upon the land, and I shewed unto hymeagane that my Lord had many good frendes in this cuntree as far furth as I knewe, and I said that bicause have more understanding of his communicacion. Then he shewing unto me, thowe shall see not long too, that John of Lincoln shall geve theme all abrekefast that oweth hyme no luff nor favour; I asking hyme that my Lord of Northumberland and he stood in condicion, he said agane he doth bot litill for as therfor we sett litill by hyme, for thou shall here tell that right good gentlemen shall take myLordes part. Can ye oght tell me howe farre I have to Sir Thomas Mallevery place for we must have hyme writing or ells send it hyme? Then I askid hyme if he wold to York, and he said, nay, I must to Hull, and if I come to York I will call upon you. I come than to Wentbrig to an in, and spird for thiez merchaunts that wold ride forward to York, and the good man of the house told me that they were sleping in their beddes and thidre I come twise to spir after theme, and I desired to hostler for to tellme where he was that rode of the hoby, and had not he bene I had there tarid long; than I departid from hyme, and than I metbetwix Daryngton and Wentbrig a man that was bowne to theservaunt of my Lord of Lincolne that lay at Wentbrig in his bedand I toke knowlage of that same man for he was somtyme of his company, for he said he had sent for hyme in grete hast with a man that was with hyme hired for to goo for hyme, and I come streght to York; then thies same merchauntes of London come unto York, and a servaunt of theires shewed me that they shuld mete the Priour of Tynmouthe at the signe of the boore in York; and I come to Master Karlill shewing unto hyme all manre of things that I had hard as afforsaid, because of my discharge and for saving of the othe that I maid to God and the King, and in no one othre wise bycause he was oone of the Kinges Chapleins: this servaunt of my Lord of Lincoln that shewed me this by the way as I come froo Doncaster hight Saunder. And I shewed unto Master Karlill the last tyme the King was here that two felows that dwelt about Middleham said that here is good gate for us to Robyn of Redesdall over the walles; and this I said, and noo word more, litill nor mekill; and the same two felows resorted to my Lord of Lincolne houshold and come thiddre to mete and drink'. Raine, *York Civic Records*, pp. 4–5 (original records fols 73–74).

21. See arguments of Davis, *Paston Letters*, p. 451, for the identity of the recipient and the year of the letter.

22. Davis, Paston Letters, pp. 451, no. 810.

23. 'Ryght wurshipfull and myn aspecyall good maister, I comaund me vonto your good masitership. Ser, it is so that ther hath ben a gret rumour and mervelous noyse of yower departing fro Yermoth, for summe seid in a Spaynessh ship and some seid in yower ship, and some seid ayein your wyll ye were departed; of wych departing my lord Steward hadde knowleche and comaunded a-noon after your old seruaunt Rychard Fitz-Water to ryde to Norwich and so to Yermoth to knowe the trowth. And at Norwich I spoke with your seid seruaunt, and ther he shewed vonto me that my lord hadde send another of his seruauntes vonto my lord of Oxynford to shewe vonto his lordship of your departyng, &c. And furthermore he shewed vonto me prevyly that my lord hath imagyned and purposed many grievous thynges ayein your maistership; for wych cawse he shewed vonto me that in ony wyse your mais-tership shuld not come that wey. And I shall shewe your maistership moch more at

your comyng, with the grace of God, whoo euer preserue your good maistership. At
Norwich the Sonday next after Sent Marke. Your seruaunt T. Balkey'.

24. Davis, *Paston Letters*, pp. 452–3, no. 811. As printed the letter is said to have been
    addressed to 'John Paston II', but this must be a misprint. John Paston II cannot pos-
    sibly have been the recipient, since he died in 1479.

25. 'As for you, ye be sore takyn in sum place, seying þat ye jntende swyche thyngys as
    ys lyke to follow gret myscheffe. I seyd I vndyrstood non swyche nor thyngys lyke
    yt. And yt ys thought ye jntende nat to go forthe thys jorneye, nor no jentylman jn
    þat quarter but Robert Brandon that hath promyseyd to go with them, as they seye.'

26. 'what jentylmen jntende to goo … and be assuryd to go to-geþer'.

27. The Earl of Oxford?

28. 'Furþermore, cosyn, yt ys seyd þat after my lordys departing to the Kynge ye ware
    mette at Barkwey, whyche ys construed that ye had ben with the Lady Lovell; but
    wrather seyd neuer well. And jn asmoche as we vnderstonde my lordys pleser, yt ys
    well doon we dele wysly þer-after. And nexte to the Kynge I answered pleynly I was
    bownde to do him seruice and to fullfylle hys comawndment to the vttermest off
    my powere, by the grace off God, who euer preserue you to hys pleser. Wretyn at
    Oxburgh the xvj day off Maye. Your cosyn E. Bedyngfeld'.

29. Davis, *Paston Letters*, pp. 455–6, no. 813.

30. Davis, *Paston Letters*, p. 455.

31. Cavell (*Heralds' Memoir*, p. 108, note 254), incorrectly states that this date fell on a
    Thursday.

32. 'At that counseill was therle of Lincolln, whiche incontinently after the said coun-
    seil departed the land and went into Flaunders to the lorde Lovell and accompanied
    hym silf with the kings rebelles and enemyes, noysing in that country that therle of
    Warwike shulde bcc in Irelande, whiche him selffe knew and dayly spake with him
    at Shene afore his departing.' Cavell, *Heralds' Memoir*, p. 109.

33. 'Thomas Grey, first Marquess of Dorset', *ODNB*.

11. Burgundian Preparations

1. Sutton, *Anglica Historia*. See Chapter 4.

2. 'the boy … crossed over to Ireland. … In those days such was the ignorance of
   even prominent men, such was their blindness (not to mention pride and malice),
   that the Earl of Lincoln … had no hesitation in believing. And, inasmuch as he was
   thought to be a scion of Edward's stock, the Lady Margaret, formerly the consort
   of Charles, the most recent Duke of Burgundy, wrote him a letter of summons.
   By stealth he quickly made his way to her, with only a few men party to such a
   great act of treason. To explain the thing briefly with a few words, the Irish and
   the northern Englishmen were provoked to this uprising by the aid and advice of
   the aforementioned woman. Therefore, having assembled an expedition of both
   Germans and Irishmen, always aided by the said Lady, they soon crossed over to
   England, and landed on its northern shore'. Sutton, *De Vita atque Gestis Henrici
   Septimi Historia*, pp. 33–4.

3. In a very complicated episode of history, 'False Dimitry II' claimed (falsely) to be
   the youngest son of Tsar Ivan the Terrible. He was then accepted as her husband
   by the surviving wife of an earlier claimant, known as 'False Dimitry I'. By her,

'False Dimitry II' then had a son, Ivan, who was briefly recognised as the heir to the Russian throne.

4. http://en.wikipedia.org/wiki/Martin_Schwartz_(mercenary), accessed December 2013.

5. J. Goy, *Le Sacre des Rois de France*, [Reims(?) no date of publication].

6. http://courseweb.stthomas.edu/jmjoncas/LiturgicalStudiesInternetLinks/ ChristianWorship/Texts/Centuries/Texts_1900_2000CE/ RCWorshipTexts1900_2000CE/Rite_of_Ordination_of_a_Bishop.htm, accessed September 2013.

7. Lord Twining, *European Regalia*, London 1967, p. 187.

8. Twining, *European Regalia*, p. 127 and note 1.

9. Hayden, 'Lambert Simnel', p. 628

10. 'Coronum quae usus est, a statua B. Mariae Virginis, in Ecclesia illius memoriae dicata, prope portam urbis, quam Dames-gate vulgo appellamus, asservata; mutuatam serunt.' J. Ware, *Rerum Hibernicarum Annales regnatibus Henrico VII, Henrico VIII, Edwardo VI & Maria*, ab anno scil MCCCCLXXXV ad annum MDLVIII, p. 9.

12. The Reign of the Dublin King

1. Cavell, *Heralds' Memoir*, pp. 109–10.

2. Cavell, *Heralds' Memoir*, p. 110.

3. Cavell, *Heralds' Memoir*, pp. 110–11.

4. Raine, *York Civic Records*, pp. 10–11 (original records, Book 6, fol. 84).

5. Raine, *York Civic Records*, pp. 13–14 (original records, Book 6, fol. 88).

6. Raine, *York Civic Records*, p. 16 (original records, Book 6, fol. 91b).

7. J.O Halliwell, ed., *Letters of the Kings of England*, 2 vols, London 1848, vol. 1, p. 171.

8. Hayden, 'Lambert Simnel', p. 628.

9. Hayden, 'Lambert Simnel', p. 630.

10. Cited in Hayden, 'Lambert Simnel', p. 627.

11. Hayden, 'Lambert Simnel', p. 627; Bennett, *Lambert Simnel*, p. 6.

12. Darcy, who had briefly studied at Lincoln's Inn in 1485, was later vice-treasurer of Ireland and held a knighthood. He was aged about 27 at the time of the Dublin coronation. See http://en.wikipedia.org/wiki/William_Darcy_(died_1540), accessed December 2013.

13. Hayden, 'Lambert Simnel', p. 629.

14. Hayden, 'Lambert Simnel', p. 627.

15. I published a paper on the coins attributed to the Yorkist pretenders five years ago (J. Ashdown-Hill, 'Coins attributed to the Yorkist Pretenders, 1487–1498', *Ricardian*, 19 2009, pp. 63–83). The evidence I then produced fairly firmly undermined the suggestion that coins and tokens were later issued in the name of the second Yorkist pretender, Perkin Warbeck / Richard of England. That evidence and conclusion still hold good. However, my earlier conclusion in respect of the alleged coinage of the Dublin King was simply that further research was required. In particular, I argued that it was necessary to seek to clarify the royal name and numeral employed by and for him. Since the present study has now come to the firm conclusion that the boy crowned in Dublin did indeed use the royal identity of 'King Edward VI', and since

very clear evidence in support of that conclusion has been presented here, my earlier views regarding the alleged coinage of 'Edward VI' do now need to be updated
somewhat.

16. A. de Longpérier, 'Perkin Werbecque', *Revue Numismatique* (1860), pp. 384–95; H.
Symonds, 'The Irish Silver Coinage of Edward IV', *Numismatic Chronicle*, series
5, no. 1 (1921), pp. 108–25; C.N. Schmall, 'Note on the "Perkin Warbeck Groat"
dated 1494', *Numismatist*, 41 (1928), pp. 219–20; R. Carlyon-Britton, 'On the Irish
Coinage of Lambert Simnel as Edward VI', *Numismatic Chronicle*, 6th series, 1 (1941),
pp. 133–5; C.E. Blunt, 'The Medallic Jetton of Perkin Warbeck', *British Numismatic
Journal*, vol. 26 (1949–51), pp. 215–16; M. Dolley, '*Tre Kronor – Trí Choróin*, a note on
the date of the "three crown" coinage of Ireland', *Numismatiska Meddelanden*, 30
(1965), pp. 103–12; P. Power, 'The History and Coins of Lambert Simnal [*sic*] and
Perkin Warbeck', *Seaby's Coin and Medal Bulletin*, no. 615 (November 1969), pp.
376–8; M. Dolley, 'Simnel and Warbeck – some recent misconceptions', *Seaby's Coin
and Medal Bulletin*, no. 616 (December 1969), pp. 424–5; G. Brady and C. Gallagher,
'The Lambert Simnel Coinage: An enquiry', *Spink Numismatic Circular*, 103, no. 8
(October 1995), pp. 301–2.
17. Edward I had briefly issued a groat, but later abandoned it.
18. Further major changes to the English coinage were introduced by Henry VII from
1489 onwards.
19. For purposes of comparison with the fluctuating weight of the Irish coinage under
Edward IV, the reformed 'light' English coinage of the same monarch had a groat
weighing 48 grains (reduced from the groat of 60 grains of the earlier 'heavy' coinage).
20. As the author and others have argued previously, there is no evidence that the so-
called 'red rose of Lancaster' was really used by any of the Lancastrian monarchs.
Roses had been used as punctuation marks in the Marian inscription (MARIA ✿
MATER ✿ GRACIE ✿) of an Anglo-Gallic jetton of Henry VI, but never as part
of the main design of a coin: see M. Mitchiner, *Jetons, Medalets and Tokens*, vol. 1, *The
Medieval Period and Nuremberg*, London 1988, p. 190. Much earlier, a rose had figured
at the neck of the tunic of Edward I on some of his English and Irish silver pennies:
S. Mitchell and B. Reeds, eds., *Standard Catalogue of British Coins*, vol. 1, *Coins of
England and the United Kingdom*, 26th edition, London 1990, p. 97, and P. Seaby and
P.F. Purvey, eds., *Standard Catalogue of British Coins*, vol. 2, *Coins of Scotland, Ireland and
the Islands*, 1st edition, London 1984, p. 111.
21. Dating was only introduced to English coins in the reign of Edward VI (son of
Henry VIII), in the sixteenth century.
22. The initial plans were actually made by the Lancastrian government of Henry VI.
23. The following summary of legislation from 1461 to 1470 (inclusive) is derived from
Symonds, 'Irish Silver Coinage of Edward IV', p. 114.
24. In the event most of the coins seem to have been struck in Dublin. Examples are
known from Waterford, but none of the other named mints is represented among
the surviving specimens.
25. This was Edward IV's second 'crown' coinage (1463–65).
26. At this date the weight of the English groat was still 60 grains.
27. Reflecting the fact that the English groat had by now been reduced to a weight of
48 grains. On this occasion, and at the time of all subsequent weight changes, earlier
Irish coins were withdrawn from circulation to enforce the new standard.

28. Seaby, *Catalogue*, p. 116. However, some would assign the cross on rose coinage to the 1470s.

29. Coins may have been issued by all the named mints, but because with each reissue of the coinage, old coins were recalled and melted down, few Irish coins of this period survive, so it is difficult to be sure. There are extant examples of the fourth coinage minted at Dublin, at Drogheda and at Trim.

30. Abbreviated to REX.ANGL.DNS.HYB.

31. Dolley, 'Tre Kronor – Trí Choróin', p. 105, citing J. Simon, *An Essay towards an Historical Account of Irish Coins*, Dublin 1749 and 1810, p. 29. The original text of the statute was no longer extant in 1965.

32. Seaby, *Catalogue*, p. 122.

33. We may also note that Dolley suggests that the rare Irish copper farthing (¼ *d*) of Edward IV, displaying a shield of arms bearing three crowns on the obverse and a *rose-en-soleil* on the reverse probably dates from about the same period. Dolley, 'Tre Kronor – Trí Choróin', p. 104. Seaby (*Catalogue*, p. 123) would date this coin somewhat earlier (1467–70).

34. Society of Antiquaries MSS 116. The text is published in Symonds, 'The Irish Silver Coinages of Edward IV', pp. 122–3, though Dolley, 'Tre Kronor – Trí Choróin', pp. 109–10 offers some corrections and demonstrates that the marginal drawings of a penny and half groat of the 'three crowns' issue which now accompanies the manuscript text of the indenture is a nineteenth-century interpolation.

35. **'Introduction to the coinage of Edward IV – Three Crowns Issue 1483– 1485'**, http://www.irishcoinage.com/HAMMERED.HTM, **accessed October 2008:**

36. On this point see Dolley, 'Tre Kronor – Trí Choróin', pp. 109–10. Such discrepancies between legislation and implementation are not unknown, however.

37. The well-known Irish harp was a later invention, which we owe to Henry VIII: 'The Arms of Ireland', http://www.heraldica.org/topics/national/ireland.htm, accessed October 2008. 'As late as 1536 the Great Seal of Ireland preserves the three crowns as the arms of Ireland', Dolley, 'Tre Kronor – Trí Choróin', p. 103, n. 2, citing *Archaeologia*, 85 (1935), plate XCI, 3.

38. One other minor design feature which varies is the form of the trefoils at the end of the arms of the long crosses. On some specimens these are formed by pellets, on others by annulets. The former are believed to be earlier in the series than the latter.

39. The title *Rex Hybernie* rather than *Dominus Hybernie* is anachronistic at this period. It has been taken by some to indicate a sovereign crowned *in* Ireland (i.e. the first Yorkist pretender), Carlyon-Britton, 'Irish Coinage of Lambert Simnel'. But this point is now generally discounted: 'Proceedings of the Royal Numismatic Society', *Numismatic Chronicle*, 7th series, 9 (1969), pp. xii–xiii. The use of the rose emblem on coinage is discussed further below.

40. See, for example, Power, 'History and Coins', p. 377 and figure 1. However, other anonymous 'three crowns' coins have been assigned to Henry VII: Seaby, *Catalogue*, 126–7; Spinks, *Coins of Scotland, Ireland and the Islands*, London 2003, pp. 139–40.

41. Based on their values as given in Seaby, *Catalogue*, and Spinks, *Coins of Scotland, Ireland and the Islands*, pp. 139–42.

42. Dolley, 'Tre Kronor – Trí Choróin', p. 111.

43. Dolley, 'Tre Kronor – Trí Choróin', p. 112.

44. For example, one published account states categorically that the Dublin King 'had

Groat coins struck by his supporters, the FitzGeralds, sometime between May and July of that year, at the Dublin and Waterford mints, in the three crowns style'. G. Petterwood, 'The Harp and the Shamrock!', *Tasmanian Numismatist*, vol. 9, no. 6 (June 2004), http://www.vision.net.au/~pwood/june04.htm (consulted October 2008).

45. See Ashdown-Hill, 'Execution of the Earl of Desmond', figure 1.

46. E. Curtis, *Cal. Ormond Papers*, vol. III (1413–1509), Dublin 1935, pp. vii, xxv, 261–3 (document 272).

47. 'Edwardus dei gratia Rex Anglie et Francie et Hibernie omnibus ad quos presents litere peruenit salute. Sciatis quod nos concessimus dilecto nobis Petro Buttyller gentilman, alias dicto Petro Buttiller filio Jacobi Buttiler gentilman, officium vice-comitis nostri comitatus Kylkenn', habendum et tenendum officium predictum prefato Petro quamdiu nobis placuerit, saluis nobis finibus et amerciamentis dicti comitatus perueniendis. Precipiendo de nobis in officio illo feodum consuetum. In cuius rei testimonium has literas nostras fecimus patentes. Teste precarissimo consan-guineo nostro Geraldo comite Kyldar' locum nostrum tenente regni Hibernie, apud Dublin', xiii die Augusti, anno regni nostri primo. Dovedalle Per breve de priuato sigillo nostro.'

48. Note, however, that – significantly – some of the 'three crowns' coins also bear the title *Rex Hibernie*.

13. The Battle of Stoke Field

1. Cavell, *Heralds' Memoir*, p. 111.

2. Raine, *York Civic Records*, p. 20 (original records, Book 6, fols 96b–97).

3. Raine, *York Civic Records*, p. 20 (original records, Book 6, fols 96b–97).

4. Raine, *York Civic Records*, pp. 20–21 (House Book 6, fol. 97 recto).

5. Raine, *York Civic Records*, p. 21 (House Book 6, fol. 97 verso).

6. "I thanke you for your luffing disposicions perseverantly shewed unto me, but spe-cially for the faithfull guyding and true disposicions shewed for your provident and sure ordring of the King our souverain lordes Citie undre your rule, for the surtie and conservacion of the same to his moost high pleaser, praying you as effectually as I can, therin to shewe your faithfull endevours with all diligence as ye, have doone, and if the caas require that occasiuon be to the contrary herof, I therof certified, who, God helping, wolbe at Poklington to morowe at evene, shall not rest ther but be with you the same nyght, like as worshipfull thes berers, chapleyns unto the Knges highnesse, kan shewe unto you, to whom I pray you to yeve credence, and upon Sonday next coming I wol not fail to be with you at the farrest, and tofore if ye think it requisite. Writyn in my Manous of Lekyngfeld the viij day of Juyn. Your lovyng frend, H. Northumberland'. Raine, *York Civic Records*, p. 21 (House Book 6, fols 97 verso and 98 recto).

7. 'Satterday, the viiij day of Juyn the yere of the reigne of our souverain lord King Herry the Sevent, at after none of the same day, the Chamberleyns sent in message unto the Lordes of Lincolne and Lovell, and othre herebifore named, come in at Mikylgate-barre, and ther shewed unto my lord the Mayre and othre his brethren being present, howe the said lordes and ther retinewe was departed on Brugh-brig, and soo streght suthward, not entending to come negh this Citie to doo any preju-

dice or hurt unto the same. And incontinently after ther comyng the Lord Clifford sent word unto my lord Maier that he might come in with his folkes and retenewe for to assiste and support the Maier and the Communaltye of this Citie, if any of the Kinges ennymes wold approche unto the same. Wherunto the Mayre consentid and graunted that he shuld soo have his entree, and causid all the stret of Mikelgate to be garnysshed with men in harnesse the nomber of DC personez and mor, and within the space of iiij houre aftre, receyved the said Lord Clifford at Mikelgate-Barre with CCCC personnez of footmen and horsmen in to the said Citie and sent unto hyme a present of wyne and according to his honour'. Raine, *York Civic Records*, p. 22.

8. Raine, *York Civic Records*, p. 22.

9. 'Also upon the tewesday after, Therl of Northumberland, Lord Clifford and many othre nobles accompanyd with vj Ml, nombred, departid suthward toward the Kinges grace at xj of the clok, and anone after his departour the Lordes Scropes of Bolton and Upsall, constreyned as it was said by there folkes, cam on horsbak to Bowthom Barre, and ther cried King Edward, and made a salt at the yates, hot the Comons being watchmen there well and manly defendid tham and put tham to flitht. … Therle of Northumberland having knowlege hereof, being within vj milez of the Citie, sent in message unto the Maier and desired hyme that lie might come and entre the Citie agane for diverse consideracions and causes hyme moveing. … And incontinently therupon, the said Erl, the lord Clifford, and othre many nobles accompayned with iiijMl men and moo, was thankfully receyved unto the said Citie, and there continued to Thursday, Corpus Christi day, and the same day at noone hastly the said lordes toke ther journey towardes the north parties'. Raine, *York Civic Records*, pp. 22–3.

10. 'Upon Corpus Christi evene, proclamacion was made thrugh the Citie that the play of the same, for diverse consideracions moveing my lord Maier, my masters Aldremen and othre of the Comune Counsailie, shuld be differd unto the Sonday next after the fest of Saint Thomas of Canterbdry. And then aftre it was differd to the Sonday next aftre the fest of Saint Petre called *Ad vincula*, because of the Kinges comyng hidder'. Raine, *York Civic Records*, p. 23. This proves, incidentally, that the York House Books were written up some time after the events reported in them took place.

11. Sutton, De Vita atque Gestis Henrici Septimi Historia, sections 54 and 55.

12. Raine, *York Civic Records*, pp. 23–4

13. Raine, *York Civic Records*, pp. 20–24.

14. Cavell, *Heralds' Memoir*, p. 117, note 327.

15. 'Cecedit comes Lincolniensis et Martinus Zwarte cum fere vm hominum, sed rex, pie cum extraneis agens, omnes de Yrlandia captives strangulari mandavit; captus quoque fuit juvenis dux Clarentiae [sic], quem suptiliter comes de Suffolc liberans transfretavit cum eo et apud Guizam se recepit.' De But, Chroniques, pp. 674–5.

16. 'Cum nonnulli ex praelatis Hiberniae, archiepiscopus scilicet Dublinensis, archiepiuscopus Armachanensis et episcope Medensis et Darensis, tam in nostri dominii quam censurarum ecclesiasticarum contemptum, rebellibus hostibusque nostris opem et juvamen impenderint, ac spurium quemdam pueram, quem victoria potiti in manibus nostris habemus, ac rebellium ipsorum et hostium nostrorum confingentium puerum ipsum ducis quondam Clarentiae filium esse in regem Angliae coronarunt, ad grave nostrum et totius regni nostril praejudicium, vestram Sanctitatem humillime imploramus ut praefatos prelates in censuras incursos eccle-

siasticas postulare velit, atque in eos de jure procedure'. Gairdner, Letters and Papers of the Reigns of Richard III and Henry VII, pp. 95–6.

Part 4 – The Aftermath

14. Lambert Simnel, Scullion and Falconer

1. Sutton / Vergil, *Anglica Historia*, http://www.vision.net.au/~pwood/june04.htm (consulted December 2013).
2. Calendar of the Carew Manuscripts preserved in the Archiepiscopal Library at Lambeth: The Book of Howth, London 1871, p. 189.
3. A.J. Otway-Ruthven, *A History of Medieval Ireland*, New York 1980, p. 406.
4. For details of the Barons of Howth, see http://en.wikipedia.org/wiki/Earl_of_Howth, accessed November 2013.
5. Smith, 'Lambert Simnel and the King from Dublin', p. 516.
6. R. Lockyer, ed., F. Bacon, The History of the Reign of King Henry the Seventh, London 1971, p. 54.
7. 'Before leaving Leicester, [Henry VII] sent Robert Willing into Yorkshire to fetch Edward Earl of Warwick, the fifteen year-old son of George Duke of Clarence, whom Richard had been holding in the castle of Sheriff Hutton'. Sutton / Vergil, *Anglica Historia*, http://www.vision.net.au/~pwood/june04.htm (consulted December 2013).
8. On this point, see also Smith, 'Lambert Simnel and the King from Dublin', p. 503.
9. In Vergil's Latin text the change in vocabulary was from the word *puer* in the published text of 1534, to the word *adolescens* in the published text of 1546. Smith, 'Lambert Simnel and the King from Dublin', p. 513 and note 103.
10. 'Lambert Simnel', *ODNB*.
11. J.S. Brewer, ed., *Letters and Papers, Foreign and Domestic, Henry VIII*, vol. 4, part 1 (1524–1526), London 1870, pp. 149–150.
12. Ibid.
13. http://www.gravestonephotos.com/public/cemetery.php?cemetery=835, accessed December 2013.
14. Simnel is not a common surname, but it does exist and seems to be geographically quite widely distributed – see above for origins – see also https://familysearch.org/search/record/results#count=20&query=%2Bsurname%3ASimnel~%20%2Brecord_country%3AEngland, accessed August 2013. 'Simnel cakes have been known since at least the medieval times. They would be eaten on the middle Sunday of Lent, Laetare Sunday (also known as Refreshment Sunday, Mothering Sunday, Sunday of the Five Loaves, and Simnel Sunday), when the forty day fast would be relaxed. More recently, they became a Mothering Sunday tradition, when young girls in service would make one to be taken home to their mothers on their day off. The word *simnel* probably derived from the Latin word *simila*, meaning fine, wheaten flour.' http://en.wikipedia.org/wiki/Simnel_cake, accessed August 2013.
15. J. Gairdner and R.H. Brodie, eds, *Letters and Papers, Foreign and Domestic, Henry VIII* vol. 15 (1540), London 1896, item 147.

15. 'Richard of England'

1. Wroe, Perkin.
2. Raine, *York Civic Records*, pp. 100–1.

16. 'A Newe Maumet'

1. D. Seward, *The Last White Rose*, London 2010.
2. Sutton, *Anglica Historia* – my emphasis.
3. Lockyer, History of the Reign of King Henry the Seventh, p. 195.
4. 'At the junction with the presently named Shorncliff Road (previously Thomas
    Street) was the bridge crossing of *St Thomas-a-Watering* over a small brook, which
    marked a boundary in the Archbishop of Canterbury's authority of the nearby
    manors in Southwark and Walworth. The landmark pub nearby, the "Thomas a
    Becket", derives its name from this connection. It was a place of execution for
    criminals whose bodies were left in gibbets at this spot, the principal route from the
    southeast to the City of London'. http://en.wikipedia.org/wiki/Old_Kent_Road,
    accessed December 2013.
5. Thomas, *Great Chronicle*, p. 289.
6. http://en.wikipedia.org/wiki/List_of_Sheriffs_of_London, accessed November
    2013.
7. https://familysearch.org/pal:/MM9.1.1/JS1T-7M7, https://familysearch.org/
    pal:/MM9.1.1/NPL3-148, https://familysearch.org/pal:/MM9.1.1/NP2W-RJ6,
    https://familysearch.org/pal:/MM9.1.1/NP2W-RMT and https://familysearch.
    org/pal:/MM9.1.1/N532-PQ5, all accessed November 2013.
8. http://london.enacademic.com/710/Black_Bull_Inn,_Bishopsgate_Street, accessed
    November 2013.
9. http://www.pepysdiary.com/encyclopedia/12498/#discussion. See also http://
    en.wikipedia.org/wiki/Bishopsgate, both accessed November 2013.

17. Catherine of Aragon and the Spanish Interest

1. los reyes católicos.
2. J. Ashdown-Hill, 'The Lancastrian Claim to the Throne', *Ricardian*, 13 (2003), p. 37.
3. Gairdner, Letters and Papers of the Reigns of Richard III and Henry VII, pp. 113–14.

18. The Third 'Prince in the Tower'

1. http://en.wikipedia.org/wiki/Edward_Plantagenet,_17th_Earl_of_Warwick,
   accessed December 2013, citing H. Pierce, *Margaret Pole, Countess of Salisbury
   1473–1541*, University of Wales Press, 2009, p. 23.
2. H. Ellis, ed., Robert Fabyan, *New Chronicles of England and France*, London 1811, p. 687.
3. As referenced in the original text: 'They were found guilty of a plot to slay the marshal of the Tower and release the earl of Warwick 18 Nov. R.L. Storey believes the
   whole episode was engineered by the king, The Reign of Henry VII (1968), 87.'
4. Kirby, *Plumpton Letters and Papers*, p. 135, no. 142.

5. Thomas, *Great Chronicle*, pp. 291–2.

6. Bisham Priory was not an abbey at the time of Warwick's burial. It only (and very briefly) became an abbey later. The Augustinian priory was dissolved on 5 July 1537, but 6 months later, on 18 December, it was refounded as a Benedictine abbey.

7. http://en.wikipedia.org/wiki/Bisham_Abbey, accessed August 2013.

8. http://www.berkshirehistory.com/churches/bisham_abbey.html, accessed August 2013.

9. S. Bentley, ed., *Excerpta Historica*, London 1831, p. 123.

10. See Ashdown-Hill, *Last Days of Richard III*; also P. Langley & M. Jones, *The King's Grave: The search for Richard III*, London 2013.

Appendix 1: Timeline

1. http://en.wikipedia.org/wiki/Thomas_Lovell. For Francis Lovell, see http://en.wikipedia.org/wiki/Francis_Lovell,_1st_Viscount_Lovell, accessed December 2013

Appendix 3: Frequency of the Occurrence of the Surname Simnel in the UK circa 1500–2000

1. http://www.findmypast.co.uk/ (consulted January 2014, and searched under the surnames Simnel and Simnell).

2. http://search.findmypast.com.au/search/australia-and-new-zealand-records?lastname=simnel&lastname_variants=true&page=10, accessed January 2014. I am grateful to Olga Hughes for her help with this.

3. http://www.findmypast.co.uk/search/all-records/results?forename=&include ForenameVariants=true&_includeForenameVariants=on&surname=Sevil&_ includeSurnameVariants=on&f, accessed January 2014.

4. http://www.findmypast.co.uk/search/all-records/results?forename=&includeFo renameVariants=true&_includeForenameVariants=on&surname=Baulsom&_inc ludeSurnameVariants=on&fromYear=&toYear=&Region=UK&Search=Search, accessed January 2014.

5. http://www.findmypast.co.uk/search/all-records/results?forename=&includeFor enameVariants=true&_includeForenameVariants=on&surname=Mineveh&_inc ludeSurnameVariants=on&fromYear=&toYear=&Region=UK&Search=Search, accessed January 2014.

Bibliography

Books

André – *see* Sutton

Annals of Ulster, vol. 3 (1379–1541), Dublin 1895

Armstrong C.A.J., ed., D. Mancini, *The Usurpation of Richard III*, Gloucester 1989

Ashdown-Hill J., *Eleanor the Secret Queen*, Stroud 2009

Ashdown-Hill J., *The Last Days of Richard III*, Stroud 2010, 2013

Ashdown-Hill J., Mediaeval Colchester's Lost Landmarks, Derby 2009

Ashdown-Hill J., Richard III's 'Beloved Cousyn': John Howard and the House of York, Stroud 2009

Ashdown-Hill J., *Royal Marriage Secrets*, Stroud 2013

Ashdown-Hill J., The Third Plantagenet, George, Duke of Clarence, Richard III's Brother, Stroud 2014

Attreed L.C., ed., *York House Books 1461–1490*, vol. 1, Stroud 1991

Bacon – *see* Lockyer

Baldwin D., The Lost Prince, the Survival of Richard of York, Stroud 2007

Benham W.G., ed., The Oath Book, or Red Parchment Book of Colchester, Colchester 1907

Benham W.G., ed., *The Red Paper Book of Colchester*, Colchester 1902

Bennett M., *The Battle of Bosworth*, Stroud 1993

Bennett M., Lambert Simnel and the Battle of Stoke, New York 1987

Bentley S., ed., *Excerpta Historica*, London 1831

Brewer J.S., ed., *Letters and Papers, Foreign and Domestic, Henry VIII,* vol. 4, part 1 (1524–1526), London 1870

Buchon J.-A., ed., *Chroniques de Jean Molinet*, vol. 2 & vol. 3, Paris 1828

Buck G., The History of the Life and Reigne of Richard the Third (1646) – see Myers

But A. de, *Chroniques* – *see* de Lettenhove

Calendar of the Carew Manuscripts preserved in the Archiepiscopal Library at Lambeth: The Book of Howth, London 1871

Calendar of Patent Rolls 1452–1461

Calendar of Patent Rolls 1467–1477

Calendar of Patent Rolls 1485–1494

Calendar of State Papers, Milan

Campbell W., ed., Materials for a History of the Reign of Henry VII, vol. 1, London 1873

Carson A., Richard III, The Maligned King, Stroud 2013

Cavell E., ed., *The Heralds' Memoir 1486–1490*, Richard III & Yorkist History Trust 2009

Cox J.C., The Sanctuaries and Sanctuary Seekers of Mediaeval England, London 1911

Crawford A., ed., The Household Books of John Howard, Duke of Norfolk, 1462–71, 1481–83, Stroud 1992

Curtis E., *Cal. Ormond Papers*, vol. III (1413–1509), Dublin 1935

Davis N., ed., Paston Letters and Papers of the Fifteenth Century, part 2, Oxford 1976

Doubleday, H.A, and Howard de Walden, Lord, *Complete Peerage* (second edition) vol. VIII, London 1932

Ellis H., ed., Robert Fabyan, *New Chronicles of England and France*, London 1811

Emden A.B., A Biographical Register of the University of Oxford to A.D. 1500, vol. 3, Oxford 1959

Fabyan – *see* Ellis

Gairdner J., History of the Life and Reign of Richard the Third, Cambridge 1898

Gairdner J. and Brodie R.H., eds, *Letters and Papers, Foreign and Domestic, Henry VIII,* vol. 15 (1540), London 1896

Gairdner J, ed., Letters and Papers Illustrative of the Reigns of Richard III and Henry VII, vol. 1, London 1861

Goy J., Le Sacre des Rois de France, [Reims(?) no date of publication]

Grainge W., The Castles and Abbeys of Yorkshire, York and London 1855

Griggs F.L., Highways and Byways in Oxford and the Cotswolds, London 1924

Halliwell J.O., ed., *Letters of the Kings of England*, vol. 1, London 1848

Hanham A., ed., *The Cely Letters 1472–1488*, London 1975

Hanham A., *The Celys and their World*, Cambridge 1985

Hardy W. and Hardy E.L.C.P, eds., J. de Wavrin, Recueil des Chroniques et Anchienne Istories de la Grant Bretaigne, à Present Nommé Engleterre, vol. 5, 1891, reprinted Cambridge 2012

Hart K., The Mistresses of Henry VIII, Stroud 2009

Hearne T., Liber Niger Scaccarii nec non Wilhelmi Worcestrii Annales Rerum Anglicarum, vol. 2, London 1774

Hicks M., *Richard III*, Stroud, 2000

Horrox R., ed., British Library Harleian Manuscript 433, vol. 4, London 1983

Horrox R. and Hammond P., eds, *British Library Harleian Manuscript. 433*, vol. 3, London, 1983

Hunnisett R.F., The Medieval Coroner, Cambridge 1961, reprinted Florida 1986

Jones M.K. and Underwood M.G., The King's Mother, Lady Margaret Beaufort, Countess of Richmond and Derby, Cambridge 1992, 1995

Kendall P.M., *Richard the Third*, London 1956

Kingsford C.L., ed., The Stonor Letters and Papers, vol. 2, Camden third series, XXX, London 1919

Kirby J., ed, *The Plumton Letters and Papers*, Camden fifth seies, vol. 8, Cambridge 1996

Kleyn D.M., *Richard of England*, Oxford 1990

Langley P. and Jones M., The King's Grave: The search for Richard III, London 2013

Lettenhove, Kervyn de, Baron, ed., Chroniques relatives à l'histoire de la Belgique sous la domination des Ducs de Bourgogne, vol. 1, Bruxelles 1870, Adrien de But, Chroniques

Letters & Papers – see Brewer; Gairdner; Brodie

Loades D, *The Politics of Marriage: Henry VIII and his Queens*, Gloucester 1994

Lockyer R., ed., F. Bacon, The History of the Reign of King Henry the Seventh, London 1971

Mackie J.D., *The Earlier Tudors*, Oxford 1952, 1983

Mancini – *see* Armstrong

Metcalf D.M., *Sylloge of Coins of the British Isles 23*. Ashmolean Museum, Oxford. Part 3, Coins of Henry VII, London 1976

Mitchell S. and Reeds B., eds., Standard Catalogue of British Coins, vol. 1, Coins of England and the United Kingdom, 26th edition, London 1990

Mitchiner M., Jetons, Medalets and Tokens, vol. 1, The Medieval Period and Nuremberg, London 1988

Molinet, Chroniques – see Buchon

Morris R.K. and Shoesmith R., eds, *Tewkesbury Abbey: History, art and architecture*, Hereford 2003, 2012

Myers A.R., ed., Buck G., The History of the Life and Reigne of Richard the Third (1646), Wakefield 1973

Nicolas N.H., ed., Privy Purse Expenses of Elizabeth of York: Wardrobe accounts of Edward the Fourth, London 1830

Otway-Ruthven A.J., *A History of Medieval Ireland*, New York 1968, 1980

Plumpton Letters – *see* Kirby

Pronay N. and Cox J., eds, The Crowland Chronicle Continuations 1459–1486, London 1986

Raine A., ed., *York Civic Records*, vol. 2, Yorkshire Archaeological Society 1941

Rerum Britannicarum Medii Aevi Scriptores – Letters and Papers illustrative of the reigns of Richard III and Henry VII, London 1857

Ross, C., *Edward IV*, London 1974, 1991

Sandford F., Genealogical History of England, London 1707

Seaby P. and Purvey P.F., eds, Standard Catalogue of British Coins, vol. 2, Coins of Scotland, Ireland and the Islands, London 1984

Seward, D., *The Last White Rose*, London 2010

Sellar W.C. and Yeatman R.J., *1066 and All That*, London 1930

Simon, J., *An Essay towards an Historical Account of Irish Coins*, Dublin 1749 and 1810

Spinks, *Coins of Scotland, Ireland and the Islands*, London 2003

Stonor Letters – *see* Kingsford

Sutton D.F., ed., Bernard André, *De Vita atque Gestis Henrici Septimi Historia*, http://www.philological.bham.ac.uk/andreas/, 2010

Sutton D.F., ed., Polydore Vergil, *Anglica Historia* (1555 version), http://www.vision.net.au/~pwood/june04.htm, 2005, 2010

Thomas A.H. and Thornley I.D., eds, *Great Chronicle of London*, London 1938

Tucker M.J., The Life of Thomas Howard Earl of Surrey and Second Duke of Norfolk 1443–1524, London 1964

Twining, Lord, *European Regalia*, London 1967

Vaughan R., Charles the Bold, the Last Valois Duke of Burgundy, Woodbridge 2002

VCH, A History of Oxford, vol. 4, The City of Oxford, Oxford 1979

Vergil – *see* Sutton

Ware J., Rerum Hibernicarum Annales regnatibus Henrico VII, Henrico VIII, Edwardo VI & Maria, ab anno scil MCCCCLXXXV ad annum MDLVIII, Dublin 1664

Wavrin (Waurin) – *see* Hardy

Weightman C., Margaret of York Duchess of Burgundy 1446–1503, Gloucester 1989

Wilkins D., Concilia Magnae Britanniae et Hiberniae, vol. 3, London 1737

Williamson A., *The Mystery of the Princes*, Gloucester 1978

Worcester – *see* Hearne
Wroe A., Perkin A Story of Deception, London 2003

Articles and Booklets

Ashdown-Hill J., 'Coins attributed to the Yorkist Pretenders, 1487–1498', *Ricardian*, 19 (2009), pp. 63–83

Ashdown-Hill J, 'The Death of Edward V – new evidence from Colchester', *Essex Archaeology & History*, 35 (2004), pp. 226–30

Ashdown-Hill J., 'The Lancastrian Claim to the Throne', *Ricardian*, 13 (2003), pp. 27–38

Ashdown-Hill J, 'Norfolk Requiem: The passing of the House of Mowbray', *Ricardian*, 12 (March 2001), pp. 198–217

Ashdown-Hill J., 'Thomas Marshall or John Beche? Who was the last Abbot of Colchester?', *Essex Archaeology & History*, 4th series, vol. 4 (2013), pp. 228–32

Ashdown-Hill J. and Carson A., 'The Execution of the Earl of Desmond', *Ricardian*, 15 (2005), pp. 70–93

Blunt, C.E., 'The Medallic Jetton of Perkin Warbeck', *British Numismatic Journal*, vol. 26 (1949–51), pp. 215–16

Brady G. and Gallagher C., 'The Lambert Simnel Coinage: An enquiry', *Spink Numismatic Circular*, 103, no. 8 (October 1995), pp. 301–2

Britnell R.H., 'The Oath Book of Colchester and the Borough Constitution, 1372–1404', *Essex Archaeology and History*, 14 (1982), pp. 94–101

Brown J. and Brown F.., 'The de la Poles, Earls and Dukes of Suffolk', Wingfield 2000.

Carlyon-Britton R., 'On the Irish Coinage of Lambert Simnel as Edward VI', *Numismatic Chronicle*, sixth series, 1 (1941), pp. 133–5

Davies C.S.L., 'A Requiem for King Edward', *Ricardian*, vol. 9, no. 114, September 1991, pp 102–05

Dolley M., 'Simnel and Warbeck – some recent misconceptions', *Seaby's Coin and Medal Bulletin*, no. 616 (December 1969), pp. 424–5

Dolley M., '*Tre Kronor – Trí Choróin*, a note on the date of the "three crown" coinage of Ireland', *Numismatiska Meddelanden*, 30 (1965), pp. 103 12

Hayden M.T., 'Lambert Simnel in Ireland', *Studies: An Irish Quarterly Review*, 4 (1915), pp. 622–38

Longpérier A. de, 'Perkin Werbecque', *Revue Numismatique* (1860), pp. 384–95

Longstaffe W.H.D., 'Misplaced Coins – Richard IV's Groat', *Numismatic Chronicle*, third series, 9 (1889), pp. 363–4

G. Petterwood, 'The Harp and the Shamrock!', *Tasmanian Numismatist*, vol. 9, no. 6 (June 2004), http://www.vision.net.au/~pwood/june04.htm (consulted October 2008).

Power P., 'The History and Coins of Lambert Simnal and Perkin Warbeck', *Seaby's Coin and Medal Bulletin*, no. 615 (November 1969), pp. 376–8

'Proceedings of the Royal Numismatic Society', *Numismatic Chronicle*, 7th series, 9 (1969), pp. xii–xiii.

Richmond C.F., 'The Death of Edward V', *Northern History*, 25 (1989), pp. 278–80

Schmall, C.N., 'Note on the "Perkin Warbeck Groat" dated 1494', *Numismatist*, 41 (1928), pp. 219–20

Smith G., 'Lambert Simnel and the King from Dublin', *Ricardian*, 10, no. 135, December 1996, pp. 498–536

Sutton A. and Visser-Fuchs L., 'Richard III and the Knave of Cards: An illuminator's model in manuscript and print, 1440s to 1990s', *The Antiquaries Journal*, 79 (1999), pp. 257–99

Symonds H., 'The Irish Silver Coinage of Edward IV', *Numismatic Chronicle*, series 5, no. 1 (1921), pp. 108–25

Unpublished Sources

Ashdown-Hill L.J.F., 'The client network, connections and patronage of Sir John Howard (Lord Howard, first Duke of Norfolk) in north-east Essex and south Suffolk', PhD thesis, University of Essex 2008

Bodleian Library, MS. Top. Glouc. d.2, Founders' and benefectors' book of Tewkesbury Abbey

Essex Record Office, *Colchester Oath Book*

Society of Antiquaries MSS 116

Electronic Sources & Internet

'The Arms of Ireland', *Heraldry in Ireland*, http://www.heraldica.org/topics/national/ireland.htm, accessed October 2008

'Irish Hammered Coinage', *Irish Coinage*, http://www.irishcoinage.com/HAMMERED.HTM, accessed October 2008

'Charmouth', *Wikipedia*, http://en.wikipedia.org/wiki/Charmouth, accessed April 2012

'The Abbot's House', http://www.abbotshouse.co.uk/index.php?id=11, accessed April 2012

'History', *Charmouth Parish Council*, http://www.charmouth.com/History.htm accessed April 2012

'Bisham Abbey', *Wikipedia*, http://en.wikipedia.org/wiki/Bisham_Abbey, accessed August 2013

'Discover your family history', *Family Search*, https://familysearch.org/search/, accessed August 2013

'Osney Abbey', *Wikipedia*, http://en.wikipedia.org/wiki/Osney_Abbey, accessed August 2013

'Oxford, St Thomas the Martyr', *Church of England*, http://www.achurchnearyou.com/oxford-st-thomas-the-martyr/, accessed August 2013

D.N. Ford, 'Bisham Priory', *Royal Berkshire History*, http://www.berkshirehistory.com/churches/bisham_abbey.html, accessed August 2013.

http://www.fpnotebook.com/endo/exam/hghtmsrmntinchldrn.htm, accessed August 2013

'Last name: Simnel', *The Internet Surname Database*, http://www.surnamedb.com/Surname/Simnel, accessed August 2013

'Rite of Ordination of a Bishop, 1968', 'John Writhe', *Wikipedia*, http://en.wikipedia.org/wiki/John_Writhe, accessed September 2013

http://courseweb.stthomas.edu/jmjoncas/LiturgicalStudiesInternetLinks/ChristianWorship/Texts/Centuries/Texts_1900_2000CE/

RCWorshipTexts1900_2000CE/Rite_of_Ordination_of_a_Bishop.htm, accessed September 2013

'Bishopsgate', *Wikipedia*, http://en.wikipedia.org/wiki/Bishopsgate, accessed November 2013

'Earl of Howth', *Wikipedia*, http://en.wikipedia.org/wiki/Earl_of_Howth, accessed November 2013

'List of Sheriffs of London', *Wikipedia*, http://en.wikipedia.org/wiki/List_of_Sheriffs_of_London, accessed November 2013

'John Wilford, England Births and Christenings, 1538–1975', *Family Search*, https://familysearch.org/pal:/MM9.1.1/JS1T-7M7, accessed November 2013

'Wilford in entry for BartholomewPhilip Wilford, England Births and Christenings, 1538–1975', *Family Search*, https://familysearch.org/pal:/MM9.1.1/NPL3-148, accessed November 2013

'Thomas Wilford in entry for Barethe Wilford, England Births and Christenings, 1538–1975', *Family Search*, https://familysearch.org/pal:/MM9.1.1/NP2W-RJ6, accessed November 2013

'William Wilford in entry for Susan Wilford, England Births and Christenings, 1538–1975', *Family Search*, https://familysearch.org/pal:/MM9.1.1/NP2W-RMT, accessed November 2013

'Thomas Wilford in entry for Bartholomew Wilford, England Births and Christenings, 1538–1975', *Family Search*, https://familysearch.org/pal:/MM9.1.1/N532-PQ5, accessed November 2013

'The Diary of Samuel Pepys', http://www.pepysdiary.com/encyclopedia/12498/#discussion, accessed November 2013

'Black Bull Inn, Bishopsgate Street', *Dictionary of London*, http://london.enacademic.com/710/Black_Bull_Inn,_Bishopsgate_Street, accessed November 2013

'High Sheriff of Berkshire', *Wikipedia*, http://en.wikipedia.org/wiki/High_Sheriff_of_Berkshire, accessed December 2013

'Old Kent Road', *Wikipedia*, http://en.wikipedia.org/wiki/Old_Kent_Road, accessed December 2013

'William Darcy (died 1540)', *Wikipedia*, http://en.wikipedia.org/wiki/William_Darcy_(died_1540), accessed December 2013

I.S. Rogers, 'Sir Henry Bodrugan of Cornwall (died 1489)', www.girders.net/Bo/Bodrugan,%20Sir%20Henry,%20(d.1489).doc, accessed December 2013

'A list of grave monuments in St Andrew Cemetery, Enfield, Middlesex, England', *Gravestone Photographic Resource*,
http://www.gravestonephotos.com/public/cemetery.php?cemetery=835, accessed December 2013

'Height measurements in children', *Family Practice Notebook*, 'Search all records', *Find My Past*, http://www.findmypast.co.uk/, accessed January 2014

http://en.wikipedia.org/wiki/Martin_Schwartz_(mercenary), accessed December 2013

http://en.wikipedia.org/wiki/Edward_Plantagenet,_17th_Earl_of_Warwick, accessed December 2013

http://en.wikipedia.org/wiki/Thomas_Lovell, accessed December 2013

Oxford Dictionary of National Biography, http://www.oxforddnb.com/

C. Given-Wilson, general ed., *PROME (Parliament Rolls of Medieval England)*, The National Archives, Leicester 2005

Index